Modes of Play in
Eighteenth-Century France

Scènes francophones:
STUDIES IN FRENCH AND FRANCOPHONE THEATER

Series Editor
Logan J. Connors
University of Miami

Dedicated to scholarship on French-language theater, *Scènes francophones* publishes theoretically and historically informed research on dramatic texts and productions from medieval France to the contemporary French-speaking world. Linguistically focused but broad in scope, this series features monographs and multi-authored volumes on dramatic literatures, theories, and practices.

Scènes francophones, which publishes in English, welcomes new research on specific playwrights or actors as well as analysis of particular theaters, dramatic repertoires, and performance spaces. Research in which theater plays a leading role among other genres, themes, or institutions is also encouraged. This series supports research on the social, economic, and cultural history of theater across time periods, from hexagonal France to the reaches of the French-speaking world today.

Titles in the Series

Modes of Play in Eighteenth-Century France

EDITED BY FAYÇAL FALAKY
AND REGINALD MCGINNIS

Bucknell | UNIVERSITY
UNIVERSITY | PRESS

LEWISBURG, PENNSYLVANIA

Library of Congress Cataloging-in-Publication Data

Names: Falaky, Fayçal, 1977– editor. | McGinnis, Reginald, 1959– editor.
Title: Modes of play in eighteenth-century France / edited by Fayçal
   Falaky and Reginald McGinnis.
Description: Lewisburg, Pennsylvania : Bucknell University Press, [2022] |
   Includes bibliographical references and index.
Identifiers: LCCN 2021008398 | ISBN 9781684483419 (hardcover) |
   ISBN 9781684483402 (paperback) | ISBN 9781684483426 (epub) |
   ISBN 9781684483433 (mobi) | ISBN 9781684483440 (pdf)
Subjects: LCSH: French literature—18th century—History and criticism. |
   Play in literature. | Games in literature. | Play—Social aspects—France—
   History—18th century. | Games—Social aspects—France—History—
   18th century. | France—Social life and customs—18th century.
Classification: LCC PQ265 .M63 2022 | DDC 840.9/357909033—dc23
LC record available at https://lccn.loc.gov/2021008398

A British Cataloging-in-Publication record for this book is available from the British Library.

www.bucknelluniversitypress.org

Distributed worldwide by Rutgers University Press

Manufactured in the United States of America

Contents

Modes of Play in Eighteenth-Century France

Introduction

Fayçal Falaky and Reginald McGinnis

Voici le temps de l'aimable Régence,
Temps fortuné, marqué par la licence,
Où la folie, agitant son grelot,
D'un pied léger parcourt toute la France,
Où nul mortel ne daigne être dévot,
Où l'on fait tout excepté pénitence.
Le bon Régent, de son palais royal,
Des voluptés donne à tous le signal.

This is the time of the lovable Régence,
A fortunate time, marked by license,
When folly, ringing its bell,
Gaily covers all of France,
Where no mortal deigns to be pious,
Where all is done except penitence.
The good Regent, in his Palais-Royal,
For the pursuit of pleasure, gives everyone the signal.

With these verses from *La pucelle d'Orléans*,[1] Voltaire announces the end of an era and the beginning of another. Following the austerity that characterized the later years of Louis XIV's reign begins a new age of jest and insouciance, sounded by a jingling bell and the regent's signal, as if to officially declare that the games have begun. Society turned to frivolity to escape all seriousness, while frivolity itself became a subject of serious reflection. As Voltaire notes in the entry dedicated to the topic in the *Dictionnaire philosophique*, the frivolous is proper to human nature: "Ce qui me persuade le plus de la providence, disait le profond auteur de *Bacha Bilboquet*, c'est que, pour nous consoler de nos innombrables misères, la nature nous a faits frivoles." (What most persuades me of the existence

1

of Providence, said the profound author of *Bacha Bilboquet*, is that to console us for our endless miseries nature has made us frivolous.)[2]

It is uncertain whether this quote is real or made up, and there is no indication that a book titled *Bacha Bilboquet* actually ever existed. The text referenced here, incorrectly, casually, or frivolously, is one that appears in Jean-Alexandre Perras's essay in this volume: Claude Cherrier's *L'homme inconnu, ou Les équivoques de la langue, dédié à Bacha Bilboquet* (1713). After the example of Monsieur Jourdain's transformation into a Mamamouchi, Cherrier, writing under the pseudonym "Chimérographe de l'Académie des Jeux Olympiques," enthrones the traditional children's toy and praises it for having conquered all of Paris: "La réputation des bilboquets est au point que rien ne la peut augmenter . . . quoique chéri des courtisans les plus distingués, vous devenez si populaire, que vous vous abaissez jusqu'aux gens du plus bas lot." (The bilboquet's repute is such that nothing can increase it . . . though cherished by the most distinguished courtiers, you have become so popular that you stoop to those of low estate.)[3] Popular though it was, the bilboquet was not the only *bacha* in town, and the quest for entertainment in eighteenth-century France came to involve many different modes of play: toys, dolls, and automata; board and card games; lotteries and games of chance; as well as *jeux de mots, jeux d'esprit*, and *jeux de rôles*, whether artistic, musical, literary or dramatic. As Louis de Jaucourt notes in his entry "Jeu" from the *Encyclopédie*, "l'amour du *jeu* est le fruit de l'amour du plaisir, qui se varie à l'infini" (the love of *play* is the fruit of the love of pleasure, which is continually varying).[4]

Following Jaucourt, we may say that it is not just the love of play but play itself that is continually varying, as is implicit in the expression "jeux de la nature," which appears as a subheading in Jaucourt's entry, referring to the abnormal and inexplicable variations produced by nature. In the supplement to the *Encyclopédie* this subheading appears as a separate entry, by Albrecht von Haller under the title "Jeux de la nature, et monstres."[5] If the monstrous is set side by side with the playful, this is because both concepts lie similarly in the interstice between the known and the unknown. Having long been frowned upon, at once marginalized and a subject of fascination, the playful—like the monstrous—became increasingly viewed in the eighteenth century as a medium for reconsidering the normative.

One need only look at the number of treatises published on the subject between 1685 and 1709 to appreciate this trend—for instance, Jean Frain du Tremblay's *Conversations morales sur les jeux et les divertissements* (1685), Jean-Baptiste Thiers's *Traité des jeux et des divertissements* (1686), Jean La Placette's *Résolution sur le jeu de hazard faite en Sorbonne* (1697) and Jean Barbeyrac's *Traité du jeu* (1709). Most notable among these are those of Frain du Tremblay and Barbeyrac. Breaking from theological or moral interpretations according to which gambling was opposed to God's Providence, Frain du Tremblay argued that there is nothing fateful or even chanceful about games of chance. We are mistaken to call these "jeux de hasard," he writes, as "Ils ne le seront qu'à l'égard de ceux qui y sont grossièrement ignorants. Car pour peu qu'un homme ait joué aux dés, par exemple, il sait en combien de façons peuvent tourner trois dés, ou, pour parler comme mathématiciens, en combien de façons les points de trois dés peuvent être combinés ensemble." (They will be so only with respect to those who are grossly ignorant of their nature. Because if a man has played dice, for example, he knows in how many ways three dice can fall, or, to speak like mathematicians, in how many ways the points of three dice can be combined.)[6] Freed from the grips of the providential or the fortuitous, chance becomes a matter of odds, no longer a fabulous "monster" but a riddle waiting to be solved.

In his *Traité du jeu*, Barbeyrac disputes a premise of theological arguments against gambling, declaring that not every throw of dice or deal of cards emanates from (or, for that matter, contradicts) God's will. If this were the case, he argues, "ceux qui jouent aux dés et aux cartes, engageraient Dieu tous les jours à se déclarer en leur faveur par des miracles perpétuels; et dans les Académies de Jeu il se ferait infiniment plus de miracles qu'il ne s'en est jamais fait dans le Temple de Dieu" (those who play at dice and at cards would ask God every day to show himself favorable to them with perpetual miracles; and in Gambling Houses there would be infinitely more miracles than there ever were in the House of God).[7] Dismissing theological interpretations of a subject deemed unworthy of God's attention, Barbeyrac considers gambling through a legal and philosophical lens and (in what might be viewed as an outline of later philosophical and political ideals) frames it as a social contract resting on the consent and the natural and moral rights of participants—specifically, liberty, equality, and fidelity.

The question of play in eighteenth-century France, which may seem distant to some readers, is perhaps no more so than the political and legal debates of that period that are recognized as having shaped our modern democracies. Frans Mäyrä, in his introduction to the field of game studies, observes that play is honored by a long history of thought with a very special place in culture. While acknowledging the influence of Roger Caillois and Johan Huizinga on late-twentieth-century theoreticians of play, Mäyrä places both these authors in "a tradition of thought reaching back to romanticism and beyond," citing Jean-Jacques Rousseau's *Émile, or On Education*, and quoting from Friedrich Schiller's *On the Aesthetic Education of Man*: "man only plays when he is in the fullest sense of the word a human being, and *he is only fully a human being when he plays*."[8] This nod to the eighteenth century echoes sentiments already expressed by Huizinga in *Homo Ludens*, remarking that "play-quality in 18th-century civilization goes deeper," and that "statecraft had never been so avowedly a game as in that age of secret cabals, intrigues and political filibustering."[9] It also reminds us of Jean de La Bruyère's assertion, "La vie de la cour est un jeu sérieux, mélancolique, qui applique: il faut arranger ses pièces. . . . [A]près toutes ses rêveries et toutes ses mesures on est échec, et quelquefois mat." (Court life is a serious, melancholic, and demanding game: we must arrange the pieces. . . . [A]fter all those musings and measures, we are put in check, and sometimes checkmated.)[10] For La Bruyère, court life may be a losing game but, during the eighteenth century, the board game and play in general became increasingly viewed as a way to rethink statecraft.

Voltaire, in another entry from the *Dictionnaire philosophique,* "Lois," similarly refers to chess in arguing that the rules governing games are often more equitable and better respected than the laws governing societies. "A la honte des hommes," he writes, "on sait que les lois du jeu sont les seules qui soient partout justes, claires, inviolables, et exécutées." (To the shame of mankind, it is well known that the laws of games are the only ones that are everywhere just, clear, inviolable and enforced.)[11] Whereas the decrees of the church, for instance, are said to be an object of horror and contempt, the rules of chess are willingly obeyed everywhere and have remained essentially unchanged five thousand years after their invention. The laws of play, in this instance, are considered more constant and more enduring because chess, contrary to what Voltaire saw in religion, was invented for people's instruction and pleasure. Similarly, in the entry "Contradictions," Voltaire decries the arbitrariness and inequality of laws other than those of gambling, stating that a man who has been a lackey, if he plays at cards with kings, will readily be paid his winnings: "Les règles du jeu sont les seules qui n'admettent ni exception, ni relâchement, ni variété, ni tyrannie. . . . [P]artout ailleurs, la loi est un glaive dont le plus fort coupe par morceaux le plus faible." (The rules of gambling are the only ones that allow neither exception, relaxation, variance, nor tyranny. . . . [E]verywhere else the law is a sword with which the weakest are cut to pieces by the strongest.)[12] Voltaire's contrasting of the laws of play with those of society is echoed two centuries later by Caillois, who observes that, for the duration of a given game, the "confused and intricate laws of ordinary life are replaced . . . by precise, arbitrary, unexceptionable rules that must be accepted as such."[13] The rules of the game may appear absurd, and the game itself may represent an illusory break from real life; but insofar as the players of this closed universe feel bound by a "social contract" to respect exact rules, the space of play can be emblematic of much more. This ludic space, whether board, court, stage or page, can serve as a microcosm, a model world, for envisioning a better, fairer society. The "author of *Bacha Bilboquet*" may have believed in providence because nature had made us frivolous. We may add, however, that, in the eighteenth century, play also reputedly came to challenge and supplant providence such that—during this period when it was often declared that all forms of faith or belief were simply outmoded—individuals might emerge from their condition of divine playthings to become players themselves.[14]

From dolls, bilboquets, and lotteries to literature and theater, this collection of essays seeks to show the prominence of play throughout the eighteenth century.

Weaving together critical perspectives from a variety of interrelated fields—
material culture, utopian spaces, natural rights, revolutionary and society theater, and critical gaming—the contributions to this volume offer new insights
into how play was used to represent and reimagine the world. These essays also
suggest how our current conceptions of play as performance or amusement often
have unexpected affinities that can be traced to Enlightenment thought.

Rori Bloom inaugurates the volume with a discussion of the fairy tales of
Marie-Catherine d'Aulnoy and Henriette-Julie de Murat. Though written for
adults, these stylish and sophisticated stories show a preoccupation with toys and
especially dolls. In Mme d'Aulnoy, dolls are beautifully and elaborately clothed
in the latest fashions, highlighting the artistry of toymakers and suggesting a
parallel with her own crafting of stories. Mme de Murat, by contrast, took a dimmer view of play, denouncing gambling and fairground entertainments while
evoking dolls in questioning the treatment of women in French society. Despite
their many differences, both d'Aulnoy and Murat use dolls as allegories of our
place in the world, be it as talented puppet masters or as tormented puppets.

In chapter 2, "The Morality of Bilboquet, or the Equivocations of Language,"
Jean-Alexandre Perras further explores the interplay between material and textual forms of play. Noting how brochures such as Pierre de Marivaux's *Bilboquet* or the anonymous *De l'antiquité et de l'usage du bilboquet* are as playful,
frivolous, and seductive as the suggestively phallic-shaped toy they celebrate, Perras illustrates the persistent linking of the fashion of bilboquet with wordplay.
As stated explicitly in the aforementioned brochure, *L'homme inconnu, ou Les
équivoques de la langue dédié à Bacha Bilboquet*, the cup-and-ball game exemplifies the equivocation inherent in calembours. A children's toy readily lending itself to sexual interpretation, the bilboquet is an object of both amusement
and seduction.

The third chapter in this volume, Zeina Hakim's "Fiction as Play: Rhetorical
Subversion in Alain René Lesage's *Histoire de Gil Blas de Santillane*," considers
how readers may be less the object of the text's seductive ploys than autonomous
agents, freely and willingly choosing to play a game of narrative illusion proposed by the author. At issue here is a playful tension between, on the one hand,
a literary process whose stated purpose is to make readers believe in the authenticity of the narrated events and, on the other, clues preventing the same readers from believing in the reality of what they are told. In Hakim's interpretation,
readers of Lesage's novel are invited to decipher narrative strategies in demysti-
fying their own relation to a providential author.

Whereas the opening chapters underline different modes of play, from the
material to the textual, chapters 4 and 5 attend to the political dimension of the
ludic and its relevance to matters of state and society. In chapter 4, "Playthings
of Fortune: Lots, Games of Chance, and Inequality in l'Abbé Prévost," Masano
Yamashita considers the role of chance in promoting social justice and redressing

inequality. Whereas in *L'histoire du chevalier des Grieux et Manon Lescaut* gambling emerges as a means of redistributing wealth, marriage by lottery is presented in *Cleveland* as an equitable way of regulating marital and social relations. Yamashita shows how in both novels the discussion of gambling and lots reflects a broader will in the eighteenth century to secularize (and tame) chance, be it Providence or Fortuna.

The role of chance in reshaping society is a question taken up again by Erika Mandarino in chapter 5, "Boundless Play and Infinite Pleasure in the Chevalier de Béthune's *Relation du monde de Mercure*." Games of chance, as reflected notably in the different lotteries played by Béthune's Mercurians, are imagined here as a means of experiencing infinite, ever-changing variety. Mirroring the diversity of the universe, this emphasis on variety offers a conceptual lens through which to question the confines of teleological uniformity. Béthune's utopian playground also allows for a reimagining of life as an endless set of permutations, akin to the limitless variations of virtual reality in present-day video games.

Whereas Béthune looked to Mercury as a mirror through which to contemplate potential reforms to French society, the librettists and composers studied in chapter 6 invoke a blatantly fictionalized Orient. In "The Politics of Orientalist Fantasy in French Opera," Katharine Hargrave analyzes two works set in Persia, Jean-Philippe Rameau and Louis de Cahusac's *Zoroastre* and Antonio Salieri and Pierre Beaumarchais's *Tarare* to illustrate how the commercial and entertainment capital of *turqueries* could be exploited to surreptitiously convey subversive sociopolitical ideologies. These operas are seen here as playing with Orientalist fantasy in creating a game of mirrors to incite political awareness and engagement. As with readers of Charles-Louis de Secondat, baron de Montesquieu's *Persian Letters*, spectators are drawn into a game in which they are invited to decode a veiled meaning behind the performance.

As with chapter 6, the following three chapters are devoted to the role of play in plays and the function of theater in mimicking or contesting social and political structures. In chapter 7, "Playing at Theater: Modes of Play in *Théâtre de Société*," Maria Teodora Comsa focuses on a form of entertainment that became fashionable in the second half of the eighteenth century. Practiced within homes of the elite, society theater was a private affair intended as a playful diversion for aristocrats who could temporarily become actors and "play" for, and with, their select *société*. This practice, which at first appears to be a frivolous pastime is, nonetheless, shown to have offered a way for participants to represent, reenact, and sometimes prolong maneuverings and social intrigues unfolding in everyday life. Due to its private nature, society theater thus offered extensive freedom to play oneself and parody "real life" while revealing the ludic and often cruelly alienating nature of the *theatrum mundi*.

Chapter 8, Annelle Curulla's "Between Play and Ritual: Profane Masquerade in the French Revolution," draws on the theories of Giorgio Agamben and Roger

Caillois in considering anti- or pseudo-religious rituals (e.g. mock processions, charivari, and iconoclastic ceremonies) during the Reign of Terror. Questioning traditional assumptions regarding the separation of the religious and secular spheres, Curulla shows how profane masquerade could function simultaneously, or alternately, as a ritual of secularization consistent with the dechristianizing policies of the Revolutionary government and as a mode of play in which the mimicking of sacred forms resulted in their refashioning or displacement rather than in their disappearance.

While there was a greater number of plays during the Revolutionary era than any decade prior, as a result of the 1791 law ending privilege and censorship, the theater of this period grew into a deeply politicized space, and performances lost many of the attributes we traditionally associate with the word *play*—in two senses: as a dramatic production (the line between theater and ritual, fiction and reality, became increasingly blurred) and as a behavior or outlook (a lighthearted distance from the drama of the present became not only difficult but perilous). In chapter 9, "The Return of Play, or the End of Revolutionary Theater," Yann Robert takes as his point of departure this withdrawal of play in considering two developments, both from the year 1797: a largely forgotten, but lengthy and fascinating, debate at the Council of Five Hundred and the Council of Ancients on the need to depoliticize the dramatic arts, and a surprising campaign in the press in favor of the lost practice of hissing actors and playwrights during performances. Together, as Robert shows, these episodes amounted to a concerted effort to revive plays as play(s).

In the tenth and final chapter, Jeffrey Leichman's "Video Games as Cultural History: Procedural Narrative and the Eighteenth-Century Fair Theater," we turn from the French Revolution to the digital age, in which computer modeling and rendering of historical spaces have allowed for ever more detailed sensory simulations of historical environments. Starting from a project aimed at re-creating the sensory environment of the eighteenth-century Paris Fair theaters, this essay explores new research paradigms potentially opened up by play. In addition to discussing this collaborative digital humanities project, Leichman suggests further implications of situating play—the unpredictable and frequently unruly performance of the gamer—as a tool for researching theories about comportment, both in the eighteenth century and the present. The game itself appears accordingly as an experimental framework allowing investigators to tweak constraints and incentives in order to test how different scenarios and sources affect real-world behaviors by gamers, with successive playthroughs providing data on how contemporary users understand and confront the challenges of eighteenth-century social environments.

Taken together, the essays assembled here remind us that play, though often perceived as frivolous, was very much alive and well during the Age of Reason, as it is today. They remind us, too, that play can offer alternative perspectives through which to consider "serious" subjects such as free will and determinism, illusions and equivocations, chance and inequality, or academic research itself.

NOTES

Unless noted otherwise, all translations are our own.

1. Voltaire, *La pucelle d'Orléans*, in *Oeuvres complètes de Voltaire*, ed. Louis Moland, 52 vols. (Paris: Garnier Frères, 1877–85), 9:211–212.

2. Voltaire, "Frivolité," in *Dictionnaire philosophique*, in *Oeuvres complètes*, 19:208.

3. Claude Cherrier, *L'homme inconnu, ou Les équivoques de la langue, dedié à Bacha Bilboquet* (Paris: Chez J. Quillau, 1713), 4.

4. Louis de Jaucourt, "Jeu," in *Encyclopédie, ou Dictionnaire raisonné des sciences, des arts et des métiers*, 17 vols., ed. Denis Diderot and Jean le Rond d'Alembert (Paris: Briasson, 1751–1765), 8:531.

5. Albrecht von Haller, "Jeux de la nature, et monstres," in *Supplément à l'Encyclopédie, ou Dictionnaire des sciences, des arts et des métiers*, 4 vols., ed. Jean-Baptiste-René Robinet (Amsterdam: Marc-Michel Rey, 1776), 3:551–559.

6. Jean Frain du Tremblay, *Conversations morales sur les jeux et les divertissements* (Paris: Chez André Pralard, 1685), 70.

7. Jean Barbeyrac, *Traité du jeu, où l'on examine les principales questions de droit naturel et de morale qui ont du rapport à cette matière* (Amsterdam: Pierre Humbert, 1709), 1:23.

8. Friedrich Schiller, quoted in Frans Mäyrä, *An Introduction to Game Studies* (London: Sage, 2008), 43, emphasis in the original.

9. Johan Huizinga, *Homo Ludens: A Study of the Play-Element in Culture*, trans. R. F. C. Hull (London: Routledge and Kegan Paul, 1949), 186.

10. Jean de La Bruyère, *Les caractères*, ed. Emmanuel Bury (Paris: Librairie Générale Française, 1995), 332.

11. Voltaire, "Lois," in *Dictionnaire philosophique*, in *Oeuvres complètes*, 19:620.

12. Voltaire, "Contradictions," in *Dictionnaire philosophique*, in *Oeuvres complètes*, 18:256.

13. Roger Caillois, *Man, Play, and Games*, trans. Meyer Barash (Urbana: University of Illinois Press, 2001), 7.

14. In Western metaphysics, as Mihai I. Spariosu, *Dionysus Reborn: Play and the Aesthetic Dimension in Modern Philosophical and Scientific Discourse* (Ithaca, NY: Cornell University Press, 1989), 29, observes, "play has often been employed in the form of a game metaphor that imagines the relationship between divinity and man as one between a player and a plaything."

CHAPTER 1

Playing with Dolls in Old Regime Fairy Tales

Rori Bloom

Although Charles Perrault's stated motive for writing his tales was "la louable impatience d'instruire les enfants" (the admirable intention of educating children),[1] scholars have long recognized the late-seventeenth-century French fairy tale as a genre aimed at adult readers.[2] The stylish, sophisticated stories written by Marie-Catherine d'Aulnoy (1650–1705) and Henriette-Julie de Murat (1670–1716) were clearly not meant for the nursery but for the salon. That said, in each of these authors' tales, the genre's origins in the nursery are not forgotten, with toys, and especially dolls, having a frequent if problematic presence. For Mme d'Aulnoy, the toymaker is a talented artist: in her tales, toys are like jewels, made of precious metals and encrusted with gems; dolls are like dressmakers' dummies, carefully clothed in scaled-down versions of the latest fashions. While her childish characters marvel at dancing dolls, d'Aulnoy invites her reader to admire the puppet master as a figure of the author in stories that seem inspired by doll weddings and tin soldier wars. Despite many similarities between their works, d'Aulnoy's contemporary, Mme de Murat, takes a dimmer view of play, making disapproving pronouncements about gambling but also denouncing fairground entertainments such as sharpshooters, acrobats, and puppet shows. Murat's critique of play is especially incisive when she evokes the weddings of doll-like princesses. Although she seems, in one tale, to applaud the marriage of young princess Marie-Adélaïde de Savoie to Louis XIV's grandson and sees her arrival at Versailles as a rejuvenation of court culture, Murat's fairy-tale depiction of the wedding of fictional princess Risette condemns the practice of arranged marriages for child brides. D'Aulnoy and Murat both transpose the childish realm of toys into the world of aristocratic leisure, but the two authors have distinct views on the value of play. Both feature childlike, doll-like heroines, but while the tales of Mme d'Aulnoy celebrate playfulness, those of Mme de Murat critique established modes of play in Old Regime France.

The presence of toys in many of Mme d'Aulnoy's tales would seem to sub-stantiate the modern view of fairy tales as children's literature,[3] yet the exqui-site beauty of the playthings she describes affords them a status similar to the most finely wrought works of the decorative arts produced and consumed by aristocratic adults in seventeenth-century France. Toys in her tales are often assimilated into a more general category of luxury objects. In "La Princesse Printanière," in her collection *Contes des fées, suivis des contes nouveaux, ou Les fées à la mode*, the king's treasure chest is also a toy chest, containing a rich head-dress and a shiny dagger as well as dolls that open and close their eyes.[4] In "Finette Cendron," the ogres' treasure consists of "meubles si riches qu'elles mouraient de plaisir" (pieces of furniture so rich that they were dying of happi-ness) but also "des poupées en abondance" (an abundance of dolls; 450). In cred-iting d'Aulnoy with inventing the term *joujou* in "La Princesse Printanière," Michel Manson refers to a probable etymology that links *joujou* to *bijou*,[5] an association affirmed by the fact that many of the toys described by d'Aulnoy are less children's playthings than jeweled accessories. In "Le dauphin," toys given as gifts to a baby prince are also made of precious materials: "une rose de pierreries . . . un lion d'or, un loup d'agate, un cheval d'ivoire" (a rose made of gemstones . . . a lion made of gold, a wolf made of agate, a horse made of ivory; 1022). In "Le serpentin vert," an invisible host provides the princess with talk-ing toys to entertain her, figurines encrusted with various jewels: "Elle vit venir à elle cent pagodes vêtus et faits de cent manières différentes; les plus grands avaient une coudée de haut et les plus petits n'avaient pas plus de quatre doigts . . . ils étaient de diamants, d'émeraudes de rubis, de perles, de cristal, d'ambre, de corail, de porcelaine, d'or, d'argent, d'airain, de bronze, de fer, de bois, de terre." (She saw coming toward her one hundred Chinese figurines dressed in one hundred different styles; the biggest were one foot high and the smallest only about four inches . . . some were made of diamonds, others of emeralds and rubies, some of pearls or crystal or amber or coral or porcelaine or gold or silver or brass or bronze or iron or wood or clay; 581–82.) These *pagodes* are amusing, but they are also decorative—not just the playthings of a child but objects made for adult consumption and collection, the kind of porce-lain figurines that might be placed on a side table in a salon or displayed in a cabinet of similar exotic objects, often imported from the Orient (as the term *pagodes* suggests) or made in France during a time when chinoiserie was fash-ionable.[6] In "Le Prince Lutin," the hero purchases dresses and jewels for the princess in Paris but also a "petit carrosse tout d'or" (little carriage all of gold; 246), an object that is made for play like a toy but made of precious metal like a jewel. The prince buys this piece "chez Dautel," owner of a curiosity shop on the quai de la Mégisserie, where clients may purchase "bijoux et vaisseaux de prix" (jeweled objects and expensive tableware; 246n29), and the toy carriage is found alongside a variety of other expensive wares in a shop that does not cater to children but to adults. Something that seems to appeal to a child is in fact intended for a sophisticated consumer, much like d'Aulnoy's tales.[7]

Just as d'Aulnoy conflates the toy (*joujou*) and the jewel (*bijou*) in her tales to revalorize the seemingly puerile object as precious, her frequent mentions of dolls equally engage the attention of children and adults, as the dolls (*poupées*) in her tales may in fact be fashion dolls (*poupées de mode*), the mannequins used to disseminate French style throughout seventeenth-century Europe. This blurring of boundaries between the child's world of play and the adult's world of fashion is abetted by the ambiguous status of the fashion doll itself: Manson asserts that *poupées de mode* were made by the same craftsmen who made toy dolls: "Nous savons l'existence de ces poupées de mode parisiennes, lesquelles ne pouvaient sortir que des ateliers qui fabriquaient les poupées jouets." (We know of the existence in Paris of these fashion dolls, which could only have been produced by workshops which made toy dolls.)[8] And Joan DeJean hypothesizes that once ladies had studied new fashions displayed on the *poupées de mode*, they would give the dolls to children as playthings.[9] While in all of her tales d'Aulnoy takes pleasure in attiring her characters in beautiful clothing, her outfitting of animals and babies combines a child's love of dolls with an adult's passion for fashion. In "La chatte blanche," the main character is a cat, but, like a doll, she is dressed in assorted tiny outfits for various occasions. She is first dressed for mourning: "[Elle] se couvrait d'un long voile de crêpe noir" (She covered herself with a long, black crepe veil; 759). And later she is dressed for hunting: "[E]lle avait quitté son grand voile et portait un bonnet à la dragonne" ([S]he had taken off her long veil and put on a tasseled cap; 762). In "Babiole," the queen buys a monkey as a plaything for her spoiled son but soon transports the animal from the nursery to the throne room, amusing herself by dressing the pet as a child would dress a doll: "On la faisait paraître [la guenon] avec une robe de velours ou de brocard en corps et en collerette; lorsque la cour était en deuil, elle traînait une longue mante et des crêpes qui la fatiguaient beaucoup." (The monkey was made to appear wearing a velvet or brocade dress with a lace collar; when the court was in mourning, she was exhausted by the weight of the heavy mourning clothes that she wore; 510.) The monkey is treated less like a live animal than a stuffed toy that comes with several specially made small outfits: one for court festivities; one for royal mourning; and finally an elaborate bridal trousseau for her wedding to the monkey king. When d'Aulnoy evokes babies, they seem only to be present in order to be dressed in delicate, diminutive attire. The baby princess in "La chatte blanche" is dressed in a particularly elaborate and expensive manner: "toutes les bandes de [son] maillot étaient faites de grosses perles" (her singlet was covered in large pearls; 779). In "L'oranger et l'abeille," baby Aimée is found "enveloppée de langes de brocard d'or" (wrapped in a gold brocade baby blanket; 336); in "Le dauphin," the baby is "habillé de brocart d'or et d'argent" (dressed in gold and silver brocade; 1022). Between baby doll and fashion doll, these aestheticized infants are less persons than things. Unlike in child's play, where the manipulated object seems to come to life, in d'Aulnoy's tale living things become objects—specifically, objets d'art.

Moreover, in evoking the tiny accessories made for dolls, animals, and babies, d'Aulnoy inspires our admiration for the expert work needed to craft them. Various elements of a baby's layette are appreciated in d'Aulnoy's tales as luxury items, and her detailed descriptions of them are celebrations of the toymaker's art. In "La biche au bois," the beautiful embroidery on the baby's blanket invites us to admire the seamstress's skill: "L'on y voyait représentés mille jeux différents auxquels les enfants s'amusent. Depuis qu'il y a des brodeurs et des brodeuses, il ne s'est rien vu de si merveilleux." (One could see embroidered on it a thousand different games at which children play. Ever since embroidery has existed, there has never been sewing so marvelous; 691.)[10] In "L'oranger et l'abeille" and "La chatte blanche," ornate cradles are less functional pieces of furniture than works of art. The baby's cradle in the former tale is described not just as a "riche berceau" (rich cradle) but as "un berceau de nacre de perle, orné de tout ce que l'art peut faire imaginer de plus galant" (a cradle made of mother-of-pearl, adorned with the most gallant ornaments that art could imagine; 336). In the latter tale, the cradle is similarly exquisite: "Ce n'était que guirlandes de fleurs et festons qui pendaient autour et les fleurs en étaient des pierreries dont les différentes couleurs . . . réfléchissaient des rayons [du soleil]" (It was all flower garlands and festoons, and the flowers were made of different colored gemstones that reflected the rays of the sun; 779). In "La biche au bois," d'Aulnoy asks us to admire a cradle not for the precious materials with which it is made but because of the art of masters in carpentry, marquetry and sculpture necessary to create this masterpiece:

> Mais quand le berceau parut, la reine s'écria d'admiration, car il surpassait encore tout ce qu'elle avait vu jusqu'alors. Il était d'un bois si rare, qu'il coutait cent mille écus la livre. Quatre petits Amours le soutenaient, c'étaient quatre chefs-d'œuvre où l'art avait tellement surpassé la matière, quoiqu'il fût de diamants et de rubis, que l'on n'en peut assez parler. Ces petits Amours avaient été animés par les fées de sorte que lorsque l'enfant criait, ils le berçaient et l'endormaient: cela était d'une commodité merveilleuse pour les nourrices.

> But when the cradle appeared the queen cried out in admiration, since it surpassed anything that anyone had ever seen. It was made of wood so rare that it cost one hundred thousand écus for a pound. The four little cupids that supported it were four masterpieces in which the artistry was of more value than the materials, although they were made out of diamonds and rubies, that people could never praise them enough. These little cupids were animated by the fairies so that each time the baby cried, they rocked him to sleep: this was marvelously useful for his nurses. (691)

The baby in this tale does not inspire the religious awe surrounding the infant Jesus (often displayed as a tiny porcelain doll in a Christmas crèche); instead, in this scene, the baby's mother and her nurses marvel at the cradle itself.[11] Although the movement of the cradle is attributed to magic, d'Aulnoy's use of the words "œuvre" and "art" point to the skill of workers and artists in making this marvelous piece of mechanical furniture.

Likewise, in her descriptions of tiny toys such as the "petits ciseaux" (little scissors) in "La Princesse Printanière" or the "petit ménage d'argent" (little tea set) in "Finette Cendron," d'Aulnoy draws our attention to the delicate touch of artisans able to scale down objects meant for adults to fit into a child's hands or a doll's house.[12] In her evocation of toy carriages, d'Aulnoy highlights the metalworker's skill as a miniaturist: in "Le Prince Lutin" the "petit carrosse tout d'or" (little gold carriage) is too small to be drawn by horses and filled with people and is pulled instead by monkeys and filled with marionettes (246); in "L'oiseau bleu" the heroine cracks a magic egg to reveal "un petit carrosse d'acier poli, garni d'or de rapport" (a little carriage of polished steel, adorned with gold inlay) drawn by six green mice and a pink rat and containing four dancing marionettes (218). That story's evil queen is amazed by this marvelous toy and "ravie de ce nouveau chef d'oeuvre de l'art nécromancien" (delighted with this new masterpiece of the magic arts; 218)—a response reminiscent of those described by Alfred Gell where wonder at a work of art emerges from the incomprehension of its mechanism.[13] When the heroine refuses the queen's offer of twenty-five sols for the tiny carriage, declaring, "demandez aux gens de lettres et aux docteurs de ce royaume ... ce qu'une telle merveille peut valoir, et je m'en rapporterai à l'estimation du plus savant" (ask men of letters and doctors of this land ... what such a marvel is worth, and I will agree with the conclusions of the most knowledgeable of them; 218), she identifies the toy as an object of value to be appreciated not just by children but by men of science. The tiny carriage is not a mere plaything but a "chef d'oeuvre," a masterpiece of skilled workmanship and manifestation of technical mastery. Toys that move provoke a specific sort of wonder in d'Aulnoy's tales, but behind the seeming magic of their animation, she often points to a mechanical cause, replacing awe for the enchanted with admiration for the technical. Whether the toy may move because of a hidden mechanism (as in the cradle), or because of the hand of the puppeteer, the magic of these seemingly enchanted objects is a product of human ingenuity that may inspire wonder in the child but should also attract the admiration of the adult.

Moreover, in her evocations of animated objects, d'Aulnoy implies a comparison between the puppeteer's dexterous performance and her own skill as a storyteller manipulating doll-like characters.[14] In "Le Prince Lutin," the princess admires the movement of a toy carriage drawn by monkeys trained by "Brioché, fameux joueur de marionettes" (Brioché, the famous puppeteer; 246); in "L'oiseau bleu" the queen is awed by another display of animated objects, since this tale's little carriage is occupied by "quatre marionettes plus fringantes et plus spirituelles que toutes celles qui paraissent aux foires Saint-Laurent et Saint-Germain: elles faisaient des choses surprenantes, particulièrement deux petites Egyptiennes qui pour danser la sarabande et le passe-pieds ne l'auraient pas cédé à Léance" (four marionettes more lively and wittier than all those one may see at the Saint-Laurent or Saint-Germain fairs: they did surprising things, particularly two little Gypsies who danced the sarabande and the passe-pieds just as well as Léance; 218). Just as d'Aulnoy's characters enjoy playing with toys, the author herself plays with her own characters as if they were dolls. In one of d'Aulnoy's first tales, the heroine appears to be playing with dolls in a scene where little figures emerge from a magic box: "elle l'ouvrit et aussitôt il en sort de petits hommes et de petites femmes, de violons, d'instruments, de petites tables, petits cuisiniers, petits plats, enfin le géant de la troupe était haut comme le doigt" (she opened it and suddenly little men and little women, and little musicians and little instruments, and little tables and little cooks, and little plates all sprang out, and the giant of the band was only as big as a finger; 171). But when Gracieuse and Percinet ride in a "petit traîneau peint et doré" (little painted and gilded sleigh; 161), this sleigh recalls the toy carriages featured in later tales, and these characters resemble the marionettes that d'Aulnoy has placed in the *petits carrosses* in "Le Prince Lutin" and "L'oiseau bleu." Similarly, in "Finette Cendron," where Finette and her sisters are portrayed as children fighting over toys (442), the heroine herself may be a toy as well: she is small and delicate, as her name suggests, and her lost slipper is like a doll's shoe, a "petite, pouponne, mignonne, jolie mule" (a little, doll-like, adorable, pretty slipper; 453). In several stories d'Aulnoy refers to infants as "poupards," a term loosely translatable as "chubby baby," thus assimilating a baby with a doll. Her fictional babies are often less lifelike than doll-like: they are the kind that never soil their lace-trimmed, gold-brocade diapers. Baby Joliette in "La bonne petite souris" is prettily perfect with her "petites menottes" (little hands) and her "bécot ver-meil" (little mouth); Aimée in "L'oranger et l'abeille" with her "joues semblables à des roses blanches mêlées d'incarnat" (cheeks the color of white and pink roses; 336), resembles a pink and white china doll, a smile fixed to her face even as she is seized by a family of ogres. As if playing with the origin of the word *marionnette*—which designates not just a puppet but, according to Antoine Furetière's *Dictionnaire universel*, a little lady—d'Aulnoy explores the ambigu-ity between animate and inanimate in her treatment of living beings as objects.[15] Just as d'Aulnoy's human characters resemble dolls, her animal protagonists often evoke toys. In "La chatte blanche," the cat is evoked with the terms "figu-rine" (760) and "bamboche" (a type of marionette; 759), as if she were a toy, and in "Babiole" the animal characters Babiole and Magot (a type of figurine) are named for decorative objects, suggesting that the story is composed by d'Aulnoy as she plays with figurines on a tabletop.[16]

In playing with her characters as a child might play with dolls, d'Aulnoy allows her reader to understand the manipulation of objects as a creative act. Moreover, the presence of children's playthings in her works is not reason to devalue d'Aulnoy's fairy tales as minor literature but instead an invitation to understand children's play as a model for adult creativity. D'Aulnoy is not asking her reader to adopt the eyes of children who believe that marionettes are magically alive but the perspective of *gens de lettres* and *docteurs* who admire puppets for the care with which they have been made and the skill with which they are maneuvered. In his preface to "Peau d'âne," Perrault concedes : "Qu'en de certains moments l'esprit le plus parfait peut aimer sans rougir jusqu'aux marionnettes." (At certain times, the most perfect mind may enjoy a puppet show without embarrassment.)[17] In *Eighteenth-Century Fiction and the Reinvention of Wonder,* Sarah Kareem explains that "wonder's allure resides in its promise that one might consume marvels while maintaining one's critical faculties."[18] In this way, puppet shows and fairy tales of seventeenth-century France could simultaneously appeal to both the child and the adult in the spectator or reader. In appealing to adults' love of fashion accessories or children's love of toys, d'Aulnoy reveals the important role of objects as an inspiration for invention and reminds us of the vital relation in her own work between the realm of the imagination and the real world of things.

Despite Mme de Murat's general emulation of the tales of Mme d'Aulnoy,[19] one element that she seems to eschew is d'Aulnoy's interest in children and their toys. When babies appear in Murat's tales they usually take the form of cupids: the little god himself appears as a character in "Jeune et belle"; in "Anguillette," drawn, painted, and sculpted cupids abound in the story's decorative scheme. Nevertheless, these babyish cupids have little to do with the real world of childhood and are present instead as emblems of adult love; even when children figure in Murat's tales, their childhoods are elided to arrive as soon as possible at the start of adult adventures. The only games mentioned in Murat are different forms of gambling, an adult amusement included along with "fêtes, divertissements, repas somptueux, bals, opéras, comédies, et appartements" (parties, entertainments, sumptuous meals, balls, operas, plays, and other gatherings) as one of many forms of aristocratic leisure.[20] Play in Murat is not for children; in her tales, aristocratic adults often enjoy gambling (lansquenet, basset, and brelan) as part of an evening's entertainment. In her final published tale, "Le turbot," Murat celebrates the beauty of an elegant game room where tokens made of rubies, emeralds, and topazes sparkle in the light of jewel-encrusted chandeliers (315), but she nevertheless goes on to condemn gambling, calling the game of basset "[le] jeu le plus détestable de tous les jeux et qui serait capable d'épuiser les trésors de toutes les fées du monde" (the most detestable of all games, as it could exhaust the treasures of all of the fairies in the world; 345). In fact, at the end of "Le turbot," the ironically named Fortuné's gambling proves ruinous, as this prince loses all of his money at cards, causing the disappearance of his fortune and of the fairy palace. Although this tale was written and published before Murat's gambling had led to her own financial ruin,[21] it shows the dark side of this glittering pastime. While Raymonde Robert sees the late-seventeenth-century fairy tale as an uncritical celebration of aristocratic leisure,[22] a view substantiated by d'Aulnoy's celebration of play, Murat's "Le turbot" condemns a major aristocratic amusement and indicates a marked skepticism toward play in her work.[23]

Along with her criticism of gambling, Mme de Murat extends her disapproval of play to her condemnation of tricksters, charlatans, and all types of fairground entertainers. In this she exemplifies Lorraine Daston and Katharine Park's characterization of those critics of wonder who see it as "disreputable . . . redolent of the popular, the amateurish, and the childish."[24] Yet Murat disdains these acrobats, dancers, and clowns not only because of the popular tinge to their art performed in the street or at the fair but also for their interest in turning a profit from their talent. She begins by bemoaning the attraction of the elite to the vulgar in "L'île de la magnificence," when a prince falls in love with the daughter of the king of the Fariboles, a people that Murat describes as

> de sottes gens [qui] ne s'amusent qu'à faire de méchants vers et des chansons pour chanter au coin des rues. Leurs discours ne sont remplis que de proverbes, de dictons, de quolibets, de plaisanteries fades et peu divertissantes. Il y en a qui courent le monde et deviennent danseurs de cordes, joueurs de marionnettes, [des] Tabarin . . . Arlequin . . . Scaramouche . . . Léance . . . Colombine.

> foolish people [who] amuse themselves by composing bad poetry and songs to sing on street corners. They speak in proverbs, sayings, taunts, and dull jokes that are not at all entertaining. Some travel the world and become tightrope walkers, puppeteers, Tabarins . . . , Harlequins . . . , Scaramouches . . . , Leances . . . or Columbines. (237–38)

The same types of spectacles that d'Aulnoy's characters admire are here denigrated as bad, dull, and not at all entertaining. Furetière's *Dictionnaire universel* confirms this negative definition of *fariboles* as "choses vaines qui ne méritent aucune considération" (vain things unworthy of any consideration).[25] Murat not only condemns fairground entertainment for its lack of artistic refinement but also attacks these entertainers for using their art as a means to make money: "Et par ce moyen ils s'enrichissent car ils sont tous gueux dans leur pays." (And in this way they get rich, since they are all beggars in their own country; 238.) Murat's condemnation of tricksters continues in "L'île de la magnificence," when the hero finds himself in a city filled with charlatans producing potions of dubious effectiveness, and in "Le roi porc," where Princess Ondine is sold by her father to King Pactole in exchange for alchemical secrets. In each case, art and science are identified as duplicity and degraded by the practitioner's desire for profit.[26]

Murat's scorn for trickery is most developed in her story "Le père et ses quatre fils," in which four princes leave their father's kingdom and return as tricksters, so debased by their adventures that the princess prefers to marry a fisherman. Prince Harangan has become a "nécromancien," a master of magical deceptions. Princes Tirandor and Facinety have also become street performers: the first can impress crowds with feats of marksmanship, and the second has become an "escamoteur" or "joueur de gobelets" (trickster or card sharp) who uses his sleight of hand to cheat anyone willing to play his game. The last son, Artidas, has become an inventor of "des jeux et des machines" (toys and machines), including ingenious objects such as "boîtes à double fond pour mettre des portraits" (boxes with double bottoms in which to hide portraits; 367) in which a married woman may place her husband's image but also to hide her lover's underneath. Artidas acknowledges the shame that should be felt by a prince who has become a craftsman, begging his royal father's forgiveness by admitting: "C'est à moi de vous demander mille pardons: je suis devenu artisan sans aucun respect pour ma naissance" (I am the one who must beg your forgiveness: I became an artisan without considering the rank into which I was born; 357). In her evocation of the *fariboles* and of the fisherman's four sons, Murat characterizes performers not as artists to be admired for their power to amaze and delight but instead as beggars and cheats, motivated by an ignoble desire for economic gain. However, as a noblewoman who is also a gambler and an artist, Murat's condemnation of play is problematic, for she is herself a composer of *fariboles*, a word whose first definition according to Furetière is "contes."[27] Yet if Murat's talent for *fariboles* allows us to identify her with the degraded figure of the fairground entertainer, Artidas's apology provides a possible alibi for her artistic practice: "Mais si la perfection diminue ma faute, vous m'en accorderez sans doute le pardon." (But if the perfection of my art diminishes my crime, then I hope that you will pardon me; 357.) The artisan is ennobled by the perfection of his or her finished work.[28]

Murat's ambivalence toward playfulness is most evident in her treatment of one of d'Aulnoy's favored toys: the doll. In Murat's "Le turbot," a baby's pink and white cheeks, his permanent smile, and his "grands yeux bleus où la gaité était peinte" (big blue eyes in which gaiety was painted; 306) resemble those of d'Aulnoy's doll-like infants. In Murat's "L'île de la magnificence," a young girl is described as if she were a doll: "une petite personne dont la taille est faite au tour" (a little person whose waist was perfectly turned), her body shaped as would be a well-turned wooden table leg. The features of her perfect pink and white face seem to be painted on: her brows are "noirs comme de l'ébène, et il semble qu'ils soient faits au pinceau" (black as ebony and seemed to be painted on with a brush; 239). But while d'Aulnoy's tales often feature gaily animated dancing dolls,

Murat's descriptions of people as dolls betray an uneasiness with the treatment of the child as an object or, more specifically, of the child bride as living doll, especially when princesses are used as pawns in the political gambit of dynastic intermarriage.[29] In "Le sauvage," Murat does appear to be celebrating the arranged marriage of Louis XIV's grandson when she relates the fairies' arrival "à Versailles justement la veille du mariage de Madame la princesse de Savoie" (at Versailles on the very eve of the wedding of the Princess of Savoy; 294). In this fairy tale, Murat's characters attend the wedding reception, eat fruits and jellies, admire the wedding gift display, see the opera *Issé*, and even jostle the king as they pass through a crowded doorway (294–95). Calling this royal wedding "le plus grand événement de nos jours" (the greatest event of our time; 293), Murat characterizes it as the advent of a new generation that gave the aging court at Versailles a second chance at childhood, for Marie-Adélaïde de Savoie was not just a sort of adopted grandchild but a plaything for the elderly Louis XIV and Mme de Maintenon. Much like the porcelain dolls that the princess in d'Aulnoy's "Serpentin vert" stuffs into her pockets, Marie Adélaïde was treated like a living doll, as Louis de Rouvroy de Saint-Simon writes in his memoirs: "le roi menait la princesse qui semblait sortir de sa poche" (the king led the princess who seemed to poke out from his pocket)" and "le roi et Mme de Maintenon firent leur poupée de la princesse" (the king and Mme de Maintenon made the princess into their doll).[30] In paintings of her wedding to the Duc de Bourgogne, the twelve-year-old and her groom are represented as doll-like figures, less than half the size of adult courtiers; moreover, as a young bride, Marie-Adélaïde would later be featured as a model for Parisian fashion illustrations, almost like a living *poupée de mode*.

Although Robert sees allusions to Marie-Adélaïde and the Duc de Bourgogne in various fairy tales as just another piece of evidence supporting her view of the genre as a celebration of court society in general,[31] a closer look at the cultural production that accompanied Marie-Adélaïde's arrival at Versailles shows her as the inspiration for the creation of art forms meant to amuse a child, including fairy tales. In *La duchesse de Bourgogne, enfant terrible de Versailles*, Fabrice Préyat introduces a collection of essays that analyze Marie-Adélaïde's effect on court culture. Préyat alludes to Marie-Adélaïde's interest in fairy tales when he notes that she reputedly applauded Florent Carton Dancourt's play *Les fées* and was the recipient of Antoine Galland's translation of *Les mille et une nuits*. But the most striking example of the creation of art to address the taste of a child is documented in Joan Pieragnoli's essay "La duchesse de Bourgogne et la Ménagerie de Versailles." Pieragnoli cites Louis XIV's letter to Jules Hardouin-Mansart—whom the king charges with the task of decorating an apartment for the Duchesse de Bourgogne inside the royal zoo—and characterizes Louis's orders to his architect as a demand for aesthetic rejuvenation inspired by the young Marie-Adélaïde's presence at Versailles. The king writes of the architect's initial project, "Il me paraît qu'il y a quelque chose à changer; que les sujets sont trop sérieux et qu'il faut qu'il y ait de la jeunesse mêlée dans tout ce que l'on fera. Vous m'en apporterez des dessins quand vous viendrez, ou du moins des pensées; il faut de l'enfance répandue partout." (It seems to me that something should be changed; the subjects are too serious and there must be more youthfulness in all that will be done. You must bring me plans when you come or at least thoughts; there must be childhood everywhere.)[32] As a result, one room is decorated with motifs from the *Fables* of Jean de La Fontaine, while another is known as "la chambre des amusements de la jeunesse où sont représentés quatre-vingt jeux d'enfants . . . l'escarpolette, ou encore la pêche" (the room of children's games where eighty-five different children's games are represented, . . . including swinging and fishing).[33] Much like the blankets embroidered with "mille jeux différents auxquels les enfants s'amusent" (a thousand different games at which children play; 92) given to the baby prince in d'Aulnoy's "La biche au bois," the young Marie-Adélaïde is surrounded by motifs of childhood in an apartment placed at the center of a zoo filled with exotic birds and animals that she can observe from her window. In this context, d'Aulnoy's tales—filled with peacocks, monkeys, toy carriages, and marionettes—are part of a broader production of art made to amuse a very young princess.[34]

If court culture at this time seems to celebrate childhood, some fairy tales do question the treatment of children at Versailles. Much as Madeleine de Scudéry depicts the king at court as a bird in a gilded cage,[35] young bride Marie-Adélaïde is a beautiful creature kept caged in the royal menagerie, a prisoner of her arranged marriage. With some of her heroines (e.g., Finette and Printanière), Mme d'Aulnoy alludes to the practice of marrying girls so young that they still play with dolls, but it is Mme de Murat who more clearly questions the treatment of child brides.[36] Psychocritical readings interpret Perrault's "Petit chaperon rouge" or Jeanne-Marie Leprince de Beaumont's "La belle et la bête," as well as several of d'Aulnoy's tales in which women are forced to marry animals,[37] as allegorized explorations of the young girl's anxiety about the prospect of her future husband's sexual appetites. While in "Le sauvage" (where the savage in question reassuringly regains his human form before marrying a princess) Murat does not explicitly criticize the marriage of Marie-Adélaïde, a doll-like girl still young enough to sleep in a bedroom decorated with scenes of children's games,[38] she paints a troubling picture of the wedding of young Princess Risette in "Le turbot." Murat's last tale directly describes the uncomfortable spectacle of a young girl's sudden sexualization on her wedding day: "Vous étiez rouge comme du feu, vous baissiez les yeux. . . . [M]ais vous ne voyiez que des gens qui avaient envie de rire, ce qui redoublait votre embarras. . . . [V]otre père vous dit d'un ton absolu: 'Princesse, finissez ces façons.'" (You were blushing a fiery red, you were lowering your eyes. . . . But you saw that everyone was laughing at you, which only doubled your embarrassment. . . . Your father declared in the firmest of tones: "Princess, stop your fussing"; 338.) As her father commands her submission to his will and to the desires of her new husband, the assembled wedding guests laugh knowingly at the innocent virgin's apprehension.

In "Le turbot," Murat makes it clear that the unwilling bride is still very much a child, with this tale illustrating a very problematic perversion of play. In order to trick the young girl into marrying an unknown man, a fairy has appealed to Risette's childish taste, luring her inside a garden pavilion (reminiscent of the menagerie apartment made for the Duchesse de Bourgogne) and then into a room designed to please a child, "tapissée que de grandes estampes enluminées représentant des singes, des figures de Callot et des marionnettes" (wallpapered with colored prints representing monkeys, puppets, and figures by [Jacques] Callot; 336). In this gaily decorated room, Risette is entertained by trained mice and rats "qui faisaient mille plaisantes postures" (who were doing a thousand funny things) as well as dwarves dressed like clowns, "s'escrimant avec des roseaux et faisant des postures grotesques" (fencing with reeds in various grotesque postures; 337). The girl is soon escorted into another room, where she is forcibly married to a stranger and then returns to the playfully decorated room to find that the figures in the paintings have come alive to dance with her: "Nous vîmes que les figures callotines, les singes, et les marionettes des estampes avaient quitté leurs places, et faisaient un bal au son de plusieurs instruments ridicules qui faisaient un charivari fort plaisant." (We saw that the figures by Callot, the monkeys and the puppets had all left their places and were dancing to the music of several ridiculous instruments which were making quite a funny racket; 339.) And yet amid all this gaiety—"la gouvernante et les deux femmes de chambre riaient à pâmer" (the governess and the two chamber maids were doubled over with laughter)—Risette, despite her name, is the only one not laughing. She is put to bed with the prince and awakens to find that the "ridicule demeure des songes" (ridiculous house of dreams; 340) has disappeared and that she is pregnant and alone. Murat's depiction of the forced marriage of a girl young enough to be fascinated by puppets and trained mice portrays wedding festivities as a dazzling distraction from an otherwise nightmarish wedding night.[39] While d'Aulnoy invites her readers to marvel at the beauty of well-made toys, Murat cautions against the abuse of childish pastimes and the exploitation of innocence.

If the fairy tale vogue of the late 1690s may be read as a response to changes in court culture, the image of court society in the tales of d'Aulnoy and Murat is not merely a flattering reflection of luxurious leisure. In admiring the beauty of well-made toys, d'Aulnoy highlights not only the good taste of their consumers but also the skill of their producers, acknowledging the essential contribution of artisans to the *art de vivre* of Old Regime aristocracy. In criticizing both aristocratic and popular forms of entertainment, Mme de Murat objects to the contamination of play by money; likewise, in her portrayal of the doll-like child bride, she condemns the perversion of childhood by economic and political forces, as well as by the forced sexualization that made children into women before their time. In the end, the reader of these fairy tales is not invited to marvel in childish wonder at the magic of fairies but to recognize as a sophisticated connoisseur the work of artists or to judge as a disillusioned cynic the dark side of life at the Sun King's court.

NOTES

Unless noted otherwise, all translations are my own.

1. Charles Perrault, preface to *Histoire ou contes du temps passé*, in *Contes*, ed. Catherine Magnien (Paris: Le livre de poche, 2006), 177.

2. This recognition is especially due to Raymonde Robert's groundbreaking book, *Le conte de fées littéraire en France* (Paris: Honoré Champion, 2002).

3. Raymonde Robert, "L'infantilisation du conte merveilleux au XVIIe siècle," *Littératures classiques* 14 (1991): 33–46, argues that d'Aulnoy herself is in large part responsible for the infantilization of the tale with her use of childish expressions such as *pipi* and *dodo*.

4. Marie-Catherine d'Aulnoy, "La Princesse Printanière," in *Contes des fées, suivis des contes nouveaux, ou Les fées à la mode*, ed. Nadine Jasmin (Paris: Honoré Champion, 2004), 274; hereafter, page numbers from this collection will be cited parenthetically in the text.

5. Antoine Furetière, "Jouet," in *Dictionnaire universel* defines *jouet* as "petit bigeou avec lequel on amuse, on fait jouer les enfants" (a little entertaining bijou with which children play). Antoine Furetière, *Dictionnaire universel, contenant généralement tous les mots français tant vieux que modernes, et les termes de toutes les sciences et des arts*, vol. 2 (The Hague: Leers, 1690). Michel Manson "Madame d'Aulnoy, les contes et le jouet," in *Tricentenaire Charles Perrault: Les grands contes du XVIIe siècle et leur fortune littéraire*, ed. Jean Perrot (Paris: Éditions In Press, 1998), 143–156), provides a complete catalog of the references to toys in d'Aulnoy's *Contes de fées*, as well as useful definitions of *joujou, marionnette*, and *babiole*. Overall, Manson responds to Robert's 1991 article about the infantilization of the tale, arguing that d'Aulnoy's stories can be about children without being childish.

6. Christine Jones, *Shapely Bodies: The Image of Porcelain in Eighteenth-Century France* (Newark: University of Delaware Press, 2013), attests to the European fascination with the pagoda at Nanjing and cites it as an inspiration for Versailles' Trianon de Porcelaine as well as for the collecting of small porcelain figurines in an Oriental style.

7. Lorraine Daston and Katharine Park, *Wonders and the Order of Nature* (Cambridge, MA: Zone Books, 1998), 19, see cities and courts as sites for a specific kind of wonder that the authors characterize as "elaborate exercises in taste and connoisseurship."

8. Manson, "Madame d'Aulnoy," 144.

9. Joan DeJean, *The Essence of Style: How the French Invented High Fashion, Fine Food, Chic Cafés, Style, Sophistication, and Glamour* (New York: Free Press, 2005), 64.

10. Just as we marvel at the embroiderers' skill in sewing motifs drawn from children's games, we acknowledge d'Aulnoy's art in transforming nursery stories into beautifully made fairy tales. Patricia Hannon, *Fabulous Identities: Women's Fairy Tales in Seventeenth-Century France* (Amsterdam: Rodopi, 1998), 150, notes this and other instances of embroidery in fairy tales as examples of the use of *mise en abîme* in writing.

11. See Yvan Loskoutoff, *La sainte et la fée: Dévotion à l'enfant Jésus et mode des contes merveilleux à la fin du règne de Louis XIV* (Geneva: Droz, 1987).

12. Manson, "Madame d'Aulnoy," 146, affirms that the toys in the tales were likely made by craftsmen who made both regular-size and miniature objects, tools, and jewels, as well as toys. In reference to the silver tea set, Manson argues that "les bimbelotiers et les orfèvres parisiens étaient tout à fait en mesure de fabriquer ces objets" (Parisian craftsmen and goldsmiths certainly had the skills to make these objects).

13. See Alfred Gell, "The Technology of Enchantment and the Enchantment of Technology," in *Anthropology, Art and Aesthetics*, ed. Jeremy Coote and Anthony Shelton (Oxford: Clarendon, 1992), 40–63.

14. While Manson's analysis of play in "Madame d'Aulnoy" posits an identification between character and reader, my reading advances an association of character and author.

15. Antoine Furetière, "Marionette," in *Dictionnaire universel*, cited in Manson, "Madame d'Aulnoy," 148.

16. Even the tale's evil fairy is named Fanfreluche, a term that, according to Furetière, designates a decorative embellishment on a garment. Antoine Furetière, "Fanfreluche," in *Dictionnaire universel*, cited in d'Aulnoy, *Contes des fées*, 507n1.

17. Perrault, preface to "Peau d'âne," in *Contes*, 133. In fact, marionettes were a source of philosophical reflection in the eighteenth century, following René Descartes's notion of the *corps machine*. Diderot will see the actor as the poet's puppet in his *Paradoxe sur le comédien*; Mme du Châtelet's *Discours sur le bonheur* will express her pleasure in watching the puppet play without looking at the strings, and Jean-Jacques Rousseau in *Émile, ou De l'éducation* will teach his pupil a lesson by explaining to him the manipulation of the puppet by the puppeteer.

18. Sarah Kareem, *Eighteenth-Century Fiction and the Reinvention of Wonder* (Oxford: Oxford University Press, 2014), 9.

19. Charlotte Trinquet, *Le conte de fées français (1690–1700): Traditions italiennes et origines aristocratiques* (Tübingen, Germany: Narr Verlag, 2012), chap. 6, demonstrates that d'Aulnoy and Murat were inspired by the same Italian sources and often wrote alternate versions of the same stories.

20. Henriette-Julie de Murat, "L'île de la magnificence," in *Contes*, ed. Geneviève Patard (Paris: Honoré Champion, 2006), 225; hereafter, page numbers from this collection will be cited parenthetically in the text. Since the happy inhabitants of Murat's "L'île de la magnificence" have no use for money—all of their desires are satisfied by magic—gambling in the tale is not a means of material gain; instead it allows a demonstration of the aristocratic ideal of disinterest. As the narrator explains, "[L'o]r monnayé ne servait qu'au jeu" (Gold coins were only used as tokens in games; Henriette-Julie de Murat, "L'île de la magnificence," in *Contes*, 232).

21. In a brief biographical sketch of Mme de Murat, prisoner of the Château de Loches, Alfred Boulay de la Meurthe notes her enjoyment of "jeux sévèrement défendus" (strictly forbidden games), including basset, and intimates that gambling was the cause of her financial ruin, "sa gêne et de ses dettes" (her difficulties and debts). See Alfred Boulay de la Meurthe, *Les prisonniers du roi à Loches sous Louis XIV* (Tours, France: J. Allard, 1911), 76.

22. Robert, *Le conte de fées littéraire*, 349, 350, calls the tales of the 1690s a "miroir de leur temps" (mirror of their time) that "renv[oit] aux lecteurs gratifiés une image d'eux-mêmes" (reflects back a gratifying image to their readers) "l'affirmation d'une conception de la vie dans laquelle le luxe et la richesse prennent une valeur absolue et ne servent plus qu'à designer l'élite" (the affirmation of a concept of life where luxury and wealth have an absolute value by which their only purpose is to designate their possessors as an elite).

23. A later tale by Mme d'Auneuil, "L'origine du lansquenet" (1703)—in which an envious fairy corrupts the court of a virtuous queen by introducing the fashion for gambling, causing the ruin of the queen's beauty through exhausting hours spent at the tables—mirrors Murat's warning against gambling's dangers. See Mme d'Auneuil, "L'origine du lansquenet," in *Contes: Mademoiselle Lhéritier, Mademoiselle Bernard, Mademoiselle de la Force, Madame Durand, Madame d'Auneuil*, ed. Raymonde Robert (Paris: Honoré Champion, 2005), 739–43.

24. Daston and Park, *Wonders and the Order of Nature*, 15.

25. Antoine Furetière, "Marionette," in *Dictionnaire universel*, quoted in Murat, *Contes de fée*, 236n2.

26. As Roger Caillois, *Man, Play and Games*, trans. Meyer Barash (New York: Schocken Books, 1979), 45, explains, play is corrupted when the players are "professional" or "cheats."

27. Antoine Furetière, "Fariboles," in *Dictionnaire universel, contenant généralement tous les mots français tant vieux que modernes, et les termes de toutes les sciences et des arts*, vol. 2 (The Hague: Leers, 1701).

28. In Jones, *Shapely Bodies*, the artisan is the hero of the story. Jones even reads the eighteenth-century fairy tale "Prince Périnet ou L'origine des pagodes" as the triumph of French ingenuity over Chinese secrets (186).

29. Like d'Aulnoy, Murat was a young bride unhappily married off by her family.

30. Louis de Rouvroy de Saint-Simon, *Mémoires du duc de Saint-Simon*, ed. Adolphe Chéruel and Adolphe Régnier, vol. 1 (Paris: Hachette, 1873), 374–75. In "Le sauvage," Murat refers to the heroine's three ugly sisters as "magottes," a type of porcelain figurine; their marriage to three misshapen suitors, including one named Magotin, can again be read as a doll wedding.

31. Raymonde Robert, "La duchesse de Bourgogne en féerie: Les contes de fées et le pouvoir au XVIIe siècle," in *Marie-Adélaïde de Savoie (1685–1712), duchesse de Bourgogne, enfant terrible de Versailles*, ed. Fabrice Préyat (Brussels: Éditions de l'Université de Bruxelles, 2014), 93–106.

32. J[oan] Pieragnoli, "La duchesse de Bourgogne et la Ménagerie de Versailles" in Préyat, ed., *Marie-Adélaïde de Savoie*, 156.

33. Pieragnoli, "La duchesse de Bourgogne," 157.

34. Jérôme de La Gorce, *Dans l'atelier des menus plaisirs du roi* (Paris: Archives nationales, 2010), 51, notes that the stage designer Gaspare Vigarini made a marionette theater to entertain Marie-Adélaïde during her pregnancy.

35. Madeleine de Scudery, quoted in Joan DeJean, *Tender Geographies: Women and the Origins of the Novel in France* (New York: Columbia University Press, 1991), 46.

36. That said, Manson, "Madame d'Aulnoy," 145, notes that d'Aulnoy often situates the action of her tales at a psychosexual juncture between childhood innocence and adult sexuality as in "La Princesse Rosette," where the heroine leaves "ses belles poupées à ses bonnes amies" (her pretty dolls and good friends) in order to go meet her husband.

37. In Murat's version of this story, "Le roi porc," the bride is saved from sleeping with a pig when her servant replaces her with a "grande poupée de carton" (a large papier-mâché doll; 205). Ironically, here a doll saves the young bride from forced passage into sexual maturity.

38. Saint-Simon, *Mémoires du duc de Saint-Simon*, 1:487–88, does note that Louis XIV was adamant about protecting the duchess's innocence and prevented the couple from consummating their marriage,.

39. Here again is an example of play corrupted, according to the theory in Caillois, *Man, Play and Games*, 135: "everyone knows that the phantasmagoria is make-believe . . . an illusion . . . that has been agreed to." In "Le turbot," Murat clearly identifies nonconsensual play as abuse.

CHAPTER 2

The Morality of Bilboquet, or the Equivocations of Language

Jean-Alexandre Perras

Recalling the charms of the ideal society he knew in Chambéry in the company of Mme de Warens and her lover Claude Anet, Jean-Jacques Rousseau underlines how the trio's constant activity helped create what he calls "une société sans autre exemple peut-être sur la terre" (a society without another example perhaps on the earth). By contrast, he attributes to idleness many of the ills that plague social gatherings:

> Selon moi, le désœuvrement n'est pas moins le fléau de la société que celui de la solitude. Rien ne rétrécit plus l'esprit, rien n'engendre plus de riens, de rapports, de paquets, de tracasseries, de mensonges, que d'être éternellement renfermés vis-à-vis les uns des autres dans une chambre, réduits pour tout ouvrage à la nécessité de babiller continuellement. Quand tout le monde est occupé, l'on ne parle que quand on a quelque chose à dire; mais quand on ne fait rien, il faut absolument parler toujours, et voilà de toutes les gênes la plus incommode et la plus dangereuse.

> In my view, lack of occupation is no less the scourge of society than of solitude. Nothing narrows the mind more, nothing engenders more trifles, malicious tales, sly tricks, teasing, lies, than being eternally shut up face to face with one another in a room, reduced to the necessity of continually babbling as one's only occupation. When everyone is occupied, one speaks only when one has something to say, but when one is doing nothing it is absolutely necessary to speak all the time, and that is the most inconvenient and dangerous of all bothers.[1]

If one must always have something to do, this is, first, to keep those who do not from speaking; for idle conversations, the nothingness of words in themselves soon gives rise to deceptions, annoyances, and barbs. To prevent these obstacles, Rousseau proposes a remedy that is at once surprising and paradoxical:

> Quand j'étais à Môtiers, j'allais faire des lacets chez mes voisines; si je retournais dans le monde, j'aurais toujours dans ma poche un bilboquet, et j'en jouerais toute la journée pour me dispenser de parler quand je n'aurais rien à dire. Si chacun en faisait autant, les hommes deviendraient moins méchants, leur commerce deviendrait plus sûr, et, je pense, plus agréable. Enfin, que les plaisants rient, s'ils veulent, mais je soutiens que la seule morale à la portée du présent siècle est la morale du bilboquet.

> When I was at Môtiers I went to make laces at my neighbors' houses; if I returned into the world, I would always have a cup-and-ball [bilboquet] in my pocket, and I would play with it all day long to de dispensed from speaking when I had nothing to say. If everyone did as much men would become less wicked, their dealings would become more reliable and, I think, more agreeable. In sum, let the jokers laugh if they wish, but I maintain that the only morality within the reach of the present age is the morality of the cup-and-ball.[2]

Rousseau's personal situation—in exile in Môtiers after being driven out of Bern and Geneva, where his works were burned—was particularly difficult, and the posture he adopted was that of a persecuted philosopher who remained silent while playing with a cup and ball and making laces.[3] As attested to in letters from 1762 and 1765, these two occupations were widely publicized to various correspondents in order to embody his new ethos.[4] Magnificent in his exile, and insensitive to quarrels, Rousseau makes laces, collects plants, and flips a cup and ball all day long. No longer writing or reading, he chooses to keep his hands busy and fend off boredom with pastimes that could readily be described as frivolous.

Indeed, in *Émile, ou De l'éducation*, Rousseau advocates for using games in the education of young children.[5] The use of the cup and ball in polite conversation, however, raises issues other than those of childhood: too frivolous to be reformed, the society Rousseau evokes has no longer the innocent malleability of childhood, but all the vices of decadence. Coming from a reformer condemned to exile, the "morality" of the cup and ball presents itself as an accusation addressed to a whole century given to idle talk, and which has often made this game the object of its passion.

What does the cup and ball stand for? Why is it better to say nothing than nothings? If we pay attention to the story staged by Rousseau, the cup and ball seems to have a supplementary function, the stakes of which will be explored in this chapter.[6] Beyond Rousseau, who takes up commonplaces long rooted in the culture of the ancien régime, the cup and ball is also associated with equivocations and wordplay, whose meanings are sometimes judged less important than the pleasant surprise they occasion. Combining skills of both body and mind, the game of cup and ball, like wordplay, belongs to French nobiliary culture, and particularly to a declining culture of gaiety performing its swan song at the end of the eighteenth century.[7] At the same time, the cup and ball is the pretext for narrative and stylistic innovations, which doubtless belong to a certain "modernity" but which above all evince a claim to a kind of "minor writing."[8]

THE ORIGINS OF BILBOQUET

One may recall how, after studying and eating, François Rabelais's young Gargantua would play games, not without having first washed his hands with fresh wine, picked his teeth with a pig's foot, and joyfully chatted with his attendants. In the Rabelaisian *paideia*, bodily care is associated with that of the mind, and play figures prominently in a young man's education. Following the pleasures of the table, games and recreation are linked to lively conversation. Of the many games played by the giant, there is one that has had a singular fortune, whose fickleness reflects its practice: the bilboquet (or *bille boucquet*, as Rabelais writes)—the cup and ball.[9] According to the *Dictionnaire historique de la langue française*, Rabelais's famous list provides the first occurrence of the game in the French language.[10]

The bilboquet, according to the *Dictionnaire de Trévoux*, is a "petit instrument fait d'un bâton creusé en rond par les deux bouts; au milieu duquel est une corde où une balle de plomb est attachée" (small instrument made from a stick hollowed out at both ends; in the middle of which is a string with a lead ball attached). This ball is thrown into the air and taken "alternativement dans ces deux creux" (alternately in these two hollows). Although it comes in other forms (one end of the cup and ball may be a spike on which one attempts to catch a slotted ball), the principle of the game stays the same, requiring much skill and agility. The word *bilboquet* refers also to "Une petite figure qui a deux plombs aux deux jambes, et qui est posée de manière que de quelque façon qu'on la tourne, elle se trouve toujours debout. C'est de là qu'on dit d'un homme qui se tient toujours debout, qu'il se tient droit comme un bilboquet; et d'un homme, dont les affaires demeurent toujours en bon état, quelques traverses qu'on lui suscite, qu'il se trouve toujours sur ses pieds comme un bilboquet. On dit familièrement d'un homme léger et frivole, que c'est un vrai bilboquet." (A small human figure with lead weights on both legs, and that is placed so that, whichever way it is turned, it always remains upright. This is why one says of a man who is always standing that he stands up like a bilboquet; and of a man whose business is always in good order, regardless of whatever misfortunes he may suffer, that he is always on his feet like a bilboquet. It is colloquially said of a silly and frivolous man, that he is a real bilboquet).[11] As the *Manuel de l'imprimeur* explains, "On appelle bilboquet ces petits ouvrages de rien, tels que sont les cartes, les affiches sur un carré, les billets de mariage, de mort, bout-de-l'an, et autres, parce qu'ils demandent peu de temps et peu de soin à composer. Ces petits bilboquets sont ordinairement d'un bon bénéfice au maître imprimeur. Ils se font en conscience." (We call bilboquet these small insignificant productions, such as cards, posters, wedding, death and other announcements, because they require little time and care to compose. These small bilboquets are usually of good benefit to the master printer. They are made in conscience.)[12]

After bilboquets entertained Henry III in the midst of the Catholic-Protestant conflict,[13] the fashion for them resurfaced at the beginning of the eighteenth century—just before the death of Louis XIV, if we are to believe the sudden proliferation of brochures, songs, and poems attesting to the enthusiasm generated by this small device—for instance, this "Chanson nouvelle, sur l'air, du Bilboquet":

> Maman je meurs d'envie
> De jouer avec Colinet
> Au jeu du Bilboquet,
> Ha! l'aimable folie:
> Six fois de suite il y met,
> Et quand la partie
> Lui parait jolie
> Il met jusqu'à sept.
>
> Quoi donc petite follette,
> Vous voulez jouer à ce jeu,
> Il est trop dangereux,
> Vous êtes trop jeunette:
> S'il vous faut de l'amusement,
> Jouez-y seulette,
> Comme une nonette,
> Fait dans son couvent.
>
> Quoique maman me conseille,
> Avec moi Colinet jouera
> A ce joli jeu-là,
> Il y joue à merveille:
> Toute seule je me déplais,
> Car la main me lasse,
> Et quoique je fasse,
> Jamais je n'y mets.

Ha Colinet qu'est-ce à dire,
Est-ce ainsi qu'on joue à ce jeu,
De grâce arrête un peu,
Je pleure au lieu de rire:
Tu as brisé mon Bilboquet,
La corde est rompue,
La balle est perdue,
Helas! qu'as-tu fait?

Quoi pour une balle égarée,
Iris je vous en offre deux,
Recommençons un peu
Ne soyez point fâchée,
Rajustons notre Bilboquet,
Et prenez, la belle,
Au lieu d'une ficelle,
Un bout de lacet.

Mommy, I am dying
To join with Colinet
In the game of Bilboquet,
Ha! Sweet folly:
Six times in a row he puts it there,
And when the game
To him seems fair
He goes up to seven.

What, then, crazy little girl,
You wish to play this game?
It is too dangerous,
You are far too young:
If you need some pleasure,
Play it on your own,
As a little nun,
Does in her convent.

Whatever Mommy may say,
Colinet with me will play
This fine game.
He plays it wonderfully:
All alone I feel unhappy,
Because my hand tires,
And whatever I do,
I never get it.

THE MORALITY OF BILBOQUET

Ha, Colinet what is this,
Is that how one plays this game,
For pity's sake, take a break,
I am crying instead of laughing:
You broke my Bilboquet,
The string is severed,
The ball is lost,
Alas! What have you done?

What, for a lost ball,
Iris, I offer you two,
Let us start over again
Do not be angry,
Let us fix our Bilboquet,
And use, my dear,
Instead of a string,
A piece of your lace.[14]

The erotic allusions in this song, depicting a tension between Iris's childish innocence and Colinet's virile prowess, are easily recognizable—notably, in the
motif of lost virginity, repaired here thanks to a lace (yet another one) taken,
perhaps, one might imagine, from the eyelets of a bodice. This song is, moreover, not the only one to highlight the erotic potential of the bilboquet (see fig. 2.1).
We have only to turn the page of this collection of songs to discover the "Chanson nouvelle du Bilboquet, sur l'air: Vous m'entendez bien," which begins,

Du jeu nouveau du Bilboquet
Je connais fort bien le secret,
De dix fois belle brune, hé bien,
Je n'en manque pas une,
Vous m'entendez bien.

Of the new game Bilboquet,
I know very well the secret,
Of ten games played, beautiful brunette, well,
I miss not one,
You understand me well.[15]

At the height of the cup-and-ball craze in 1714, a sixteen-page anonymous brochure titled *De l'antiquité et de l'usage du bilboquet* was published, as well as an
allegorical tale by Marivaux, *Le bilboquet*.[16] Like so many other eighteenth-
century narratives that abound in facetious stories featuring the invention of
the innumerable follies embraced by a public in love with novelty,[17] both of these
texts evoke the origin of the bilboquet. Although different in style, both tales

Figure 2.1. "Air sérieux de M. R. Marais," in *Recueil d'airs sérieux et à boire* (Paris: Ballard, 1713), 159. © Bibliothèque nationale de France.

insist more or less explicitly on the relation of the cup and ball with sexual matters.

In Marivaux's brochure, the game of bilboquet appears first as an obstacle to love.[18] This allegorical tale is told to a friend by a lover who is frustrated that his mistress prefers to play bilboquet rather than spend time with him. The lover tells how Madness, Stupidity, and Ignorance, at war with Love, Spirit, and Reason, are plotting to dethrone their rivals—a plan that consists of bringing into the world the child of Madness and the god of Ridicule, a "petit monstre" (a little monster) named Bilboquet. One morning, Ridicule and Madness bring Bilboquet to the door of a rich and spiritual young man, Lysidor, whose servants pick up the child as he is making a "bruit épouvantable avec une espèce de machine de bois avec laquelle il se jouait" (terrible noise with a kind of wooden machine he [is] playing with). After this introduction, the story recounts the social ascent of the game of bilboquet, from servants to serious magistrates, and its disruption of Lysidor's love affair. Indeed, Lysidor's mistress, Lysie, is entirely absorbed in the pleasure of playing with her new toy. One scene exploits the undertones of erotic equivocation suggested by the shape and action of the bilboquet: Lysie rushes to show her friend Philis her bilboquet, but refuses to let her use it:

Lysie lui en parle comme un trésor de plaisir; ah ma chère, que j'en joue: donne, s'écrie Philis. Lysie ne peut se résoudre de lui confier si tôt cette machine, elle en veut auparavant jouer à ses yeux pour mettre son amie à un point d'impatience et d'ardeur digne du jeu charmant dont elle va lui faire part.

Lysie joue, Philis étouffe; la parole lui manque par la précipitation de parler: la présence de cette machine l'accable, et semblable à ces anciennes prêtresses, elle paraît agitée d'un mouvement convulsif, qui ne lui laisse que la liberté de bredouiller.

Lysie speaks of it as a delightful treasure: "Ah, my dear, let me play with it: give it to me," cries Philis. Lysie cannot yet resolve to hand over the machine to her; she first wants to play with it in front of her friend to bring her to a point of impatience and ardor worthy of the delightful game she is going to share.

As Lysie plays, Philis chokes; she is speechless in her haste to speak: the presence of the machine overwhelms her, and like the priestesses of antiquity, she seems shaken by a convulsive movement which leaves her only the freedom to stutter.[19]

As Sylvie Dervaux has clearly shown, however, this is only one of the registers deployed in the tale, whose multiple digressions and pastiches form a stylistic *mise en abîme* playing on the homonymy of the narrative and its object: the bilboquet—both the story and the device—is a child of Madness.[20]

Such is not the case with *De l'antiquité et de l'usage du bilboquet*, which hinges entirely on erotic ambiguity and, unlike Marivaux's tale, attributes "the excellence of bilboquets" to their antiquity:

Il est donc très constant que dès le temps de l'âge d'or on jouait à ce joli jeu, et il me souvient d'une vieille chronique en caractère gothique, dont je saurai montrer l'original aux incrédules, qui remonte bien avant dans ces temps délicieux où il est parlé de la *Bilboqueterie* comme d'une chose qui était alors très usitée parmi le monde. . . . On ne s'en cachait pas, on le faisait sur l'herbe, et tout à l'air, aussi le faisaient-ils sainement et leur faisait du bien; point de mère qui dépeignit à sa fille un *Bilboquet* comme un instrument du Diable et les *Bilboqueteurs* comme les suppôts de Satan, ô temps heureux! point de Vestales grillées, à qui sous peine du feu on interdisit le doux plaisir du *Bilboquet*; tout *Bilboquetait* sur la terre et sur l'onde à bouche que veux-tu et croyez que le premier âge du monde qui a été surnommé d'or, n'a été ainsi appelé ni pour les fleuves de lait et de miel qui coulaient par les prairies, ni pour les gâteaux et les petits pâtés, qui se trouvaient tout chauds sur le bord des grands chemins et aux branches des arbres, mais par ce que les hommes tous frais et dans leur printemps, pleins de vigueur, *Bilboquetaient* avec plus de délices, plus suavement et à coups bien plus réitérés qu'on n'a fait depuis, ô siècles ingrats, etc.

It is thus entirely certain that this lovely game was played as early as the golden age, and I am reminded of an old chronicle in Gothic characters, the original of which I can show to unbelievers, which goes back long before, in those delicious times when *Bilboqueterie* was spoken of as widely used throughout the world. . . . No one hid from it and it was done on the grass, in plain sight. So they did it healthily and it did them good. No mother portrayed a *Bilboquet* to her daughter as an instrument of the Devil and the *Bilboqueteurs* as Satan's accomplices. Oh happy times! No roasted Vestals, to whom the sweet pleasure of *Bilboquet* was forbidden under penalty of being burned. Everything on land and at sea was *Bilboqueting* to its heart's content. You must know that the first age of the world was called the golden age neither for the rivers of milk and honey that flowed through the meadows, nor for the cakes and pies which were found ready-made next to the roads and on the branches of the trees, but because men, all fresh in their youth and full of vigor, *Bilboqueted* with more delight, more gracefully and much more repeatedly than we have done since. Oh! ungrateful times, etc.[21]

The burlesque spirit of the narrative, which combines the codes of antiquarian erudition with those of bawdy Rabelaisian comedy, is maintained throughout the brochure's sixteen short pages, which can be read by replacing the word *Bilboquet*, written in italics throughout the text, with the word *foutre* or other similar terms. Due to its size and shape, the bilboquet invites such substitutions: "C'est assez parler de l'excellence des bilboquets, disons deux mots de la manière de s'en servir et sur leur taille." (That is enough about the excellence of bilboquets, let us say two words about how to use them and about their size.)[22] This is what was called in the previous century *envelopper les ordures* (wrapping filth),[23] a practice of which Pierre Bayle wrote, in 1696, "Quand on ne marque qu'à demi une obscénité, mais de telle sorte que le supplément n'est pas malaisé à faire, ceux à qui l'on parle achèvent eux-mêmes le portrait qui salit l'imagination. . . . Ainsi ces prétendus ménagements de la pudeur sont en effet un piège plus dangereux. Ils engagent à méditer sur une matière sale, afin de trouver le supplément de ce qui n'a pas été exprimé par des paroles précises." (When you only half state an obscenity, but in such a way that the supplement is not difficult to provide, those to whom one speaks complete the picture that soils their imagination. These so-called considerations of modesty are thus indeed a more dangerous trap. They oblige us to meditate on a filthy matter in order to find the supplement of what has not been expressed in precise words.)[24] The bilboquet thus *supplements* sexual matter, whether it is, as in Marivaux, a diversion from love, or, as in *De l'antiquité et de l'usage du bilboquet* and the various songs composed on this theme, a lexical substitution based on the analogy of the two practices and the fact that the bilboquet consists of two parts, one concave, the other convex: "Mais ce n'est que moitié de l'ouvrage de rejoindre la par-

Figure 2.2. François de Poilly, *Le jeu du bilboquet*, etching based on a painting by Jacques Courtin. © Royal Academy of Arts, London.

tie concave avec la partie convexe, il faut l'y laisser le plus qu'on peut." (But it is only half of the work to join the concave part with the convex part, one must leave it there as long as possible.)[25] This affinity of the bilboquet with eroticism appears in an engraving based on a canvas by the painter Jacques Courtin, where one observes a languidly smiling woman holding a bilboquet and pointing at its ball as it hangs between her legs (see fig. 2.2).

Conceptions and representations of bilboquets throughout the eighteenth century include criticism of contemporary modes of play. A few decades after the 1714 fashion for bilboquets, Denis Diderot and Jean le Rond d'Alembert's *Encyclopédie* underlines the moral issues of play, in line with the Catholic narrative warning against the dangers of excessive or immoral play. Indeed, *jouer* (to play) "se dit de toutes les occupations frivoles auxquelles on s'amuse ou l'on se délasse, mais qui entraînent quelquefois aussi la perte de la fortune et de l'honneur" (refers to all frivolous occupations involving fun or relaxation, but which sometimes also lead to the loss of fortune and honor).[26] This warning against the excesses to which bilboquets can lead was already in Marivaux's brochure. The intrinsic immorality of bilboquets differs, however, from gambling, which stimulates greed and cupidity. A frivolous occupation or a bizarre activity with no obvious purpose, the game of bilboquet needlessly occupies the hands of both children and adults. Its frenetic activity is driven not by the want of something (money, for instance) but by the frail and endlessly renewable satisfaction of succeeding in something at once difficult and useless. On the other hand, bilboquet is a game of skill, and in this sense, it enhances the player's ability, as do billiards, *jeu de paume* (real tennis), bowling, or ball games. Like *jeu de paume*, whose virtues were praised in Baldassare Castiglione's *The Courtier*, the game of bilboquet draws attention to the proper positioning of the body,[27] develops self-control, contributes to loosening the wrist of those who handle the sword, and helps to regain freedom of spirit.[28] It exalts and exhibits the virtues of the noble body, and readies it for its main purpose: war. But as this idealized representation of gentry is gradually called into question at the end of the ancien régime, the bilboquet comes to embody the uselessness of a class no longer ascribed to the kingdom's glory but rather devoted to distinguishing itself purely for distinction's sake.

THE CALEMBOUR CRAZE

The cup and ball, however, requires not only physical skills but also seems to involve a particular kind of wit. In 1713, around the same time the fashion of the bilboquet was at its height, there appeared a book titled *L'homme inconnu, ou Les équivoques de la langue dédié à Bacha Bilboquet*—a facetious portrayal of a fictional being whose interest consisted entirely of a particular sort of equivocation.[29] Through the use of a genitive, the author associated words with generally used expressions, even if the latter had no connection whatsoever with the context of the narrative. Thus, the "description chimérique d'un être de raison, fabriqué de pièces rapportées, habillé d'une étoffe à double sens, lequel fut construit par une assemblée d'équivoques, assistées du génie burlesque" (chimerical description of a rational being, made of patches, dressed in an ambiguous fabric, and put together by an assembly of equivocations, assisted by a burlesque genius) includes expressions such as "corps de garde" (guardroom), "des membres de période" (parts of a discursive section), "une tête d'armée" (a head of the army), and "une face de théâtre" (a stage front).[30] The dedicatory epistle, signed "Chimérographe, de l'Académie des Jeux Olympiques" and addressed to a certain "Bacha Bilboquet," serves as pretext for a comic description of the fashion of bilboquets:

> La réputation des BILBOQUETS est au point que rien ne la peut augmenter: les boutiques des plus fameux parfumeurs n'ont rien de comparable à l'odeur de votre renommée; Quoi qu'élevé dans les forêts, vous faites les divertissements de la plus grande ville du monde; Qu'on vous regarde par la taille, vous avez une figure qui nous charme tous, et les aveugles même avoueront que vous êtes fait au tour.

> The Bilboquet's repute is such that nothing can increase it: the shops of the most famous perfumers have nothing comparable to the smell of your fame; although raised in a forest, you entertain the greatest city in the world; a look at your waist, and we are all charmed by your figure; and even the blind would admit that you are nicely turned out.[31]

The author of the preface, who calls upon the figure of the "friendly reader," fully assumes the burlesque vein in which the book is written, anticipating the criticisms he will face. To this, however, he answers "par avance qu'il ne vient pas du génie de Socrate, mais que c'est un travail d'enfant de la joie, que son imagination l'a conçu, et que la folie lui a servi de sage-femme" (in advance that the book does not come from the genius of Socrates, but that it is the work of a joyful child, that his imagination has conceived it, and that madness has served as his midwife).[32]

The author of this work, the Abbé Claude Cherrier, is, to say the least, as ambiguous as the "unknown man" he describes. He worked as a censor for the police lieutenant, signing his approval, sometimes a bit offhandedly, under the pseudonym Passart, as we read in a letter from the marquis d'Argenson.[33] It is in this capacity and under this pseudonym that Cherrier, alias Passart, signed in 1713 the permission to print Marivaux's *Bilboquet*,[34] as well as his own *Homme inconnu*.

Although ostensibly downplaying the importance of his equivocal puns (even as he claims to be relatively innovative),[35] Cherrier's *L'homme inconnu* was popular enough with readers to assure a numerous progeny. One such example is *Chimérandre l'antigrec, fils de Bacha Bilboquet, ou Les équivoques de la langue française*, a burlesque portrait published in 1766. Dedicating his work to the members of "toutes les académies du royaume" (all the academies of the kingdom), its author, a certain Cerfvol, justified this undertaking by a desire to purify the French language of its equivocal and ambiguous terms, but also, paradoxically, by the particular witty skill required to produce such puns: "Nous avouons que cette manie [celle de faire des pointes] n'élève pas l'esprit, et que les prétendus bons mots ne sont souvent que des avortements du génie; mais au moins c'est le rapprochement de deux idées, et il faut une certaine combinaison pour opérer et sentir dans l'instant ce rapport." (We admit that this craze [of producing puns] does not elevate the mind, and that so-called witticisms are often but instances of stifled genius; but at least there is a convergence of two ideas, and it takes a certain mind to sense and show this relation instantly.)[36] Although they have their share of critics, equivocal puns surprise and enliven the mind, instill good cheer at social gatherings, and dissipate feelings of languor. They belong first to the realm of orality and conversation, which finds the pinnacle of its refinement (or decadence, depending on one's perspective) in the more or less libertine world of salons or *petits soupers*.[37]

Wearing the legacy of Bacha Bilboquet, Cerfvol also feeds this "craze" of ornamenting burlesque descriptions with equivocal puns like so many useless embellishments: "Ceux qui n'aiment pas les équivoques pourront supprimer, en lisant, tout ce qui est écrit en lettres italiques" (Those who do not like equivocations may remove, while reading, everything written in italics.)[38] Equivocal puns are a cheerful supplement, but only if they appeal to the reader's taste. Although part of the narrative, they are perfectly superfluous, adding nothing to the meaning—which, on the contrary, is purposely obscured.

A few years after the publication of Cerfvol's *Chimérandre*, the art of equivocal puns was to find its most illustrious master and theoretician in François-Georges Maréchal de Bièvre, a member of the King's Musketeers, knight of the Royal Order of Saint-Louis, and reputedly one of the most conspicuous fops in the city of Paris.[39] In 1770 he published a brief brochure titled *Lettre écrite à Madame la Comtesse Tation, par le Sieur de Bois-Flotté, étudiant en droit-fil*. Following in the footsteps of Bacha Bilboquet, the brochure abounds in equivocations on the thin pretext of a narrative entirely subordinated to the production of puns: "Oui, Madame la Comtesse, j'ai su l'intérêt vif et sensible que vous avez pris aux faits et gestes *de main*, et à la mort *de faim* du Bacha Bilboquet, vous et beaucoup d'autres dames *polonaises,* connues par leur goût déclaré pour les contes *de Lyon* à dormir debout *et de crachat*." (Yes, Madame Countess, I learned of the keen and sensitive interest you took in the actions and *hand* gestures, and in the *starvation* to death of Bacha Bilboquet, you and many other *Polish* ladies, known for their declared taste for the tales [counts] *of Lyon* to sleep *upright and spitting*.)[40]

As we can see in this short but significant excerpt, the production of a pun relies on its pronunciation; it is formed by adding a set expression to the word it plays on, without regard to the meaning nor the value of what is created. For example, *de Lyon* plays on the homophony between *comte* (count) and *conte* (tale)—the Count of Lyon was the cathedral's canon; and *de crachat* plays on the equivocation between *debout* (upright) and *de boue* (muddy)—a house made *de boue et de crachats* (from mud and spit) is a house built of poor materials.

Immediately after its publication, the brochure was met with great success,[41] much to the chagrin of a journalist from the *Correspondance littéraire*:

> Un mousquetaire dont le nom ne me revient pas, a publié, il y a quelque temps, une *Lettre écrite à madame la comtesse Tation par le sieur de Bois-Flotté.* . . . Ce titre vous met au fait du genre de plaisanterie qui règne dans cette brochure. . . . Qu'un mousquetaire s'amuse à faire des platitudes si misérables et à les imprimer, le mal assurément n'est pas grand . . . mais que cette insipide et exécrable rapsodie ait fait dans le public plus de sensation qu'aucun des ouvrages publiés dans le cours de l'hiver, qu'on en ait fait plusieurs éditions en très peu de semaines, et que pendant plus de quinze jours on n'ait parlé que de la comtesse Tation, voilà une *note d'infamie* qui tombe directement sur le public, et dont il ne se relèvera pas de sitôt dans mon esprit.

> A musketeer, whose name I do not remember, published some time ago a letter written to the *Comtesse Tation* by the *Sieur de Bois-Flotté.* . . . This title tells you all you need to know about the kind of jokes to be found in this brochure. . . . That a musketeer amuses himself making and printing such miserable platitudes is assuredly of no great harm . . . but that this insipid and execrable rhapsody has caused a greater public sensation than any of the works published in the course of this winter, that several editions have been printed in the span of a few weeks, and that for fifteen days one has spoken only of the *Comtesse Tation*, is a *weight of infamy* that falls directly upon the public, and from which it will not recover anytime soon in my mind.[42]

Nevertheless, the Marquis de Bièvre's burlesque muse seems inexhaustible. That same year he published a tragedy titled *Vercingentorixe*, composed of alexandrines replete with puns of the same caliber, and two years later a historical novel titled *Les amours de l'ange Lure*, a set of ambiguous variations on the erotic theme of the fée Lure and her celestial yet ardent lover. These were followed by a number of reworkings and imitations of this accommodating genre, to the delight of readers who kept asking for more. Bièvre was sought after in salons, was a fixture at court, and was soon made a marquis by the king. The fashion of wordplay brought its most illustrious practitioner to the pinnacle of fame.

Noting the French taste for fashion and novelty, one of the editors of *Le radoteur*, which included none other than Cerfvol, author of *Chimérandre*, writes these lines about the new fashion of equivocal puns he had helped revive and that now bore the name Calembourg: "La Nation Française est de tout temps en possession de saisir les objets avec enthousiasme, de s'en occuper jusqu'à la satiété, et de s'en dégoûter avec mépris, dès que le charme de la nouveauté est épuisé." (The French nation has always been inclined to take up objects with enthusiasm, to busy itself with them for a time, and turn away in disgust once the charm of novelty is exhausted.)[43] But, he adds, thanks to the "rotation du cercle" (rotation of the circle), fashions come back after a period of twenty or thirty years; thus, "le Public les ressaisit encore avec chaleur, et sans avoir l'honneur de l'invention, l'on peut néanmoins se faire un nom dans une carrière abandonnée, et que l'on semble ouvrir" (the Public grasps them again with enthusiasm; and without having the honor of invention, an author can nevertheless make a name for himself by following an abandoned path which seems to be of his making). Everything returns, then, and sometimes under a new name. Such was the case of the calembour, the new craze that consumed the city and the court alike, and of which Bièvre prides himself on being the inventor.

In addition to excelling in the practice of calembours, reportedly to the point of a woeful obsession, Bièvre was an enlightened theorist. He is the author of the article "Kalembour, calembour" in the *Supplément à l'Encyclopédie*. Defined as "l'abus que l'on fait d'un mot susceptible de plusieurs interprétations" (the abuse of a word open to several interpretations),[44] calembours are described as the offspring of gaiety, chance, and opportunity. Above all, one must not be concerned by meaning or the accuracy of spelling. The essence of the calembour is to carry "tout à coup l'imagination fort loin du sujet dont on parle, pour ne lui offrir qu'une puérilité piquante et curieuse" (the imagination suddenly far away from the object at stake, offering but a funny and surprising puerility)—and this, much to the displeasure of purists:

> Il est toujours sûr de son effet, même en dépit de l'orthographe, lorsqu'il est assaisonné de quelque sel, ou qu'il présente à l'esprit quelque contraste vraiment plaisant. Il fallait être de bien mauvaise humeur pour condamner ces deux vers qui sont dans la bouche de Vercingentorixe:
>
>> *Je sus*, comme un cochon, *résister à leurs armes,*
>>
>> *Et je pus*, comme un bouc, *dissiper vos alarmes.*
>
> Ceci est exécrable, disait-on à l'auteur, vous écrivez je *sus* et je *pus* avec un *s* à la fin, il faudrait qu'on pût y mettre un *e* pour que le kalembour fût exact. Celui-ci répondit au censeur: *Eh bien! monsieur, je ne vous empêche point d'y mettre le vôtre* (un nez pour un é).

Calembours are always certain of their effect, regardless of the spelling, when they are seasoned with salt, or when they present to the mind some truly amusing contrast. Whoever condemned these two verses pronounced by Vercingentorixe must have been in a very bad mood:

> I knew how [/ I sweat], like a pig, to resist their arms,
>
> And I could [/ I stink], like a goat, dispel your alarms.

"This is terrible," they told the author, "you write *je sus* and *je pus* with an *s* at the end; you should have written them with an *e* for the calembour to be accurate." The author replied, "Well, sir, I am not stopping you from putting yours (a *nez* for an *é*)."[45]

If a calembour can in itself silence the criticisms addressed to it, this is because it nullifies the meaning of the words it plays on: all that remains is the material- ity of language—emptied, as it were, of the imperative to signify.[46] This is per- haps where the antipathy of philosophers for equivocations comes from, as their fundamental ambiguity is a source of obscurity and misunderstandings. But, we read in the supplement to the *Encyclopédie*, "aujourd'hui que nous sommes assez éclairés pour qu'il [le calembour] ne puisse nous donner que matière à rire . . . , il faudrait avoir bien de la rancune pour le bannir absolument de la société" (now that we are enlightened enough for the calembour to give us only something to laugh about . . . one must be truly resentful to want to banish it completely from society).[47]

Calembours, like all puns, are particularly criticized by authors who strongly condemned everything relating to the faux bel esprit.[48] Because they played superficially with words, calembours were, notably, deemed untranslatable by Louis de Jaucourt, who made translation the criterion for evaluating the quality of witticisms.[49] Voltaire later picked up this denunciation of the gleaming trin- kets of the *faux esprit*; and in the entry "Esprit," which he wrote for the *Encyclo- pédie*, he censured false and recherché thoughts whose sole purpose was to call attention to themselves, noting, "cette petite vanité produit les jeux de mots dans toutes les langues; ce qui est la pire espèce de faux bel-esprit" (this little vanity produces wordplays in every language; which is the worst kind of false wit).[50] In 1765, citing the "profond auteur de *Bacha Bilboquet*" (profound author of *Bacha Bilboquet*), Voltaire paradoxically (and bitterly) sang the praises of frivolity, which he considered a social virtue that contributed to lightness and forgetful- ness.[51] When he returned to Paris in 1778, however, in the middle of the calem- bour craze, a shocked Voltaire allegedly looked at them as "le fléau de la bonne conversation, l'éteignoir de l'esprit" (the plague of good conversation, the extin- guisher of wit). Bièvre, who quotes this remark, replies:

> Si, malgré cet anathème, il est encore quelque esprit pointu qui veuille retomber dans le même péché, nous lui donnerons une règle générale pour la fabrica- tion des jeux de mots: c'est d'avoir très peu d'égards au sens des paroles, mais l'oreille fort attentive au son et à la prononciation des mots, de tâcher surtout d'oublier l'orthographe. Nous prétendons qu'avec ces principes on aura l'avantage de briller parmi les diseurs de riens, et de couper la parole à toutes les personnes qui voudraient s'aviser de parler raison.

> If, despite this anathema, there is still some sharp wit inclined to relapse into this sin, we shall give him a general rule for making puns: it is to have very little regard for the meaning of words, but rather to pay attention to their sound and pronunciation; and to try, above all, to forget their spelling. We declare that with these principles, one will have the advantage of shining among idle talkers, and of cutting off all those who would take it into their head to talk reason.[52]

In becoming a theorist of calembours and puns, the Marquis de Bièvre took up the defense of French gaiety, as evidenced by a letter addressed to the authors of the *Bibliothèque universelle des romans*,[53] in which he inveighs against the moody spirit of those who "répandent des nuages sombres sur toutes les branches de la philosophie" (cast dark clouds over all branches of philosophy). Bièvre considered cheerfulness to be "philosophie par excellence" and thought there was nothing like calembours to combat the melancholic mood of reasoners: "Le goût des calembours n'est point une maladie chez moi, mais une ressource innocente pour repousser l'ennui ou pour rappeler la gaieté" (My taste for calembours is not an illness, but an innocent resource to repel boredom or to summon gaiety).[54]

In a similar vein, the journalists of *Le nouvelliste littéraire* recall, on the occasion of the 1799 publication of the *Biévriana*, that the genre of calembours is part of an old French tradition of *pointes* (puns), *lazzis* (taunts), wordplays, amphigories, "et autres jolies choses semblables" (and other such pretty things) of which the Marquis has made an "étude sérieuse" (serious study). Despite their insignificance—in terms of both lack of value and meaning—puns are indeed a genre, which, although minor, has its history and theorists; and Bièvre is one of its most famous representatives. There is thus a double paradox here: first, that "pareilles folies" (such follies) endure and that people persist in maintaining their practice; second, that they continue to make people laugh, "bon gré mal gré, quoi que pourtant on n'ait pas trop sujet de rire aujourd'hui. Et je crois que M. de Bièvre ne rirait guère lui-même s'il vivait encore" (in spite of themselves, although we do not have too much to laugh about today. And I believe M. de Bièvre would hardly laugh himself were he still alive).[55] Nothing is less certain, however, since the *calembourdiste* indicates the contrary in his *Dissertation sur les jeux de mots*:

> La révolution qui est en train de produire tant de changements n'a presque rien opéré sur le caractère français. Même frivolité, même goût pour le bel esprit. Paris, ce pays si fertile en contrastes, offre en ce genre des excès d'extravagance. Tandis que tout est en combustion, le Parisien joue sur les mots, et se console avec des calembours.

> The revolution that is producing so many changes has had almost no effect on the French character. The same frivolity, the same taste for the bel esprit. Paris, this land so fertile in contrasts, offers in this genre extravagant excesses. While everything is in turmoil, the Parisian plays with words, and consoles himself with puns.[56]

He notes, "les calembours se soutiennent encore malgré nos orages politiques" (calembours still endure in spite of our political storms), adding that "ce goût piquant a paru et s'est éclipsé à plusieurs reprises, et l'on doit croire qu'il reviendra toutes les fois que l'amour de la frivolité prendra le dessus" (this enticing fashion has appeared and disappeared several times, and one must believe that it will return every time love of frivolity takes over). As with the time of cherries, the love of frivolity periodically comes back and brings with it the rage for puns, as well as for the cup and ball.

Indeed, fashions come and go, and sometimes overlap. Regarding the 1771 publication of the *Almanach des calembourds*, the journalist of the *Mercure de France* made the following connection between the fashion of the cup and ball and that of puns:

> Lorsque la mode amena les bilboquets à Paris, cette plaisanterie niaise, appelée Calembourd, eut aussi une espèce de vogue. Mais on n'avait pas imaginé alors de donner un *Almanach des Calembourds*. Cette nouveauté était réservée à un ingénieux écrivain, qui cependant a eu la modestie de garder l'anonyme.

> When fashion brought the cup and ball to Paris, this foolish joke, called calembourd, also became something of a fad. But we did not think then to give an *Almanac of Calembourds*. This novelty was reserved for an ingenious writer, who nevertheless had the modesty to remain anonymous.[57]

Bilboquets and calembours were made for each other; is it any wonder that Bièvre excelled in both? Extremely witty, the man known as the Marquis Bilboquet had an unusual skill: "Il jouait supérieurement au bilboquet: celui dont il se servait présentait d'un côté une surface plane et à chaque coup la balle y retournait sur son axe. Cette adresse rare lui valut le titre de Marquis Bilboquet." (He played cup and ball better than anyone: the one he used had a flat surface on one side and every time the ball would return to its axis. This rare skill earned him the title of Marquis Bilboquet.)[58] In her *Mémoires*, written in the middle of the following century, the Baronne de Bawr tells how calembours and bilboquet were two equally irrepressible passions for the Marquis:

> Quant à M. de Bièvre, il était fort rare qu'il pût parler cinq minutes à qui que ce fût, même à la reine, sans laisser échapper un calembour. En outre, il jouait du bilboquet mieux que personne au monde, le jetant à distance, le lançant au plafond, sans jamais manquer de le ressaisir, la boule sur la petite pointe, ce que l'on considère comme la perfection de l'art. Grâce à ces deux talents, il arrivait que le marquis de Bièvre, en dépit de sa naissance et de sa fortune, jouait souvent dans le monde le rôle d'un homme fait pour amuser la société.

> As for Mr. de Bièvre, it was very rare that he could speak for five minutes to anyone, even the queen, without making a calembour. In addition, he played bilboquet better than anyone in the world, throwing it to the ceiling, never failing to catch it again, with the ball fixed on the small tip, which is considered perfection in this art. Thanks to these two talents, it happened that the Marquis de Bièvre, despite his birth and fortune, often played the role of a man born to entertain.[59]

One day, when he learned that a diplomat among his friends was to go to Italy in a mission to the Pope, Bièvre expressed his desire to accompany him. The diplomat agreed on the condition that Bièvre would give his oath not to play bilboquet nor make calembours. Until Lyon, everything went well; but invited to a salon where all the nobility of the city was to be found, Bièvre could no longer resist:

> La première chose que le marquis de Bièvre aperçut en entrant, fut un bilboquet placé sur la cheminée. Bien résolu à ne pas s'en approcher, il causait tranquillement avec quelques-uns des convives, lorsque l'un d'eux prit l'instrument fatal pour s'en servir fort maladroitement. M. de Bièvre n'y tint plus; il s'élance, enlève le bilboquet des mains du novice, et, comme s'il eût voulu regagner le temps perdu, il exécute une suite de tours de force qui excite l'admiration générale. On fait cercle autour de lui, on l'accable de compliments, de bravos répétés.—Oh! monsieur, s'écrie l'un des spectateurs, que je voudrais avoir votre adresse!—Mon adresse, monsieur? répondit-il, place des Terreaux, hôtel des Trois-Rois.

> The first thing the Marquis de Bièvre saw upon entering was a bilboquet placed on the mantelpiece. Firmly resolved to stay away from it, he was quietly chatting with some of the guests, when one of them took the fatal instrument and used it very clumsily. M. de Bièvre could no longer contain himself; he rushed forward, took the bilboquet out of the novice's hands, and, as if to make up for lost time, he performed a series of feats that aroused everyone's admiration. People gathered around and overwhelmed him with compliments and repeated bravos.—Oh sir, shouted one of the spectators, I would like to have your address!—My address, sir? he replied, Place des Terreaux, Hotel of the Three Kings.[60]

An etching, placed at the beginning of the *Biévriana* (see fig. 2.3), depicts a medallion portrait of Bièvre, decorated underneath with a fool's bauble intertwined with a bilboquet.[61] While the bauble—which was used in some societies of the ancien régime as a grotesque subversion of the royal scepter—has long been associated with madness, making an attribute out of the bilboquet was unheard of. No one but Bièvre could bring the two together. As a motto, two verses are juxtaposed to form a pun: "Beverley n'aurait pas éprouvé tant de maux, s'il eût passé sa vie à *jouer* sur les mots" (Beverley would not have experienced so much pain if he had spent his life *playing* with words). Edward Moore's bourgeois drama *The Gamester* (1753), which represented the misfortunes that come with gambling, had been adapted in 1768 by Bernard-Joseph Saurin under the title *Beverley*. The mania for puns and bilboquet is distinguished from that for gambling due to the former's benign nature; here again, cheerfulness is life's only teacher, unraveling drama and misfortune thanks to witticism.

Beverley n'auroit pas éprouvé tant de maux S'il eût passé sa vie à Jouer sur les mots().

Figure 2.3. *Beverley n'aurait pas éprouvé tant de maux s'il eût passé sa vie à jouer sur les mots*, etching, ca. 1799–1800. © Bibliothèque nationale de France.

The skills of body and mind are united together in Bièvre, who here appears as an anti-Rousseau: for him, the bilboquet is not the opposite of chatter, but the very incarnation of wit. A complete fop, a man of the day, idle talker and champion of the moment, he left an ambiguous legacy (to say the least), attached to a waning century and a noble ethics of gaiety whose death knell would be sounded by the mania of rising patriotism. Calembours, like the bilboquet with which they have so often been associated, are certainly factors of disorder; but they require for their enjoyment a tranquil and carefree admiration, an excessive and vain *otium*, and a "love of frivolity" that are at odds with the march of progress. But beyond the carefree posture intrinsic to wit or mundane gaiety, the art of the calembour, whose playful ethics was perfectly crystallized in the vain but brilliant practice of bilboquet, is also the result of imagination freed from the constraints of moral, aesthetic, and philosophical norms.

NOTES

Unless noted otherwise, all translations are my own. I would like to warmly thank Fayçal Falaky and Reginald McGinnis for their help in the delicate translation of the French calembours into English.

1. Rousseau, *Les confessions*, ed. Raymond Trousson (Paris: Honoré Champion, 2010), 299; translated by Christopher Kelly as *The Confessions*, in *The Collected Writings of Rousseau*, ed. Christopher Kelly and Roger D. Masters, vol. 5, *The Confessions and Correspondence, including the Letters to Malesherbes* (Hanover, NH: University Press of New England, 1995), 169.

2. Rousseau, *Les confessions*, 300, and *The Confessions*, 170.

3. About laces, Rousseau writes in his *Confessions* that, to support the "inanity of the babbling" of Môtiers' inhabitants, he began to make his visits with a needlework cushion: "That I might not live like a savage, I took into my head to learn to make laces." Rousseau, *The Confessions*, 589. Rousseau gave his laces as a gift to young women who were about to get married, provided they were breastfeeding their children; see Rousseau's correspondence, 1762–63, and in particular the letter to Anne Marie d'Ivernois on September 13, 1762, in Rousseau, *Correspondance complète*, ed. R.A. Leigh, vol. 13 (Geneva: Institut et Musée Voltaire, 1973), 60. In the eighteenth century, laces were mainly used to tie corsets, as well as for the backs of men's gilets; for the rest—shirt collars, sleeves, trousers, and garters— ribbons were used instead. I thank Élise Urbain-Ruano for this information.

4. See, for instance, the letter Rousseau wrote to François Henri d'Ivernois on July 20, 1765, in *Correspondance complète*, ed. R.A. Leigh, vol. 26 (Geneva: Institut et Musée Voltaire, 1976), 105: "Je vous remercie aussi du livre de M. Claparède. Comme mes plantes et mon bilboquet me laissent peu de temps à perdre, je n'ai lu ni ne lirai ce livre que je crois fort beau. Mais ne m'envoyez plus de tous ces beaux livres : car je vous avoue qu'ils m'ennuient à la mort, et que je n'aime pas à m'ennuyer." (I also thank you for M. Claparede's book. As my plants and my cup and ball leave me little time to lose, I have not read or will not read this book, which I think is very beautiful. But do not send me any more of these beautiful books because I confess to you that they bore me to death, and that I do not like to be bored.)

5. See Jean-Jacques Rousseau, *Emile, or On Education*, in *The Collected Writings of Rousseau*, ed. Christopher Kelly and Roger D. Masters, vol. 13, *Emile, or on Education (Includes Emile and Sophie; or the Solitaires)*, trans. Christopher Kelly and Allan Bloom (Hanover, NH: University Press of New England, 2010).

6. The question arises—even if they are not directly mentioned in these terms—of whether laces and the cup and ball are for Rousseau a "supplement," in the sense developed by Jacques Derrida, *De la grammatologie* (Paris: Minuit, 1967); see also Jean-Claude Coste, "Les suppléments de Jean-Jacques Rousseau," *L'en-je lacanien* 1, no. 4 (2005): 33–45.

7. See Jocelyn Huchette, *La gaieté, caractère français? Représenter la nation au siècle des Lumières (1715–1789)* (Paris: Classiques Garnier, 2015).

8. See Edward Nye, "Bilboquet, Calembours, and Modernity," *Studies on Voltaire and the Eighteenth Century* 8 (2000): 179–86; Robin Howells, "Marivaux's *Le bilboquet* (1714): The Game as a Subversive Principle," *Studies on Voltaire and the Eighteenth Century*

8 (2000): 175–78; and Christelle Bahier-Porte and Régine Jomand-Baudry, eds., *Écrire en mineur au XVIIIe siècle* (Paris: Desjonquères, 2009).

9. On the history of the bilboquet, see Françoise Rubellin, "Préface," in Pierre de Marivaux, *Le bilboquet*, ed. Françoise Rubellin (Paris: Centre national de la recherche scientifique, 1995), 25–50.

10. *Dictionnaire historique de la langue française*, vol. 1, ed. Alain Rey (Paris: Le Robert, 2010).

11. *Dictionnaire universel français et latin: Vulgairement appelé Dictionnaire de Trévoux*, vol. 6, (Paris: Compagnie des libraires associés, 1771), 902.

12. Antoine-François Momoro, *Traité élémentaire de l'imprimerie, ou Le manuel de l'imprimeur* (Paris: Momoro, 1793), 74–75.

13. As Pierre de L'Estoile, *Registre-journal du règne de Henri III*, vol. 5, ed. Madeleine Lazard and Gilbert Schrenck (Geneva: Droz, 2001), 39–40, notes, "En ce temps, le Roy commencea de porter un billeboquet à la main, mesmes allant par les *rues*, et s'en jouoit comme font les petits *enfans*." (At that time [August 1585], the King began carrying a bilboquet, and even went through the streets playing with it as little children do.)

14. "Chanson nouvelle, sur l'air, du bilboquet" (n.p. 1724), 4–5 [p. 400–401 of the manuscript], YE-10661, Bibliothèque nationale de France, Paris.

15. "Chanson nouvelle du bilboquet, sur l'air: Vous m'entendez bien," 6 [402].

16. *De l'antiquité et de l'usage du bilboquet, par Monsieur C**** (Lucerne: n.p., 1714); Pierre Carlet de Chamblain de Marivaux, *Le bilboquet* (Paris: Pierre Prault, 1714). References to the latter text will be taken from Rubellin's aforementioned 1995 edition.

17. Worth mentioning are *L'origine des cabriolets, conte allégorique et méchanique, orné de notes, attribué à Michel Marescot, à l'isle des chimères chez tout le monde* (Paris: Prault, 1755); *L'origine du fard, ou Métamorphoses d'Hébé en vieille* (Paris: Pierre Cot, 1709); and *L'origine des puces* (London: n.p., 1709). See also Christophe Martin, ed., *Fictions de l'origine, 1650–1800* (Paris: Desjonquères, 2012).

18. For an analysis of the tale, see Rubellin, "Préface"; and Sylvie Dervaux, "La chambre d'enchantement: *Le bilboquet* de Marivaux (1714)," *Studies on Voltaire and the Eighteenth Century* 323 (1994): 247–69.

19. Marivaux, *Le bilboquet*, 96.

20. See Dervaux, "La chambre d'enchantement," and in particular page 264: "En posant l'extravagance comme principe esthétique, *Le Bilboquet* constitue une réponse fort astucieuse, de la part de Marivaux, aux critiques de son temps qui condamnent le roman pour sa folie, et ses lecteurs pour leur frivolité." (By posing extravagance as an aesthetic principle, *Le Bilboquet* is a very clever response, on the part of Marivaux, to the critics of his time who condemn the novel for its madness, and its readers for their frivolity.)

21. *De l'antiquité et de l'usage du bilboquet*, 4–6.

22. *De l'antiquité et de l'usage du bilboquet*, 14.

23. See Michel Jeanneret, "'Envelopper les ordures'? Érotisme et libertinage au XVIIe siècle," *Littératures classiques* 55, no. 3 (2004): 157–68.

24. Pierre Bayle, "Éclaircissement sur les obscénités," in *Dictionnaire historique et critique*, vol. 4 (Amsterdam: Brunel, 1740), 655.

25. *De l'antiquité et de l'usage du bilboquet*, 14–15.

26. Denis Diderot, "Jouer," in *Encyclopédie; ou Dictionnaire raisonné des sciences, des arts et des métiers*, ed. Denis Diderot and Jean le Rond d'Alembert, 17 vols. (Paris: Briasson, 1751–1765), 8:884.

27. Baldassare Castiglione, *The Book of the Courtier*, trans. George Bull (New York: Penguin Classics, 1976), 63.

28. See Élisabeth Belmas, *Jouer autrefois: Essai sur le jeu dans la France moderne (XVIe–XVIIIe siècle)* (Paris: Champ Vallon, 2006), 65; and Jean-Marie Lhôte, *Histoire des jeux de société: Géométries du désir* (Paris: Flammarion, 1994), 286.

29. Claude Cherrier, *L'homme inconnu, ou Les équivoques de la langue dédié à Bacha Bilboquet* (Paris: Jacques Quillau, 1713).

30. Cherrier, *L'homme inconnu*, 11.

31. Claude Cherrier, "Épître dédicatoire," in *L'homme inconnu*, n.p. In French, *fait au tour* means at once "very well made," "good looking," and "made on a wood lathe."

32. Claude Cherrier, "Préface," in *L'homme inconnu*, n.p.

33. Regarding Cherrier's career as a censor, see F. Guessart, "La censure au commencement du XVIIIe siècle: L'abbé Cherrier, lettres inédites," *La correspondance littéraire: Critique, beaux-arts, érudition* 2, no. 4 (1858): 71–83.

34. On the circumstances of the obtention of Marivaux's *Bilboquet* privilege, see Rubellin, "Préface," 15–24. Rubellin does not make the connection between the censor, Passart, and the Abbé Cherrier, but the pages that Rubellin dedicates to the history of the game of bilboquet are extremely valuable.

35. The journalist of the *Bibliothèque universelle des romans* (Paris: n.p., 1776) retraces the history of equivocal narratives and what he calls the "satiric, comic and bourgeois novels" to Rabelais, but especially to Étienne Tabourot, author of *Les bigarrures et touches du Seigneur des Accords*, published in 1560.

36. Cerfvol, *Chimérandre l'antigrec, fils de Bacha Bilboquet, ou Les équivoques de la langue françoise* (n.p.: Balivernipolis, 1766), 7–8. The author claims that the book was composed by Bacha Bilboquet's son and entrusted to a "literary society," which suggests that it was written by several hands.

37. See Marine Ganofsky, ed., *Petits soupers libertins* (Paris: Société française d'étude du dix-huitième siècle, 2016).

38. Cerfvol, *Chimérandre*, 24.

39. See François-Georges Maréchal de Bièvre, *Calembours et autres jeux sur les mots d'esprit*, ed. Antoine de Baecque (Paris: Payot, 2000); Benoît Melançon, "Oralité, brièveté, spontanéité et marginalité: Le cas du marquis de Bièvre," in *Les marges des Lumières françaises (1750–1789)*, ed. Didier Masseau (Geneva: Droz, 2004), 215–24; and Gabriel Maréschal de Bièvre, *Le marquis de Bièvre, sa vie, ses calembours, ses comédies, 1747–1789* (Paris: Plon-Nourrit, 1910).

40. Bièvre, *Calembours*, 63.

41. According to Antoine de Baecque's introduction to Bièvre's *Calembours*, there were about fifteen editions in three years.

42. Friedrich Melchior Grimm, Denis Diderot, and Jacques-Henri Meister, *Correspondance littéraire, philosophique et critique de Grimm et de Diderot, depuis 1753 jusqu'en 1790*, vol. 6, ed. Jules-Antoine Taschereau and A. Chaudé (Paris: Furne, 1829), 402–3.

43. *Le radoteur, ou Nouveaux mélanges de philosophie, d'anecdotes curieuses, d'aventures particulières, etc., publié et mis en ordre par M. de C***, auteur de plusieurs ouvrages connus*, vol. 1 (Paris: Jean-François Bastien, 1777), 369–79. The authors of this journal, published between 1775 and 1776, were Cerfvol, Jean-Henri Marchand, and Jean-Baptiste Nougaret.

44. François-Georges Maréchal de Bièvre, "Kalembour, calembour," in *Supplément à l'Encyclopédie, ou Dictionnaire des sciences, des arts et des métiers*, vol. 3, ed. Jean-Baptiste-René Robinet (Amsterdam: Marc-Michel Rey, 1777), 680–81; See also Bièvre, *Calembours*, 39.

45. Bièvre, *Calembours*, 40.

46. See Barbara Cassin and Michel Narcy, *La décision du sens: Le livre "Gamma" de la Métaphysique d'Aristote, introduction, texte, traduction et commentaire* (Paris: Vrin, 1989); and Barbara Cassin, *L'effet sophistique* (Paris: Gallimard, 1995).

47. Bièvre, "Kalembour, calembour," 681.

48. Dominique Bouhours, *La manière de bien penser dans les ouvrages d'esprit: Dialogues* (Paris: Mabre-Cramoisy, 1687); Nicolas Boileau Despréaux, *Art poétique*, in *Œuvres diverses du Sieur D***; avec Le traité du sublime; ou, Du merveilleux dans le discours* (Paris: Lacoste, 1674); Nicolas Boileau Despréaux, *Satire XII sur l'équivoque* (n.p: n.p., 1711). On the condemnation

of puns in seventeenth-century France, see Mercedes Blanco, *Les rhétoriques de la pointe: Baltasar Gracián et le conceptisme en Europe* (Paris: Honoré Champion, 1992).

49. See Louis de Jaucourt, "Pointe," in Diderot and d'Alembert, eds., *Encyclopédie*, 12:876: "Le moyen de découvrir si une pointe est bonne ou mauvaise, c'est de la tourner dans une autre langue; lorsqu'elle soutient cette épreuve, on peut la regarder pour être de bon aloi; mais c'est tout le contraire quand elle s'évanouit dans l'opération." (The method to evaluate a witticism is to turn it into another language; when it withstands this ordeal, you can view it as good; it is the opposite if it falls apart in translation.) See also Walter David Redfern, *Calembours, ou Les puns et les autres: Traduit de l'intraduisible* (Oxford: Peter Lang, 2005).

50. Voltaire, "Esprit," in Diderot and d'Alembert, eds., *Encyclopédie*, 5:974.

51. Voltaire, *Nouveaux mélanges*, vol. 3 (Geneva: Cramer, 1765), 165.

52. François-Georges Maréchal de Bièvre, *Dissertation sur les jeux de mots*, in *Biévriana, ou Jeux de mots de M. de Bièvre*, 3rd ed., ed. Albéric Deville (Paris, Maradan, 1814), 57. Savinien de Cyrano de Bergerac had already said that the pun (*la pointe*) "n'est pas d'accord avec la raison; c'est l'agréable jeu de l'esprit, et merveilleux en ce point qu'il réduit toutes choses sur le pied nécessaire à ses agréments, sans avoir égard à leur propre substance" (does not agree with reason; it is the pleasant play of the mind, and wonderful in that it reduces all things to the level necessary for its pleasures, regardless of their own substance). Savinien de Cyrano de Bergerac, "Entretiens pointus," in *Œuvres complètes*, vol. 2, ed. Madeleine Alcover, Luciano Erba, Hubert Carrier, and André Blanc (Paris: Honoré Champion, 2000), 295.

53. François-Georges Maréchal to the authors of the *Bibliothèque universelle des romans*, quoted in Mareschal de Bièvre, *Le marquis de Bièvre*, 82–83.

54. François-Georges Maréchal to the authors of the *Bibliothèque universelle des romans*, quoted in Mareschal de Bièvre, *Le marquis de Bièvre*, 83.

55. J. F. Morin and A. Lenoir, *Le nouvelliste littéraire* 91, no. 30 (1799): 5.

56. Bièvre, *Dissertation sur les jeux de mots*, 142–43.

57. *Mercure de France*, 1771, 166.

58. "Notice sur la vie et les écrits de M. de Bièvre," in *Biévriana*, 25.

59. Alexandrine-Sophie Goury de Champgrand, Baronne de Bawr, *Mes souvenirs* (Paris: Passard, 1853), 142.

60. Goury de Champgrand, *Mes souvenirs*, 144–45.

61. Louis Petit de Bachaumont, *Mémoires secrets pour servir à l'histoire de la république des lettres en France, depuis 1762 jusqu'à nos jours, ou Journal d'un observateur*, vol. 11 (London: Adamson, 1778), 33.

CHAPTER 3

Fiction as Play

RHETORICAL SUBVERSION IN ALAIN-RENÉ LESAGE'S
HISTOIRE DE GIL BLAS DE SANTILLANE

Zeina Hakim

Alain-René Lesage's *Histoire de Gil Blas de Santillane* entertains a paradoxical relationship with reality: while the author wishes us to "believe" his story—enough, at least, for us to enter into the fiction—the historical and geographical setting, as well as the composition and enunciation, suggest nonetheless that he does not actually aspire to have his work pass for true. There exists, then, in *Gil Blas*, a tension between, on the one hand, literary devices whose stated purpose is to induce belief in the authenticity of events and, on the other hand, clues aimed at preventing us from accepting as true what we are told. This tension is not intended to deceive; it allows for the reader not to be fooled and to derive a certain pleasure in recognizing the fictional process as such. Indeed, the accreditation and legitimation of a narrative are two sides of the same coin: the novel is both accredited by hiding its fictionality and legitimated by revealing it.

The reader of these texts is thus constantly wavering between two positions—of "being immersed in fiction" and, inversely, endlessly pulled out of it, placed at a distance, and kept from believing what he reads. The text thus becomes a space of play in which the author invites the reader to participate actively, a game of illusion in which the author both satisfies and deceives the reader's expectations. Literary reading invariably entails a reciprocity between illusion and lucidity, between conformity and dissent, between the values of classical order and those of modern subversion, between the acceptance and refusal of stereotypes. The contradiction one might see in a reader's adherence to a fictive reality thus only exists if one fails to consider reading as a game, and that playing also implies both illusion and lucidity. The phenomenon of fiction depends precisely on this tension between two incompatible positions that are constantly brought together in the practice of reading.

Lesage is, of course, not the only one at the time using his text as a space of play; we can think of the authorial games of the Abbé Prévost in *Cleveland* or his *Mémoires et aventures d'un homme de qualité*, or of Pierre de Marivaux in *La vie de Marianne*, whose tongue-in-cheek references to literary convention often feel very playful. What stands out with Lesage, however, is that the literary game he sets up concerns every aspect of his narration: the temporal dimension, the geographical frame, the composition, and even the enunciation.

Beginning with the question of temporality in his work, one may observe that the paradoxical nature of *Gil Blas* stems in part from its many temporal indications, which ultimately produce narrative indeterminacy rather than the contrary. Indeed, while Lesage provides a detailed division of time in enumerating the daily activities of his character (getting up, dining, going to bed, etc.), and while many temporal indications (after, for a long time, later, morning, afternoon, evening, etc.) punctuate the story, to the extent that the reader might feel overwhelmed by the sheer density of information, this surplus of chronological detail has the paradoxical effect of *saturating* the text, which is to say that the reader is ultimately left with no precise indication. The author explains offhandedly, for instance, in the preface to the third volume that he had mistaken one Spanish reign for another:

> On a marqué dans ce troisième tome une époque qui ne s'accorde pas avec l'histoire de don Pompeyo de Castro qu'on lit dans le premier volume. Il paraît là que Philippe II n'a pas encore fait la conquête du Portugal, et l'on voit ici tout d'un coup un royaume sous la domination de Philippe III sans que Gil Blas en soit beaucoup plus vieux. *C'est une faute de chronologie dont l'auteur s'est aperçu trop tard, mais qu'il promet de corriger dans la suite*, avec quantité d'autres, si l'on fait une nouvelle édition de son ouvrage.

> This third tome depicts a period which does not agree with the story of Don Pompeio de Castro included in the first volume. It appears there that Philip II has not yet conquered Portugal, and one finds here suddenly a kingdom under the domination of Philip III without Gil Blas being hardly any older for it. *This is a chronological error which the author recognized too late, but which he promises to rectify eventually*, along with many others, if there is a new edition of his work.[1]

If it is in fact in 1580 that Philip II united Portugal with Spain (*L'histoire*, 3.7.156–62; *Adventures*, 131–35), the story of Don Pompeio, which mentions a king of Portugal, takes place under the reign of Philip III. Lesage claims to have noticed this confusion between two Spanish reigns but does little to rectify it,[2] promising only to do so in a future edition. The chronological error is corrected so clumsily that the passage in question loses all plausibility, and the reader cannot take the author's good faith seriously.

While cursory and inconsistent in the first two volumes of the novel, the historical temporality nonetheless becomes more precise in the third, at the moment when the fate of the character appears to merge for a while with that of the Spanish dynasty.[3] Yet even here it is difficult to reconcile these historical references with the overall chronology of the novel, whose coherence remains most often questionable.[4] The points of contact with history are thus only incidental, as if Lesage were in this way mocking authorial claims aiming to impose historical time on the narrative. Here, on the contrary, the (defective) chronology is treated in parody, and all that matters ultimately is the *game* the author plays with the expectations of the reader.

The chronological inconsistencies of the novel may be viewed incidentally as evidence of a textual game. For instance, when addressing his son in chapter one of the first book, the father of Gil Blas indirectly reveals the latter's age: "Le temps de ton enfance est passé: tu as déjà dix-sept ans, et te voilà devenu habile garçon." (The time of your youth has passed: you are now seventeen and a clever fellow; *L'histoire*, 1.1.24; *Adventures*, 12.) Yet, two days after his departure, Gil Blas sighs, "comme si ce n'était pas assez d'être enterré tout vif à dix-huit ans" (as if it was not enough to be buried alive at the age of eighteen; *L'histoire*, 1.6.40; *Adventures*, 26), thereby contradicting his father's assertion without there being any events to justify the skipping of a year. Similarly, at the end of his stay in the Tower of Segovia, Gil Blas declares to Don Alphonso, "Il n'y a pas quatre mois que j'occupais à la cour un poste assez considérable. J'avais l'honneur d'être secrétaire et confident du duc de Lerme." (Something less than four months ago, I held a quite considerable post at court, having had the honor to be secretary and confident to the Duke of Lerma; *L'histoire*, 10.10.460; *Adventures*, 409.) Yet he will later say to Philip IV that he was "six mois à la tour de Ségovie" (six months in the Tower of Segovia; *L'histoire*, 12.2.541; *Adventures*, 487) and that the king was kind enough to release him. These inconsistencies, among others, prevent the reader from considering chronology as a referential value in the novel but emphasize instead the author's nonchalant, or even indifferent, attitude regarding this subject. A similar offhandedness is also visible in the actual narration. Realizing, for instance, that his character, at the time of his second marriage, must be more than eighty years old, Lesage simply dodges the issue and has Gil Blas say, "Quoique je ne parusse pas avoir mon âge, et que je pusse me donner dix bonnes années de moins que je n'en avais." (Although I looked younger than I was, and could have taken ten full years off my age; *L'histoire* 12.14.607; *Adventures*, 545.)

Spatial representation in *Gil Blas*, by contrast, appears more realistic: the objective geographical data are many and place names frequent; each chapter specifies in which city the plot unfolds (Madrid, Salamanca, Valencia, etc.), and even small towns where the hero only stops in passing are mentioned.[5] Locations, itineraries, and distances are carefully specified,[6] revealing Lesage's strong familiarity with Spanish topography.

This diligence becomes suspect, all the same, given the proliferation of geographic details of every sort along with spatial indications strewn indiscriminately throughout the novel. Thus, in book 1, Gil Blas's journey leads him from Oviedo to Peñaflor, then to Cacabeolos, and Astorga, and finally to Burgos. In book 2 the action takes place in Valladolid, but it is on his way to Madrid via Segovia that Gil Blas decides to follow the journeyman barber to Olmedo. In book 3 Gil reaches Madrid, while in book 4 he is in Salamanca, then Toledo. In book 5 it is not only Madrid that is conjured up in the story of Don Raphael but also the island of Cabrera, then Algiers, Livorno, and Florence, before the character finds himself again in Spain with Barcelona and Valladolid. Finally, book 6 mentions again the names of several small Spanish cities, such as Buñol and Segorbe.

The listing of names of cities where the hero has stayed doubtless adheres to picaresque convention and thus would seemingly meet the readers' expectations. But one may equally view this cataloging of place names as having a different function in transforming semirealistic description into signs of fiction that are immediately decipherable as such to readers. Episodes follow one another in loosely connected sequence, as if to mimic the peregrinations of the protagonist, wandering wherever he is taken by the circumstances and the people he meets. The titles of chapters are emblematic of a nonchalance in composition since so many of them emphasize the fact that their unity depends entirely on chance: "par quel hasard Gil Blas sortit enfin de prison" (by what accident Gil Blas was set at liberty at last; *L'histoire* 1.13.141); "par quel hasard il rencontra le licencié qui lui avait tant d'obligation" (his accidental meeting with the litentiate who had been so much obliged to him; *L'histoire* 7.5.235); "par quel hasard, dans quel endroit et dans quel état Gil Blas retrouva son ami Fabrice" (by what accident, in what place and condition, Gil Blas found his friend Fabricius; *L'histoire* 11.7.311); "Gil Blas rencontre par hasard le poète Nunez" (Gil Blas meets by accident the poet Nunez; *L'histoire* 11.10.476); "Gil Blas rencontre encore Fabrice par hasard" (Gil Blas meets Fabricius again by accident; *L'histoire* 12.7.505).

A brief discussion with Fabricius, similarly, leads Gil Blas to renounce his original plan; his subsequent abduction by bandits tears him away from his education in Salamanca; then his meeting a barber becomes the occasion for yet another change of course; and, finally, Don Bernard de Castil Blazo, Aurora, and the secretary for the Marchioness of Chaves each request in turn that he leave their respective places, thereby forcing him repeatedly to revise his itinerary. Gil Blas himself points out the erratic nature of his life, and how he is passively carried along by chance,[7] which undoes even his most elaborate plans:

Ô vie humaine! m'écriai-je quand je me vis seul et dans cet état, que tu es remplie d'aventures bizarres et de contretemps! Depuis que je suis sorti d'Oviedo, je n'éprouve que des disgrâces. À peine suis-je hors d'un péril, que je retombe dans un autre. En arrivant dans cette ville, j'étais bien éloigné de penser que j'y ferais bientôt connaissance avec le corrégidor. (*L'histoire*, 1.12.57)

O life! (cried I, when I found myself alone in this condition) how full of capricious accidents and disappointments art thou! Since I left Oviedo, I have met with nothing but misfortunes! Scarce had I got out of one danger, when I fell into another! and when I came into this town, I was far from thinking that I should so soon become acquainted with the Corregidor. (*Adventures*, 42)

This wandering is assuredly linked to the genre to which Lesage's work belongs—the picaresque novel often depicting a character who repeatedly falls prey to the twists of fate and is set on the path of his adventures by pure chance. Nonetheless, the way that Lesage treats the "unity" of action in *Gil Blas* suggests that this indeterminacy pertains above all to a *general* questioning of literary practice. The linking of episodes is, indeed, often unnatural, and several anecdotes could be moved without visibly altering the novel's structure. In this way Lesage pays little attention to transitions in simultaneously developing several story lines: "Laissons-là mon mariage pour un moment. L'ordre de mon histoire le demande et veut que je raconte le service que je rendis à Don Alphonse, mon ancien maître. J'avais entièrement oublié ce cavalier, et voici à quelle occasion j'en rappelai le souvenir" (I should leave my marriage for a moment, to recount the service which I did to Don Alphonso my old master, whom I had entirely forgotten till now, that I remembered him on this occasion; *L'histoire*, 10.2.430; *Adventures*, 381.)

If, moreover, on a number of occasions Lesage uses the word *étoile* (star) to symbolize the destiny of his characters, this term appears to refer less to a guardian deity than to serve as a simple expression of flattery. As an admirer of Gil Blas remarks, "Je sais trop bon gré à mon étoile de m'avoir fait rencontrer l'illustre Gil Blas de Santillane, pour ne pas jouir de ma bonne fortune le plus longtemps que je pourrai." (I am too much obliged to my kind stars for having thrown me in the way of the illustrious Gil Blas, not to enjoy my good fortune as long as I can; *L'histoire*, 1.2.28; *Adventures*, 15.) The exaggerated nature of this exclamation comically defuses the connotations normally associated with such vocabulary. There is seemingly no higher power determining the destiny of the hero, who is unable to carry any resolution he may have made. Several plans of Gil Blas and his companions actually fall through, as in this instance: "Nous nous remîmes en chemin, toujours résolus, quand nous serions à Valence, de profiter de la première occasion qui s'offrirait de passer en Italie. *Mais le Ciel disposa de nous autrement.*" (We betook ourselves again to the road, still resolved, when we should arrive at Valencia, to take the first opportunity of a passage into Italy. *But heaven disposed of us otherwise*; *L'histoire*, 6.3.309; *Adventures*, 267; emphasis added.) These unkept resolutions reveal a hero led more by the course of events—or by the author's game—than by his own will.

Moreover, Lesage takes this game to its limits by leaving to chance the actual conclusion of the story. If indeed all of the hardships endured by Gil Blas after leaving Oviedo are resolved, it appears as if the hero is not the driving force behind the outcome:

> Eh bien! Monsieur, reprit le fils de la Coscolina, vous devez vous applaudir de l'aventure, au lieu de vous en plaindre: vous êtes encore dans un âge où il n'y a point de ridicule à brûler d'une amoureuse ardeur, et le temps n'a point assez flétri votre front pour vous ôter l'espérance de plaire. Croyez-moi, quand vous reverrez don Juan, *demandez-lui hardiment sa sœur....* Vous avez des lettres de noblesse, cela suffit pour votre postérité: lorsque le temps aura mis sur ces lettres le voile épais dont il couvre l'origine de toutes les maisons, après quatre ou cinq générations, la race des Santillane sera des plus illustres. Scipion *m'encouragea par ce discours à me déclarer amant de Dorothée*, sans songer qu'il m'exposait à essuyer un refus. *Je ne m'y déterminai* néanmoins qu'en tremblant. Quoique je ne parusse pas avoir mon âge et que je pusse me donner dix bonnes années moins que je n'en avais, je ne laissais pas de me croire bien fondé à douter que je plusse à une jeune beauté. *Je pris pourtant la résolution* d'en risquer la demande sitôt que je verrais son frère. (*L'histoire*, 12.13–14.606–7; emphasis added)

> Well, Sir, (replied Coscolina's son) you ought to rejoice, instead of complaining, at the adventure: there is nothing ridiculous in a man of your age being in love; and time hath not as yet so furrowed your brow, as to deprive you of the hope of pleasing. Take my advice, and when next you see Don Juan, *boldly demand his sister in marriage....* You have letters of nobility, and that is enough for your posterity, when time shall have shrouded these letters with that thick veil which covers the origin of all great families: after four or five generations, the race of Santillane will be most illustrious. Scipio, by this discourse, *encouraged me to declare myself the lover of Dorothea*, without considering that he exposed me to the risk of a refusal: *I could not, however, determine upon it* without trembling: for, although I looked younger than I was, and could have sunk ten good years at least of my age, I could not help thinking I had good reason to doubt of my pleasing a young beauty. *I resolved, nevertheless*, to risk the demand, as soon as I should see her brother. (*Adventures*, 544–45; emphasis added)

In the end, Gil Blas resolves to make a decision—"Je [ne] m'y déterminai" (I [could not] determine upon it) and "Je pris la résolution de" (I resolved)— but he does so only *after* it is proposed to him, without it being his own initiative.

Much has been written concerning the composition and the unity of *Gil Blas*,[8] so I will limit myself here to a few observations. If some chapters forecast

adventures that Lesage abandons immediately after presenting them, it is interesting to note inversely that Lesage sometimes returns to events that he has
previously neglected to mention. This is the case, for instance, with the encounter of the protagonist and Fabricius, which could have been reported in the
opening chapter (devoted to the birth and education of Gil Blas) given that they
are "compagnon[s] d'école" (schoolmate[s]). This character, however, is only
introduced belatedly in chapter 17 in a rather artificial meeting:

> Comme je sortais de chez le lapidaire, il passa près de moi un jeune homme qui
> s'arrêta pour me considérer. Je ne me le remis pas d'abord, bien que je le con-
> nusse parfaitement. Comment donc, Gil Blas, me dit-il, feignez-vous d'ignorer
> qui je suis? Ou deux années ont-elles si fort changé le fils du barbier Nunez,
> que vous le méconnaissiez? Ressouvenez-vous de Fabrice, votre compatriote et
> votre compagnon d'école. Nous avons si souvent disputé chez le docteur
> Godinez sur les universaux et les degrés métaphysiques. (*L'histoire*, 1.17.72)

> As I came out of the jeweler's house, a young fellow, who was passing, stopped
> to consider me. Not being able to recall him at first, although I had formerly
> been intimate with him: "How, Gil Blas! (said he) do you pretend ignorance
> of me, or have two years altered the son of barber Nunez so much, that you do
> not know him? Don't you remember Fabricius, your companion and school-
> fellow, with whom you have so often disputed, at the house of doctor Godi-
> nez, upon predicables and metaphysical degrees? (*Adventures*, 55)

This reference to a prior episode of which the reader was unaware, and which
appears somewhat unnatural, reveals a degree of what we may call diegetic dis-
persion. More important, though, is that this device has a definite effect on the
reader, who finds himself obligated, as Marc Escola puts it, to accept the fact that
he must "'retrouver' un personnage qu'il n'a jamais vu" ("reencounter" a character he has never seen).[9] Escola concludes that this is "un signe de l'instabilité
du rapport que le roman entretient avec ce passé narratif dont il se défait régu-
lièrement" (a sign of the instable relation the novel maintains with this narrative past from which it is constantly departing).[10] The very idea of a stable
narrative is in this way challenged by an author who plays on an arrangement
that appears, a priori, deficient.[11]

Yet, this arrangement is perhaps only seemingly deficient, and a closer look
suggests that Lesage's discrepancies in regard to the overall composition of his
novel are less the product of clumsiness or oversight than the result of a deliberate approach. The large number of secondary characters encountered throughout the narrative, for instance, seems to have an important structural function:
it organizes the relation among the different chapters and the books. In describing this process, Cécile Cavillac points out a "coordination serrée et somme
toute assez complexe qui s'exerce à différents niveaux" (a strict and all in all rather

complex coordination exerted on various levels).[12] So it is with the presence of Laure, whom Gil Blas meets while employed by Don Mathias (3.5), and who helps him enter into the service of Arsenia (3.9). Cavillac notes also that the presence of Gregorio Rodriguez at the beginning of book 4 allows for its linking with book 3, while the second appearance of Joseph Navarro in chapter 3 of book 11 ensures the cohesion of the final volumes. The causal sequence and attention to construction are thus much greater than one might at first imagine, suggesting, it would seem, a specific intention of the author.

Jacques Robichez observes, moreover, the almost complete absence of description in *Gil Blas*: "Le héros parcourt les provinces espagnoles en tout sens, du Nord au Sud, de l'Est à l'Ouest, d'Oviedo à Grenade, de Valence à Mérida. Mais ce ne sont pas les Espagnes, c'est toujours la même. Même climat identique, mœurs immuables. Mêmes auberges, mêmes prisons, avec des aubergistes, des alguazils et des geôliers interchangeables." (The hero wanders throughout the Spanish provinces in all directions, from North to South, from East to West, from Oviedo to Granada, from Valencia to Merida. But these are not different places. It is always the same Spain: the same climate, immutable customs, the same inns, the same prisons, with interchangeable innkeepers, alguacils and jailers.)[13] Alexandre Cioranescu attributes this stereotypical representation of a conventional Spain to the fact that Lesage never visited the country he writes about: "Son habileté d'écrivain dissimule ou atténue les effets de son ignorance: il ne sait que trop que le bât blesse et il prend soin d'éviter les descriptions de paysages, de villes ou de monuments." (His skill as a writer hides or attenuates the effects of his ignorance: he is well aware of this weakness and is careful to avoid descriptions of landscapes, cities and monuments.)[14] Other critics see in this absence of details regarding the country in question a result of "la mobilité chronique du narrateur [qui] lui interdit de s'attarder en descriptions et considérations historiques" (the constant mobility of the narrator [which] keeps him from lingering over descriptions and historical considerations), or again of the age of the hero, who is very young and "plus intéressé par le spectacle des hommes (et des femmes) que par la beauté des monuments" (more interested in the spectacle of men (and women) than in the beauty of monuments), or finally proof that "un roman n'est pas un récit de voyage" (a novel is not a travel narrative).[15]

But one may also see in this attitude exhibited by Lesage an unwillingness to offer the reader the means of identifying with the narrative, or at least of entering into it and "believing" in its reality. Indeed, the parodic game played throughout the entire novel seems to suggest that it is more a way of appealing to the reader's imagination as the narrative unfolds but, ultimately, only so as to deceive it more completely. The reader is consequently compelled to understand the rules of the game, which ultimately are shown to be the rules of her own participation. Fiction must thus be outmaneuvered (*déjouée*) to the extent that its deception is to be undone and identified as such by the reader.

The reader may thus remain perplexed, for instance, when Gil Blas remarks, in leaving Madrid for Toledo, "J'avais particulièrement envie de voir Tolède. J'y arrivai au bout de trois jours. . . . J'en partis un jour au lever de l'aurore." (I longed, in particular, to see Toledo, whither I arrived at the end of three days. . . . I left it one morning by break of day; *L'histoire*, 4.9.232; *Adventures*, 199.) Yet the hero will tell us nothing about this city that he was nonetheless delighted to discover. And the same goes for Valence: "Pour moi, plein d'impatience de voir une ville dont j'avais souvent entendu vanter la beauté, je sortis du palais du gouverneur dans le dessein de me promener dans les rues." (I, impatient to see a city, the beauty of which I had heard so much extolled, went out of the governor's palace, with a design to stroll through the streets; *L'histoire*, 10.4.482; *Adventures*, 437.) Yet we learn nothing more of this city. Finally, Madrid is given the same treatment, even though Gil Blas "souhait[ât] passionnément être dans cette superbe ville, qu'on [lui] avait vantée comme l'abrégé de toutes les merveilles du monde" (longed passionately to see that august city, which had been extolled to me as the epitome of all the wonders of the world; *L'histoire*, 2.6.102; *Adventures*, 83). Once in the capital, the narrator remains quite vague as to what he sees: "Je passai le jour à courir les rues en m'amusant à regarder les choses qui étaient nouvelles pour moi. Ce qui ne me donna pas peu d'occupation. Le soir, quand j'eus soupé." (I spent the day strolling about the streets, diverting myself with looking at everything that was new to me, and this gave me sufficient employment. In the evening, after having supped; *L'histoire*, 3.1.128; *Adventures*, 106.)

This lack of description in *Gil Blas* is, to say the least, disconcerting. It seems to stem nonetheless, given the recurrence of the phenomenon, from a conscious refusal on the part of the author. As Robichez notes, "Ce ne sont pas des occasions *manquées*, mais des occasions *écartées*." (These are not *missed* opportunities, but *dismissed* opportunities.)[16] We can think of two emblematic passages in which Lesage boasts specifically of not describing. The first of these occurs when Gil Blas is preparing to introduce himself to the Archbishop of Granada:

Si j'imitais les faiseurs de romans, je ferais une pompeuse description du palais épiscopal de Grenade. Je m'étendrais sur la structure du bâtiment. Je vanterais la richesse des meubles. Je parlerais des statues et des tableaux qui y étaient. Je ne ferais pas grâce au lecteur de la moindre des histoires qu'ils représentaient: mais je me contenterai de dire qu'il égalait en magnificence le palais de nos rois. (*L'histoire*, 7.2.322)

Here, was I to imitate the authors of novels, I would give a pompous description of this episcopal palace of Grenada: I would enlarge upon the structure of the building, extol the richness of the furniture, describe the statues and paintings, and not spare the reader the least tittle of the stories they represented: but I shall content myself with observing, that it equaled our royal palace in magnificence. (*Adventures*, 285)

Lesage thus agrees to play the game admitting that his narrative, although "true," still belongs to literary convention. He draws the reader's attention to clichés of the fictional genre from which he ultimately wishes to distance himself.

Elsewhere, Raphael, on a vessel bound for Majorca, expresses himself similarly:

> À peine fûmes-nous hors du golfe d'Alicante, qu'il survint une bourrasque effroyable. J'aurais dans cet endroit de mon récit une occasion de vous faire une belle description de tempête, de peindre l'air tout en feu, de faire gronder la foudre, siffler les vents, soulever les flots, *et caetera*. Mais, laissant à part toutes ces fleurs de rhétorique, je vous dirai que l'orage fut violent, et nous obligea de relâcher à la pointe de l'île de la Cabrera. (*L'histoire*, 5.1.263)

> Scarce had we cleared the gulph of Alicant, when a terrible tempest arose. I might, in this place of my relation, take an opportunity to make a fine description of the storm; to paint the air all on fire, to make the thunder roar, the winds whistle, the mountainous billows roll, etc. But all these flowers of rhetoric apart, I assure you the hurricane was violent, and obliged us to bear away for the point of the island of Cabrera. (*Adventures*, 227)

Here Lesage refers to the topos of epic narrative, which abounds with descriptions of storms,[17] rejecting the *flowers of rhetoric* and the embellishments typically used in these sorts of descriptions. Indeed, as Jacques Proust recalls, "depuis l'*Odyssée* et l'*Énéide* jusqu'aux *Voyages de Gulliver*, en passant par les *Actes des Apôtres* et le *Tiers Livre* de Rabelais, tout récit de voyage en mer inclut *nécessairement* la relation d'une tempête" (from *The Odyssey* and *The Aeneid* to *Gulliver's Travels*, not to mention *The Acts of the Apostles* and [François] Rabelais's *Third Book*, any narrative of sea travel *necessarily* includes the account of a storm).[18] The laws of the novel thus require a narrative of a sea voyage to include the various enumerations that form the description of a storm. Lesage, however, mocks such accumulation by juxtaposing specific details so that one cannot be described without the other.

By choosing *not* to describe, Lesage consequently reveals the position he has taken with respect to the rhetorical code, situating description in what Hélène Cussac calls a "processus métaficionnel" (metafictional process).[19] These "descriptions" are thus actually organized in Lesage's writings in accordance with the traditional laws of the novel, only a contrario. This style, as is well known, would later be adopted by Denis Diderot in *Jacques le fataliste*: "Je vous fais grâce de toutes ces choses que vous trouverez dans les romans, dans la comédie ancienne et dans la société." (I will spare you all these things which you can find in novels, in ancient comedies and in society.)[20]

Lesage says nothing different, which is why the rare descriptions of place he offers all conform to a poetic topos that the reader can easily recognize. Such is the case with the thieves' den, which illustrates the topos of the world upside down, or with the island of Cabrera, which inverts the utopian narrative, immediately identifiable by the reader as a sign of fictionality.

It is nonetheless the model of the *locus amœnus*, on which Lesage bases several of his landscapes, that turns out to be the most readily identifiable—as we see, for instance, in the refuge where Gil takes shelter near the end of book 4:

> C'était une grande et profonde grotte que le temps avait percée dans la montagne, et la main des hommes y avait ajouté un avant-corps de logis bâti de rocailles et de coquillages et tout couvert de gazon. Les environs étaient parsemés de mille sortes de fleurs qui parfumaient l'air; et l'on voyait auprès de la grotte une petite ouverture dans la montagne, par où sortait avec bruit une source d'eau qui courait se répandre dans une prairie. (*L'histoire*, 4.9.233)

> It was a large deep grotto that time had scooped in the rock, to which the art of man had added a kind of front, built of pebbles and shell-work, and quite covered with turf: the adjacent field was strewed with a thousand sorts of flowers which perfumed the air, and hard by the grotto, we perceived a little opening in the rock, from whence issued with an agreeable noise, a spring of water that run winding along a meadow.[21] (*Adventures*, 200)

The landscape that Lesage compels himself for once to describe is nonetheless difficult to take seriously given his stereotypical use of the motif—so much so, as Robichez wryly suggests, that "cette innocente retraite abrite deux voleurs de grands chemins déguisés en vénérables anachorètes" (this innocent retreat shelters two highway robbers disguised as venerable anchorites).[22] Cussac, for her part, speaks of "ingrédients" in describing Lesage's borrowings from religious withdrawal: "l'aspect physique repris à frère Juan décédé, la 'charité,' l'accueil, et un dîner austère offert aux voyageurs que sont Gil et don Alphonse" (the physical appearance taken from the deceased brother John, 'charity,' hospitality, and an austere meal offered to the travelers, Gil and Don Alphonso): all of these features, according to Cussac, are "trop parfaits pour prendre le lecteur au piège" (too perfect to fool the reader).[23] The site depicted is thus an assemblage—even a collage, made from a mix of different archetypes. Through his parodic use of such commonplaces, the author questions novelistic invention itself.

In concluding *Gil Blas*, the reader is ultimately left puzzled and unsettled. By deliberately playing on temporal constraints, by breaking the illusion through geographical overdetermination, and by staging a compositional technique that is impossible to define once and for all, Lesage scoffs at our expectations and upsets our demands as readers. Before Diderot's *Jacques le fataliste*, Lesage presents us with a deceptive narration in questioning the absolute power traditionally granted to the author. In this context, to write is to take into account a person addressed and to share the game with her. A veritable exchange is thus established between the author and the reader, who agree to pretend that the universe described is a temporarily valid one.

Freed from novelistic dogma (eliciting belief in the authenticity of the story told, offering the reader the expected ending to the plot), the novelist chooses here the ludic aspect of the art of poetry so as to render explicit the affected, or even misleading, nature of literary practice. Recognizing his companions beneath the clothes of brother John and Antoine, Gil thus exclaims, in a metadiscursive nod to the reader, "Vive Dieu . . . je suis ici, à ce que je vois, en pays de connaissance" (Good God! . . . I find I am among my acquaintance here; *L'histoire*, 4.11.245; *Adventures*, 212.) The character humorously reveals in this way that he has in mind traditional scenes of recognition in the novel. Recourse to a novelistic topos is openly admitted, as if to signal to the reader that representation is a deciphering game.

It is this ironic double game that is described in narratological terms by Jacques Wagner: "La voix narrative (seconde) raconte alors moins une histoire qu'elle n'évalue les effets comiques et inacceptables sur le genre romanesque." (The [second] narrative voice is thus less telling a story than evaluating the unacceptable comic effects on the novelistic genre.)[24] The author thus places his reader in a position that requires a distant attitude while simultaneously allowing the reader to take pleasure in fiction's expected clichés. What plays out here is akin to a collaboration, or even a complicity, between partners placed on an equal footing in their respective roles. The author effectively writes a biography which he pretends to consider authentic. The reader, for his part, and to play the game properly, effectively reads a story he pretends to consider authentic. The author and the reader do not pretend to effect a speech act, but pretend to effect an act of faith in the reality of an imaginary content.

Lesage aims in this way to reconcile critical awareness with the pleasure of stories, and does so beginning with the foreword: "Ami lecteur . . . si tu lis mes aventures sans prendre garde aux instructions morales qu'elles renferment, tu ne tireras aucun fruit de cet ouvrage; mais, si tu le lis avec attention, tu y trouveras, suivant le précepte d'Horace, l'utile mêlé avec l'agréable." (Friendly reader . . . if thou perusest my adventures, without perceiving the moral instructions they contain, thou wilt reap no harvest from thy labour: but if thou readest with attention, thou wilt find in them, according to the precept of Horace, profit mingled with pleasure; *L'histoire*, foreword, 21; *Adventures*, foreword, 9.) If Lesage's foreword is itself presented as a commonplace, it is also an exhortation to the reader to read "well" and to benefit from the instructions the author will give in the pages that follow. Yet these instructions are offered in a climate of "destruction dans la joie" (gleeful destruction), to adopt a saying of Jean-Paul Sermain,[25] given how laughter subverts the world for just a fraction of a second and becomes a means of revealing the truth. In making a mockery of literary conventions, the author continually encourages a dialogic reading. This is doubtless what accounts for the many comments addressed to the reader, which render the two enunciative levels complicit: "Nous sortîmes du cabinet, après y avoir si bien fait notre main, et alors, *pour une raison que le lecteur devinera fort aisément*, Monsieur l'inquisiteur tira son cadenas qu'il voulut attacher lui-même à la porte; ensuite il y mit le scellé." (After having done our business so successfully, we came out of the closet, and, *for a reason that the reader will easily guess*, master Inquisitor took out his padlock, and fixed it to the door with his own hand, then applying the seal; *L'histoire*, 6.1.305; *Adventures*, 264; emphasis added.) The entire novel is governed by this call to complicity that is inscribed, not without irony, even in the final lines of the text: "Il y a déjà trois ans, ami lecteur, que je mène une vie délicieuse avec des personnes si chères. Pour comble de satisfaction, le ciel a daigné m'accorder deux enfants dont l'éducation va devenir l'amusement de mes vieux jours, et dont je crois pieusement être le père." (For three years, gentle reader, I have led a delicious life with people whom I love so much; and to crown my felicity, heaven has blessed me with two children, whose education shall be the amusement of my old age, and whom I piously believe to be my own; *L'histoire*, 12.14.609; *Adventures*, 548.) The text thus combines two distinct interpretive modalities—a certain form of immersion in the universe of a possible world and a distancing that allows the reader to know at every moment that she is being told a story. These repeated reversals between illusion and its conscious neutralization contribute greatly to the pleasure of reading.

Narrative contradictions, temporal distension, fragmented structure, and discontinuous writing: these are some of the compositional models on which this chapter has invited reflection in examining the reading experiences such literary forms produce.

Marc Escola and colleagues observe that, unlike many nineteenth-century novels that set their characters "dans des trajectoires conformes à leur condition et à leur situation et qui répondent aux exigences classiques de cohérence, d'exemplarité et d'économie" (on paths consistent with their conditions and situations and which follow classical demands for coherence, exemplarity, and organization), seventeenth- and eighteenth-century novels are characterized by "le goût d'un matériau hétérogène, dont les liens sont souvent imprévisibles" (the taste for diverse subject matter in which connections are often unforeseeable). The narrative traces no clear line and the conclusion is often confused or evasive; the discovery of the outcome and the retrospective grasping of the overall plot provide only an uncertain light.[26]

Lesage's novel, as analyzed here, fully reflects this approach: refusing to follow a set program, the author delights in exploiting the liberties of incompletion, watering down the action in digressive episodes and unsettling the reader by withholding the expected outcome. The polyphony of narrative voices and divergent points of view within this work, moreover, break the linearity of the narrative and create an interference that prevents any clear and definitive interpretation.

And yet, while the reader is disconcerted by such offhandedness, she is none-theless not fooled as the effects of interference remain distinct from a willing-ness to deceive. The sophisticated game Lesage indulges in ends up being rather the expression of a deep skepticism regarding the notion of truth and a demand for hermeneutical involvement on the part of the reader; the author provides *signs of truthfulness*, which the reader must recognize for what they are—namely, the simple *appearance of truth*.

For it is, in fact, the notion of recognition that is brought into play with these texts, which require the reader to identify a number of themes or structures in order to see herself as "appartenant à une communauté de *happy few*" (belong-ing to a community of *the happy few*), to take up the expression Jean-Luc Mar-tinet borrows from Stendhal's *The Red and the Black*.[27] This recognition is made possible by the use of stylistic devices (ellipses, allusions, or irony to mention only a few) that allow the reader to engage in an active reading.

But while these fictions require the reader's collaboration in the production of meaning, what can be said when this meaning is lacking? In other words, is the reader of these texts obliged to solve the meaning or experience the difficul-ties of constructing a meaning? There is a notable tension here between, on the one hand, an exhortation for a participatory readership and, on the other, the refusal of a hermeneutic readership.

Martinet observes about Stendhal that the novelistic is built by "*mettant à distance* les éléments qui relèvent d'une topique romanesque conventionnelle" (*placing at a distance* elements pertaining to conventional novelistic topoi).[28] And this is precisely what is at stake in Lesage, who diverts preconceptions regard-ing the reading of novels to the extent where what is properly novelistic is shifted or treated elusively. Indeed, Lesage constantly plays on his own frame of refer-ence and delights in endlessly exploiting the principle of "mensonge et vérité romanesques" (novelistic lying and truth) aimed at destabilizing the reader.[29] This approach effectively prevents the reader's adhesion and renders undecid-able the truth value of any claim, which may always be called into question in the merging of different ways of telling and interpreting a given event. The inter-est of a text lies precisely in this shifting from one point of view to another, in this *play*—both in the ludic and in the mechanical sense—of wavering and inde-cision between truth and fiction. *Gil Blas* corresponds to this aesthetic of fragmentation and indetermination, which results—above all—in the specific pleasure we take in reading it.

Intertextuality in the work, as in metanarrative discourse, leads the reader to decipher elements of fiction, thus placing its reading in a properly ludic space. Such is the case for the reader of *Gil Blas*, a work that not only thematizes play but offers directions for its deciphering. The modernity of Lesage's work resides in its exhibiting the processes involved in its own genesis, attesting thereby to a self-reflexive awareness.

NOTES

Translated by Matthew E. Hayden with the collaboration of the editors. Unless noted otherwise, all translations of quotations are our own.

1. This reference appears in the "Avertissement" at the beginning of the third volume of Lesage's novel, published in 1724; emphasis added. All other quotations are from René Lesage, *L'histoire de Gil Blas de Santillane*, ed. Roger Laufer (Paris: Garnier Flammarion, 1977); translations are from *The Adventures of Gil Blas of Santillane*, ed. O. M. Brack Jr. and Leslie A. Chilton, trans. Tobias Smollett (Athens: University of Georgia Press, 2011). Some passages from Smollett's translation have been revised to match more closely the original French. Hereafter, citations appear parenthetically in the text; sections and page numbers from the French edition (as *L'histoire*) will appear first, followed by page numbers for the English translation (as *Adventures*).

2. Roger Laufer, *Lesage ou Le métier de romancier* (Paris: Gallimard, 1971), 287, observes that even Lesage's rectifications in the 1747 edition are quite superficial: he simply replaces Lisbon with Warsaw, Portugal with Poland, and the Duke of Almeida with Prince Radzivil. Laufer also observes, somewhat comically, that the bullfight remains, but takes place in Warsaw.

3. On the question of history and problems of dating and periodization in *Gil Blas*, see Cécile Cavillac, *L'Espagne dans la trilogie "picaresque" de Lesage: Emprunts littéraires, empreinte culturelle*, 2 vols. (Talence, France: Presses universitaires de Bordeaux, 1984), 1:277–317.

4. The team of researchers writing under the pseudonym Hubert de Phalèse (i.e., Henri Béhar, Jacques Berchtold, Michel Bernard, Baptiste Bohet, Jean-Pierre Goldenstein, and Jean-Paul Sermain) highlights, for instance, Don Alphonso's having served in the Netherlands prior to the peace treaty: "J'allai servir dans les Pays-Bas: mais la paix se fit fort peu de temps après, et l'Espagne se trouvant sans ennemis, mais non sans envieux, je revins à Madrid." (I went to serve in the Netherlands, but the peace being concluded soon after, and Spain rid of her enemies, though not of those who envied her prosperity, I returned to Madrid; 4.10.235; 197.) According to them, this passage could only refer to the Twelve Years' Truce of 1609, whereas the rest of the chronology is situated in March–April 1608. See Hubert de Phalèse, *Les bons contes et les bons mots de* Gil Blas (Paris: Nizet, 2002), 58.

5. For instance, Ponte de Mula (1.13.60; 44–45) or Olmedo (2.9.123; 100).

6. Cavillac, *L'Espagne*, 1:247, underlines, moreover, that the novelist "surpasse de très loin en minutie géographique tous les auteurs espagnols . . . : il se veut en somme plus Espagnol qu'Alemán" (far exceeds in geographic detail any Spanish author . . . : in short, he wants to be more Spanish than Alemán).

7. Gil Blas often presents himself as a victim of fate rather than blaming his own behavior—an attitude of which he is nonetheless sometimes conscious: "Au lieu de n'imputer qu'à moi ce triste incident, et de songer qu'il ne me serait point arrivé si je n'eusse pas eu l'indiscrétion de m'ouvrir à Majuelo sans nécessité, je m'en pris à la fortune innocente et maudis cent fois mon étoile." (Instead of ascribing this unlucky adventure to myself; and considering that it would not have happened to me, had I not been so indiscreet as to unbosom myself unnecessarily to Majuelo; I imputed all to innocent fortune, and cursed my fate a thousand times; 1.16.71; 54.)

8. See, in particular, Jean Molino, "Les six premiers livres de l'*Histoire de Gil Blas de Santillane*," *Annales de la Faculté des lettres et sciences humaines d'Aix* 44 (1968): 88–101; Henri Coulet, *Le roman jusqu'à la Révolution*, vol. 1 (Paris: Armand Colin, 1967), 306–9; René Démoris, *Le roman à la première personne: Du classicisme aux Lumières* (Geneva: Droz, 2002), 347–49; and Christelle Bahier-Porte, *La poétique d'Alain-René Lesage* (Paris: Honoré Champion, 2006), 491–93.

9. Marc Escola, "Récits perdus à Santillane," in *D'une gaîté ingénieuse: "L'histoire de Gil Blas," roman de Lesage*, ed. Béatrice Didier and Jean-Paul Sermain (Louvain, Belgium: Peeters, 2004), 274.

10. Escola, "Récits perdus à Santillane," 274–275.

11. Similarly, some characters are abandoned, only to reappear later, through a simple analepsis, as is the case for instance of Rolando who rehearses what he has done since Gil Blas's escape (3.3.132–33; 113).

12. Cavillac, *L'Espagne*, 2:674.

13. Jacques Robichez, "Le refus de la description dans *Gil Blas*," *Travaux de linguistique et de littérature* 13, no. 2 (1975): 483.

14. Alexandre Cioranescu, *Le masque et le visage: Du baroque espagnol au classicisme français* (Geneva: Droz, 1983), 517. Frédéric Mancier, *Le modèle aristocratique français et espagnol dans l'œuvre romanesque de Lesage: L'histoire de Gil Blas de Santillane, un cas exemplaire* (Fasano, Italy: Schena, 2001), 49, observes also that Lesage has a "connaissance médiate, essentiellement livresque" (a mediate, essentially bookish, knowledge) of Spain.

15. François Raviez and Éloïse Lièvre, *"Gil Blas" de Lesage: Livres I–VI* (Paris: Atlande, 2002), 50.

16. Robichez, "Le refus de la description," 486, emphasis in the original.

17. Hélène Cussac, *"L'histoire de Gil Blas de Santillane* ou Une littérature du refus," in *L'assiette des fictions: Enquêtes sur l'autoréflexivité romanesque*, ed. Jan Herman, Adrien Pachoud, Paul Pelckmans, and François Rosset (Louvain, Belgium: Peeters, 2010), 298, reminds us of this in citing the example of Virgil (*Aeneid*, 1.1) and Lucan (*Pharsalia*, bk. 5).

18. Jacques Proust, "Lesage ou Le regard intérieur: Recherches sur la place et la fonction de la 'description' dans *Gil Blas*," in *Beiträge zur französischen Aufklärung und zur spanischen Literatur*, ed. Werner Krauss and Werner Bahner (Berlin: Akademie-Verlag, 1971), 299, emphasis in the original.

19. Cussac, *"L'histoire de Gil Blas*," 299.

20. Denis Diderot, *Contes et romans* (Paris: Gallimard, 2004), 680.

21. Critics have routinely expressed surprise at the amount of dialogue in *Gil Blas*. One may also be surprised at the homogeneity of the narrative fabric (as here) inserted between dialogues, which is one of Lesage's specificities.

22. Robichez, "Le refus de la description," 488.

23. Cussac, *"L'histoire de Gil Blas*," 300.

24. Jacques Wagner, "L'ironie des voix superposées dans le *Gil Blas* de Lesage," *Cahiers de narratologie* 10, no. 2 (2001): 510.

25. Jean-Paul Sermain, "Introduction," in Didier and Sermain, eds., *D'une gaîté ingénieuse*, 3.

26. Jan Herman, "Préface générale," in *La partie et le tout: La composition du roman, de l'âge baroque au tournant des Lumières*, ed. Marc Escola, Jan Herman, Lucia Omacini, Paul Pelckmans, and Jean-Paul Sermain (Louvain, Belgium: Peeters, 2011), 5–6.

27. Jean-Luc Martinet, "La marquise et la femme de chambre: Le romanesque stendhalien," *Acta fabula* 8, no. 4 (2007), http://www.fabula.org/revue/document3485.php, emphasis in the original.

28. Martinet, "La marquise et la femme de chambre," emphasis added.

29. Here I am paraphrasing René Girard, *Mensonge romantique et vérité romanesque* (Paris: Grasset, 1961).

CHAPTER 4

Playthings of Fortune

LOTS, GAMES OF CHANCE, AND INEQUALITY
IN L'ABBÉ PRÉVOST

Masano Yamashita

Early modern jurists and moralists debated the intertwining of play and Providence by engaging with the meaning of play in natural law, parsing the differences between *sort extraordinaire* and *sort ordinaire,* and warning of the deleterious consequences of confusing profane and sacred lots and games of chance. These ideas circulated in writings such as Jean Barbeyrac's *Le traité du jeu,* Pierre de Joncourt's *Quatre lettres sur les jeux de hazard,* and Jean La Placette's *Traité des jeux de hazard défendu contre les objections de Mr. de Joncourt, et quelques autres.* The French Protestant theologian Joncourt, among others, worried whether the use of lots and games had not devolved into an abusive understanding of divine Providence. According to Joncourt, their increased prevalence in ordinary life ran the risk of cheapening the original sanctity of lots, which, in biblical texts, had been used parsimoniously by God as a method of expressing divine election. There is, Joncourt admonishes, "un poison secret dans tous les Jeux, où l'on cherche à gagner, qui les rend très dangereux et très nuisibles; mais outre cela, il y a dans la plus grande partie *un abus du Sort* qui les rend profanes et criminels" (a secret poison in all games where gain is sought, which makes them very dangerous and very harmful; but beyond that, there is in most games an abuse of chance that renders them profane and criminal).[1]

Louis de Jaucourt reminds readers of the *Encyclopédie* that lots in the sacred tradition presented an equitable method for reaching decisions: "Sort, (*Critiq. sacr.*) manière de décider les choses par le hasard. Cet usage est très convenable dans plusieurs occasions, surtout dans celles où il n'y a aucune raison de préférence." (Sortition. A way of deciding things by chance. This custom is most appropriate in many instances, especially in those where there is no reason for preference.)[2] Drawing on the biblical tradition of sortition, Charles-Louis de Secondat, baron de Montesquieu advocated for the fairness of lots by arguing that lotteries are, in contradistinction to choice-based elections, fundamentally democratic practices.[3] Outside of a strictly religious framework, the use of lots fulfilled an important social function: they allowed for decision-making that ensured the equal treatment of all participants.

In the context of the ancien régime, lots and *jeux* could also be seen to unleash a potential for social subversion that undermined the traditional French society of orders, prompting some, as Jean Sgard has shown, to condemn the creation of egalitarianism through play as "immoral" rather than moral.[4] The transition from a wealth structure that could be controlled through inheritance and rank to the redistribution of wealth through chance was deeply unsettling to some. Since aspirational play (a means to cheat systems of hierarchy) could affect the scrambling of social differences, it is no wonder that gambling and lots were made an object of university debates, legal scrutiny, and heavy policing.[5] Barbeyrac thus admonished his readers against the practice of playing games with people of a lower social condition lest they start conducting themselves as if all were equal.[6] The larger financial context of John Law's speculative system during the Regency arguably transformed everyday economics into a matter of risky gambling.[7] Depending on whether one was on the winning side or not, these financial changes could be welcomed as a sign of Providence or condemned as nonsensical chance. Montesquieu's Persian travelers thus noted the sudden changes in the lives of masters and servants by elaborating the metaphor of Fortune's wheel:

> Il n'y a point de pays au monde où la fortune soit si inconstante que dans celui-ci. Il arrive tous les dix ans des révolutions qui précipitent le riche dans la misère et enlèvent le pauvre, avec des ailes rapides, au comble des richesses. Celui-ci est étonné de sa pauvreté; celui-là l'est de son abondance. Le nouveau riche admire la sagesse de la Providence; le pauvre, l'aveugle fatalité du destin.[8]

> There is no country in the world where fortune is as fickle as she is in France. Every ten years there are revolutions, which precipitate the rich into the deepest poverty and raise up the poor, on rapid wings, to the greatest wealth. The first is astonished by his penury, the second, by his plenty. The upstart is amazed by the wisdom of Providence, the newly poor by the blind reversals of destiny.[9]

The linkage between chance and Providence thus highlighted two important tensions: the competition between religious and secular perspectives on randomness and the underlying politics of social change.

The convergence and discord between sacred and profane traditions of lots and games of chance prompted the defrocked Benedictine monk l'Abbé Prévost to reflect on the valuations of play and fortune in legislation and moral life, and more broadly, guided his reflections on crises of authority. The focus of this essay will be on two novels by Prévost that, at first, appear very different. *L'histoire du Chevalier des Grieux et de Manon Lescaut* 1731 (revised in 1753) tells the story of a young couple from different social backgrounds who experience the temptations of the capital of gaming, Paris. Manon, the central female protagonist, is "passionnée pour le plaisir" (passionately fond of pleasure) and ends up being banished to colonial Louisiana.[10] At the heart of *Manon Lescaut* are the Chevalier des Grieux's hesitations between a secular and Providentialist outlook in making sense of a chance-filled destiny. The second novel, *Le philosophe anglais ou Histoire de M. Cleveland, fils naturel de Cromwell*, is set in the context of the seventeenth-century English civil wars and follows the story of Oliver Cromwell's bastard sons: Cleveland and his half brother Bridge. Amid the bastard sons' dramatic life stories, one *micro-récit* is notable for its depiction of lots in deciding human fate. The interpolated story of Bridge in book 3 features a utopian Protestant colony near the island of St. Helena, which resorts to marriage by lots in an attempt to balance the gendered demographics of its community. In spite of their differences in tone, subject matter, and historical period, both novels share common reflections on the significance of the drawing of lots and play as a double-edged sword in ordering and disordering society, and as a literary trope for weighing the influence of Fortune on human destiny. They reflect on chance and cheating as a method for taming the arbitrary, as vital resources for human agency and for redressing injustice even if this redressment often takes the guise of Providential purpose.

In Prévost's tragic worldview, lots and games of chance provide a unique opportunity to highlight the various ways individuals considered their willingness to submit to chance or, conversely, challenge their destinies. Once he encounters and becomes enamored of Manon, Des Grieux understands himself to be a plaything of Fortune, unable to control his passion.[11] In *Manon Lescaut* the literary trope of humans as *jouets de la Fortune* emphasizes the competing influences of Fortuna and Providence, which could be understood as the conflict between a profane or pagan view of life and a Christianized worldview of the divine direction of human life. In the account of his love story that he delivers to the Marquis de Renoncourt, Des Grieux describes himself as quickly surrendering himself to Fortune: "Vénus et la Fortune n'avaient point d'esclaves plus heureux et plus tendres." (Never were slaves of Venus and Fortune happier nor more fond; *Manon Lescaut*, 66; *The Story*, 46.) Yet, contrary to his fun-loving mistress, Des Grieux displays little, if any, instinct for play. His family had initially chosen for him the contemplative path of studying, an estimable choice for a younger son of a noble provincial family, to be followed by entry into an "académie" as the last step before joining the Order of Malta. He thus begins the story as a model pupil who completed his "études de philosophie" (studies in philosophy) in Amiens, where "mes maîtres me proposaient pour l'exemple du collège" (my teachers held me up as an example to the entire college; *Manon Lescaut*, 17; *The Story*, 11–12). Meeting Manon quickly derails his family's ambitions and, from that point onward, Des Grieux religiously starts to obey her whims instead of his religion, abrogating in the process his ideal of "une vie sage et chrétienne" (a good and Christian life; *Manon Lescaut*, 40; *The Story*, 28). Upon learning that their money and belongings have been destroyed in a house fire in Chaillot, the wayward chevalier wonders whether scheming might not present an auspicious opportunity to lift the couple from their dire straits. Reasoning that cheating the wealthy is sanctioned by Providence and, inspired by "Le Ciel" (Heaven), Des Grieux contemplates resorting to ruse (*industrie*) to recover his losses. He goes on to justify his willingness to game the system as a strategy for economic equalization:

> *Le Ciel* me fit naître une idée, qui arrêta mon désespoir. Je crus qu'il ne me serait pas impossible de cacher notre perte à Manon, et que, *par industrie, ou par quelque faveur du hasard*, je pourrais fournir assez honnêtement à son entretien, pour l'empêcher de sentir la nécessité.... Combien de personnes vivent à Paris, qui n'ont ni mon esprit, ni mes qualités naturelles, et qui doivent néanmoins leur entretien à leurs talents, tels qu'ils les ont! *La Providence*, ajoutais-je, en réfléchissant sur les différents états de la vie, n'a-t-elle pas arrangé les choses fort sagement? La plupart des grands et des riches sont des sots: cela est clair à qui connaît un peu le monde. Or, il y a là-dedans une *justice admirable*: s'ils joignaient l'esprit aux richesses, ils seraient trop heureux, et le reste des hommes trop misérables. Les qualités du corps et de l'âme sont accordées à ceux-ci, comme des moyens de se tirer de la misère et de la pauvreté. Les uns prennent part aux richesses des grands, en servant à leurs plaisirs; ils en font des dupes.
>
> ... Et de quelque façon qu'on le prenne, c'est un fonds excellent de revenu pour les petits, que la sottise des riches et des grands.

> *Heaven* inspired me with an idea that saved me from despair. I thought it would not be impossible for me to conceal the loss from Manon and, *through some ingenious scheme or favourable turn of events*, to provide for her honourably enough myself to keep her from suffering from want.... Think how many people live in Paris who have neither my wit nor my natural qualities and who nevertheless depend for their livelihood on their talents, such as they are! Has not *Providence*, I added, reflecting on the different conditions in life, arranged things very wisely? The great and the wealthy are, for the most part, fools; this is obvious to anyone who knows anything of the world. And is there not an *admirable justice* in this? If, as well as wealth, they also had wit, they would be too fortunate and the rest of mankind too wretched. Qualities of mind and body have rather been given to these latter, so that they may use

them as a means of extricating themselves from wretchedness and poverty. Some of them acquire a share of the wealth enjoyed by the great by procuring them their pleasures, and so make dupes of them ... whichever way you look at it, the foolishness of the great and the wealthy is an excellent source of revenue for the humble. (*Manon Lescaut*, 53–54; *The Story*, 38; emphasis added)

Several assumptions are made in this reasoning. First, Des Grieux appeals to Christian Providence as a counterforce to the erratic ways of pagan Fortuna. In the *Manuel lexique*, Prévost defined *Fortune* as synonymous with chance. He elaborates his definition thus: "Les Anciens représentaient la Fortune sous la forme d'une femme, tantôt assise, tantôt debout, tenant un gouvernail, avec une roue à côté d'elle, pour marquer son inconstance; et dans sa main une corne d'abondance." (The Ancients represented Fortune in the guise of a woman, sometimes sitting, sometimes standing, holding a rudder with a wheel next to her, to show her inconsistency; and in her hand, a cornucopia.)[12] Fortune toys with human destiny and operates blindly, in complete disregard of merit and human effort. Jaucourt reminds readers of the *Encyclopédie* of Fortune's cruel randomness in the ancient tradition: "Fortune, (Mythol. Littér.) fille de Jupiter, divinité aveugle, bizarre, et fantasque, qui dans le système du Paganisme presidait à tous les événements, et distribuait les biens et les maux selon son caprice." (Fortune, daughter of Jupiter, a blind divinity, bizarre and fanciful, who in the pagan system presided over all events, and distributed goods and misfortunes according to her whim.)[13] If Fortune appears in *Manon Lescaut* as an indomitable force that toys with human destiny and thwarts individual agency (the couple encounters a series of unfortunate events that dampens their prospects of enjoying themselves in Paris: the Chaillot fire is quickly succeeded by another loss of their belongings, due to theft), Providence can be counted on, according to the chevalier, to be a more equitable life force.

In conventional early modern wisdom, chance (or Fortune, since the two are interchangeable in Prévost's lexicon) has, in effect, limited meaning from a providential perspective. God unfolds his plan in people's lives in a way that may not appear legible to humans. From the perspective of Providence, chance is, in a sense, fundamentally specious. Des Grieux appears to take up a critical stance toward chance rather than merely accept to be its victim. In the passage previously cited, he rather facilely claims as certain that Providence is guiding him to engage in scheming. Scheming counteracts chance and acts, according to Des Grieux's rather dubious reasoning, as the organ of Providence. Egged on by Manon's brother, Des Grieux resolves to recover their money by gambling "comme [le] moyen le plus facile et le plus convenable à [sa] situation" (as the easiest means and one of the best suited to [his] situation; *Manon Lescaut*, 56; *The Story*, 39). He chooses this route, however, not as a way of using chance (gambling) to counteract chance (the misfortune of having been the victim of a damaging fire), but by cheating at cards and negating the core aleatory principle of games of *alea* (chance):

> J'acquis surtout beaucoup d'habileté à faire une volte-face, à filer la carte, et m'aidant fort bien d'une longue paire de manchettes, j'escamotais assez légèrement pour tromper les yeux des plus habiles, et ruiner sans affectation quantité d'honnêtes joueurs. Cette adresse extraordinaire hâta si fort les progrès de ma fortune, que je me trouvai en peu de semaines des sommes considérables, outre celles que je partageais de bonne foi avec mes associés. (*Manon Lescaut*, 64)

> I acquired, above all, great facility in handling cards, in flipping, foisting, and palming them, and, with the assistance of a long pair of cuffs, in making them disappear and reappear so dexterously as to deceive the keenest eye and to ruin, without ceremony, any number of honest players. This extraordinary skill brought about so rapid an improvement in my fortune that, within the space of a few weeks, I had accumulated considerable sums of money, apart from those I shared in good faith with my associates. (*The Story*, 44–45)

Des Grieux combats chance by controlling his participation in *jeux de hazard*, choosing *industrie* (ruse) and "adresse extraordinaire" (extraordinary skill; *Manon Lescaut*, 64; *The Story*, 44) over passively waiting for a "faveur du hasard" (favourable turn of events; *Manon Lescaut*, 53; *The Story*, 38). He is quick to convince himself that gambling and even being a card sharp are morally acceptable activities since they allow for an alternative redistribution of wealth. According to this line of reasoning, it is simply unfair that wealth should be concentrated in the hands of a few. More specifically in regard to his personal situation (and class-inherited sense of entitlement), Des Grieux sees being a card sharp as morally justifiable when it restores his fortunes to what he believes they should rightly be. In other words, his poverty is an injustice that should be rectified by any means available.

There is an historical analogue to this argument for social justice by economic redistribution, or "restitution" achieved through play.[14] Parisian *maisons de jeu*, such as the Hôtel de Transylvanie, mentioned in *Manon Lescaut* as the *lieu de rendez-vous* for Des Grieux's gambling activities, were in effect authorized by the police starting in 1722, provided that they pay a fee of two hundred thousand livres that would then be used to aid the poor.[15] Instead of condemning gambling houses as dens of social corruption and erosion, government officials realized that *tripots* could perhaps more fruitfully be used as a socioeconomic corrective to unequal distributions of wealth. Similarly, the popularity of charitable lotteries throughout the eighteenth century demonstrated the prevalence of the idea that lotteries and games could be utilized for philanthropic purposes.[16] Although Des Grieux's gambling takes place several years before the 1722 police toleration of *maisons de jeu* in Paris, Prévost wrote his story in 1731, informed by the shifts in social attitudes toward gambling during the *Régence*.

While pursuing this analogy between Des Grieux's advocacy of social justice through gaming and the legal history that links the allowance for *académies de jeu* with assistance for the poor, it is equally important to highlight the significant material differences between the indigent population of Paris and the merely relative poverty of Des Grieux. In the passage previously noted, Des Grieux counts himself as newly belonging to the poor. Poverty, of course, can only be grasped in relative terms in his tale. As the younger son of a provincial family of *petite noblesse*, the chevalier does not have access to the wealth of the bankers of the novel, but even at his poorest (including the exile in the colonial settlement of New Orleans), Des Grieux manages to maintain two domestic servants by his and Manon's side.[17] Des Grieux can thus hardly be placed among the *indigents* whose destitution (sometimes tied to their inability to work) could be alleviated only by charitable donations. Further, his cheating is not philanthropic, as the gains he makes as a card sharp serve solely to maintain his and Manon's lifestyle rather than being shared with a larger circle of *malheureux*. Des Grieux cannot be compared to the brigand Louis Dominique Cartouche, who famously stole from the rich in order to give to the poor.[18] Rather, the chevalier's justification for cheating reeks of the interested cynicism of Denis Diderot's scoundrel, Rameau's nephew, whose hedonistic existence was based on stealing from his students and scheming against the wealthy whenever the opportunity arose. Yet for "Lui," the parasitic exploitation of his patrons was still "social justice" in action:

> On dit que *si un voleur vole l'autre, le diable s'en rit*. Les parents regorgeaient d'une fortune acquise, Dieu sait comment; c'étaient des gens de cour, des financiers, de gros commerçants, des banquiers, des gens d'affaire. Je les aidais à restituer, moi, et une foule d'autres qu'ils employaient comme moi. Dans la nature, toutes les espèces se dévorent; toutes les conditions se dévorent dans la société. *Nous faisons justice les uns des autres, sans que la loi s'en mêle.* La Deschamps, autrefois, aujourd'hui la Guimard venge le prince du financier; et c'est la marchande de modes, le bijoutier, le tapissier, la lingère, l'escroc, la femme de chambre, le cuisinier, le bourrelier, qui vengent le financier de la Deschamps.[19]

> You know that saying: "if one thief steals from another, the devil laughs." The parents were dripping with money acquired God knows how; they were courtiers, tax farmers, wholesalers, bankers, businessmen. I helped them to make restitution, I and countless others who, like me, were employed by them. In nature all the species prey on one another; in society all the classes do the same. We mete out justice to one another without benefit of the law. La Deschamps in the past, and today la Guimard, avenge the King by cheating the

tax farmer; it's the dressmaker, the jeweller, the upholsterer, the linen maid, the swindler, the lady's maid, the cook, the harness-maker, who avenge the tax farmer by cheating la Deschamps.[20]

Des Grieux likewise considers cheating and stealth as alternative paths for the distribution of wealth, but his misappropriation of the wealth of others differs from Lui's Epicureanism on one significant point—namely, that it is undertaken to satisfy his mistress's taste for pleasure rather than for himself. He does not describe any shared scenes of material enjoyment, for his passion (which he understands in the etymological sense of suffering) rests in his all-consuming attention to Manon. In other words, he enters the clandestine world of gambling only because of his dutifulness toward his beloved rather than out of self-interest.

As suggested by the name of its organization, the Ligue de l'Industrie, which Des Grieux joins, professionalizes and organizes the world of card sharps. In the shady, mixed social world of *tripots*, gambling represents leisure for some and business for others. Des Grieux's *industrie* merits further scrutiny. *Industrie*, in the eighteenth century, as mentioned earlier, points to ruse or trickery, in addition to indicating the modern sense of industriousness. It signals a shortcut to work in its tactical (and perhaps classist) avoidance of effort in the face of adversity and economic need. The *Dictionnaire de l'Académie* elaborates: "On appelle en plaisantant, *Chevaliers d'industrie, ou Chevaliers de l'industrie,* ceux qui n'ayant point de bien vivent d'adresse." (*Knights of Industry* is said in jest of those who possessing no assets, make a living out of ruse and inventiveness.)[21] *Industrie* also typifies the perversion (in the etymological sense of diversion and indirection) that many nobles found necessary to introduce in their disdainful treatment of any work or effort that is nonmilitary or nontheological. Frédéric Deloffre and Raymond Picard further point out that the order of the Chevaliers d'Industrie, joined by Des Grieux, parodies the Order of Malta with its gradations of "novices" and "chevaliers" (*Manon Lescaut*, 63). Des Grieux thus explains, "Enfin, on rendit graces à M. Lescaut d'avoir procuré à l'Ordre un novice de mon mérite, et l'on chargea un des chevaliers de me donner, pendant quelques jours, les instructions nécessaires." (Finally they thanked M. Lescaut for having procured a novice of such merit for the Order, and they assigned one of the chevaliers to give me the necessary instruction during the next few days; *Manon Lescaut*, 66; *The Story*, 44.)

Furthermore, Des Grieux's *industrie* should be placed within the context of the other kinds of work mentioned in the novel. It appears in contrast to the abundant wealth generated by the invisible work of Manon's patrons—the tax collectors and other financier types—the practical details of which are left unmentioned in the novel (partially, perhaps, because Prévost is at pains to underline how alien the secret world of high-stakes finance would have been to a young, studious provincial man of *petite noblesse*). The chevalier's *industrie* appears linked with the clandestine work of morally dubious characters: Manon's dabblings in being a courtesan, and her brother's side gig as a gamester (his official métier is "guardsman," an occupation he fulfills in a typically brutish manner).[22] These illicit activities result in compromising Des Grieux by association—his "fraternité avec Lescaut et Manon" (fraternal resemblance to Manon and Lescaut; *Manon Lescaut*, 84; *The Story*, 59) showing how few substantive differences there can be between the actions of a nobleman and commoners. Thanks, though, to the socially sanctioned, ludic nature of the *académies de jeu*, Des Grieux is able to conceal his professional endeavors as a leisure activity and manages to pass as a genteel player: "On prétendit qu'il y avait beaucoup à espérer de moi, parce qu'ayant quelque chose dans la physionomie qui sentait l'honnête homme, personne ne se défierait de mes artifices." (They claimed that a great deal was to be hoped for from me, since, with something in my physiognomy that proclaimed a man of honour, no one would suspect me of guile; *Manon Lescaut*, 62–63; *The Story*, 44.) Here Des Grieux finally appears as a player—an actor— simulating various social roles (the gentleman gambler, the dutiful son, the remorseful friend, etc.). More broadly speaking, he plays with language rhetorically (arguing, for instance, that Providence is on his side as God defends the poor). His sense of play—rhetorical and performative—proves to be more layered and formally complex than Manon's frank taste for pleasure. Des Grieux's and Manon's divergent modes of play perhaps indicate the way in which the social identity of each is molded differently by their respective historical circumstances. Des Grieux, coming from an old provincial family, presents the burden of the past. In an act of noblesse oblige, he responds to gambling equivocally by downplaying his personal involvement in the compromising world of *tripots*, *agioteurs*, and games of chance. Manon's fun-loving inclinations are less complicatedly posited as an essential part of her "nature." Her character is treated synecdochically as an organic part of Paris itself, as is her brother, Lescaut, who is described as knowing Paris "parfaitement" (intimately; *Manon Lescaut*, 54; *The Story*, 39).

Jean Sgard qualified Manon's taste for enjoyment as a "deterministic sensualism" suggestive of agentless automation,[23] and Naomi Segal, borrowing the framework of modern psychology, speaks of the couple's "addiction" (Des Grieux's love addiction, and Manon's addiction to fun).[24] Nonetheless, Manon's penchant for play does possess a unique quality in that it emphasizes her "caractère extraordinaire" (extraordinary character; *Manon Lescaut*, 61; *The Story*, 43). Hers is a hedonism without materialism that avoids the conventional moral vices (greed, avariciousness, and interestedness) linked to the expenditure of capital:

> C'était du plaisir et des passe-temps qu'il lui fallait. Elle n'eût jamais voulu toucher un sou, si l'on pouvait se divertir sans qu'il en coûte. Elle ne s'informait

pas même quel était le fonds de nos richesses, pourvu qu'elle pût passer agréablement la journée; de sorte que n'étant, ni excessivement livrée au jeu, ni capable d'être éblouie par le faste des grandes dépenses, rien n'était plus facile que de les satisfaire, en lui faisant naître tous les jours des amusements de son gout. Mais c'était une chose si nécessaire pour elle d'être ainsi occupée par le plaisir, qu'il n'y avait pas le moindre fond à faire, sans cela, sur son humeur et sur ses inclinations. (*Manon Lescaut*, 61)

What she needed was pleasure and diversion. She would never have wanted a single *sou*, if only amusement could be had free of charge. The general state of our finances was of no interest to her, so long as she could spend the day in some agreeable fashion; so that, since she was neither excessively prone to gambling, nor likely to be dazzled by extravagant displays of wealth, nothing was easier than to make her happy, by continually devising entertainments that were to her taste. But such was her need for constant pleasure that, if it was not forthcoming, there was no relying on her temper or mood. (*The Story*, 43)

As a working mistress, Manon accepts labor as the necessary precondition for her enjoyment of Paris's delights, yet the métier of a grisette presents certain traps. Manon is doubly condemned to remain a virtual prisoner, enslaved to her own and her male patrons' pleasures. Prévost, however, includes a rare reference to an idyllic moment of female, collective enjoyment. In a remarkable passage, Des Grieux describes Manon's group outings with female companions who gamble in part as a way of funding travel for their *parties de campagne* in the Bois de Boulogne:

Elle se lia, dans le voisinage, avec quelques jeunes personnes que le printemps y avait ramenées. La promenade et les petits exercices de leur sexe faisaient alternativement leur occupation. Une partie de jeu, dont elles avaient réglé les bornes, fournissait aux frais de la voiture. Elles allaient prendre l'air au bois de Boulogne, et le soir, à mon retour, je retrouvais Manon plus belle, plus contente, et plus passionnée que jamais. (*Manon Lescaut*, 118)

She made friends with several young women, whom the fine weather had brought back to our neighbourhood. Walks and other little pastimes appropriate to their sex kept them occupied. A game of cards, whose limits they set in advance, would furnish the means to hire a carriage. They would go together to take the air in the Bois de Boulogne and, when I returned in the evening, I would find Manon waiting for me, happier, more beautiful, and more passionate than ever. (*The Story*, 83–84)

The women's collective enjoyment has for the most part been largely ignored by most Prévost scholars, who prefer to focus instead on the libertinism that takes places in the forest via the Italian prince's encounter with Manon in the park. Deloffre and Picard, however, provide an invaluable gloss of Manon's group outings in their 1964 edition of the text, explaining the custom of pooling gambling losses into a fund for travel expenses: "Les pertes de chaque joueuse vont à un fonds commun, qui est employé à l'entretien collectif d'un carrosse." (The losses of each player go to a common fund, which is used for the collective maintenance of a carriage; *Manon Lescaut*, 118n4.) This custom transforms gambling losses into a counterpleasure—converting the stereotypical Parisian vice of gambling into an occasion for women's group leisure. Individual losses in gambling are thus channeled for the benefit of a social collective.

Another unexpected usage of chance occurs in the last part of the novel, which covers Manon's deportation to Louisiana (*Manon Lescaut*, 165; *The Story*, 118). Punished for leading Des Grieux astray, Manon is exiled to colonial New Orleans, where Des Grieux follows her. Prévost follows history in this episode. Starting in August 1719, young *indésirables* (vagabonds, prostitutes, or young people sent away by their relatives) were forcibly sent to Louisiana and married off to French settlers.[25] Des Grieux refers to the colonial administration of marriages and the custom of marrying by lots: the governor "donna les plus jolies aux principaux et le reste fut tiré au sort" ([gave] the prettiest to the more prominent among them, and lots were drawn for the rest; *Manon Lescaut*, 186; *The Story*, 133).[26] Marriages are thus twice decided by chance. First, they are based on physical appearance (Laclos's Marquise de Merteuil had famously derided such a chance-ridden event: "une belle figure" (a pretty face) is, after all, a "pur effet du hasard" (purely a matter of chance); and second, the remaining women are distributed by lot.[27] Manon is saved from these arbitrary rules thanks to the ship captain's mistaken impression that she and Des Grieux are already married to one another and his recognition of their merit. The governor of New Orleans thus informs them, "J'apprends du capitaine, nous dit-il, que vous êtes mariés et qu'il vous a reconnus sur la route pour deux personnes d'esprit et de mérite." (I understand from the captain, he said, that you are married, and that during the voyage he has found you to be people of intelligence and merit; *Manon Lescaut*, 186; *The Story*, 133.) Their good works, revealed through their assistance to fellow community members in New Orleans, seem to momentarily indicate that their lives could be improved by their moral choices rather than rest on Fortune and chance.[28] In other words, the New World promises to compensate the characters for their actions rather than reflect the aleatory bent of their social life in Paris. Although provisionally taken for the exception to the French rule of chance (as noted earlier, Manon escapes marriage by lottery—the governing mechanism imposed by the colonial administration), the couple face retribution when the truth about their unwedded state comes to light, and Des Grieux announces his return back to France following Manon's death in the American wilderness. Fate refuses him the right to die and provides instead the opportunity to "réparer, par une vie sage et réglée, le scandale de ma conduite" (rectify, by a wise and well-ordered life, the scandal of my past conduct; *Manon Lescaut*, 202; *The Story*, 145).

———

In *Cleveland, ou Le philosophe anglais*, marriage by lots also serves to highlight the conflict between choice and chance. Cleveland's half brother Bridge takes up residence on a colony-island close to St. Helena where a community of Huguenot refugees has found sanctuary following the Siege of La Rochelle (1627–28). Their community is abundant in natural resources, but has one fatal flaw: by some strange accident men are outnumbered by women by four to one, so that a substantial cohort of nubile women have no one to marry.[29] Bridge is recruited to the colony by a Frenchwoman, Mme Eliot, alongside five other men, as a potential future husband for one of the hundred young women "qui étaient dans le besoin du mariage" (who were in need of husbands; *Cleveland*, 193). Nature has played a cruel joke on the island: all of the young women have been graced with good looks. Mme Eliot emphasizes the wasteful, anti-utilitarianism of nature in the French colony: "Il est vrai que nos filles sont des créatures toutes parfaites; il semble que la nature, en les formant, mette en charmes tout ce qu'elle aurait dû employer de plus pour produire un garçon." ('Tis true indeed that the females are amiable creatures and one would imagine that nature in creating them, had employed all her graces and charms; *Cleveland*, 189; *The Life*, 75.) Prévost had used the suggestive metaphor of "jeux de la nature" (whims of nature) to speak of the implausible natural space of wonder (an isolated cavern by the mountains of Devonshire insulated from the ravages of history) in which Cleveland and his mother sought refuge following the bastard's birth.[30] In the case of the *colonie rochelloise*, nature's implausibility and ironic dispensation of gendered bodies and beauty is met with a playful human countertactic.

Marriage by lots is presented as an equitable way of organizing the community: if chance decides who gets married to whom, then no one can be accused of being given preferential treatment. As Mme Eliot explains to Bridge, "La résolution qu'on avait prise était de faire dépendre du sort à qui la préférence serait accordée; car il ne faut rien ici, ajouta-t-elle, qui blesse la loi de l'égalité." (It had been resolved that preference would be decided by drawing lots, as there must be nothing here, she added, that offends the law of equality; *Cleveland*, 193; *The Life*, 180.) The use of lots is justified, moreover, as being only seemingly random: according to *le ministre*, this "ceremony" allows for the expression of divine will (*Cleveland*, 199; *The Life*, 186–87)—a point that will immediately come under question as Bridge soon discovers the tyrannical ways of the administrator in charge of the island's laws. Bridge balks at the entire process; he does not want to cede his right to choose a spouse—construed by him as a *human right*—and

he fears the possibility of being assigned a homely wife. Bridge apprehends the
risk of being the exception to the rule—that is, of being paired with the only plain
woman in the colony:

> Je me sentais un fonds de délicatesse qui ne s'accomoderait point d'une épouse
> dont je ne serais redevable qu'au hasard. Mon cœur demandait à choisir, et je
> commençai à craindre de ne pas trouver dans l'île tout le bonheur qu'on y
> promettait, si j'étais contraint de vivre avec une femme que je ne pusse goûter.
> (*Cleveland*,193)

> I was quite shocked and found myself unwilling to take up with a spouse allot-
> ted to me merely by chance. My heart required that I should be permitted to
> choose, and I began to fear that I would not find on the island all the happi-
> ness that was promised me if I were forced to live with a woman. (181)

The will to choose is echoed by the other five male recruits: "Ils sentaient comme
moi beaucoup de douleur de se voir condamnés à recevoir leur épouse du hasard.
Nous sommes les premiers, dit l'un d'eux, nous avons le droit de choisir." (Like
myself, they felt much pain at being condemned to take a wife at random, as
determined by chance. "We came first ashore," said one of them, "we have the
right to choose"; *Cleveland*, 194; *The Life*, 181.) The question of choice is couched
in slightly reductive terms: the six men all object to receiving a spouse "du
hasard" (at random) owing to a libidinal "penchant" (inclination)—specifically,
their wish for an attractive spouse. The broader use of lots in the political life of
the colony is also emphasized in the organization of the government, since the
officials of the island are elected by drawing lots: "Chaque année, nous élisons
au sort quatre gouverneurs, qui sont chargés de veiller continuellement au bien
public." (Every year, we elect by lots four governors, who are charged with continually overseeing the public good; (*Cleveland*, 195; *The Life*, 182.) The seemingly
oxymoronic formulation—electing chance—is noteworthy. Lots have a history
of being used when sharing becomes a community imperative. When human
resources (including women) and land require evenhanded distribution, lots present a means of arbitration on behalf of the common good. This "blind" method
of justice brings to mind—and is correlated with—the allegory of Justice, who
since the fifteenth century has often been represented blindfolded.[31] As Denis
Grélé, Robert Mauzi, and Jean-Michel Racault have shown, however, Bridge and
his fellow recruits stand as individualists, who refuse to let go of their own will
and desire.[32] Further, the election—the consensual acceptance—of chance in the
colony avers to be illusory and self-defeating. The professed adherence to equality unveils systemic inequality and loyalty to social hierarchy, while the division
of labor is maintained along strict class lines. Every inhabitant is expected to obey
the *ministre*'s iron rule, and domestic servants perform the work while their masters enjoy the fruits of their labor.[33] Bridge and his companions rebel and opt to

clandestinely marry their own *épouses de cœur,* making them legal adulterers (*Cleveland,* 258; *The Life,* 253). In turn, nature appears to play a trick on Bridge by making him the only man to impregnate his chosen wife, making his culpability visible to all. This biological outcome is read in different ways. In the eyes of the other men, who have also followed their own hearts, Bridge's illegal wife's pregnancy appears as a "disposition du Ciel" (indulgence of Providence) and "une confirmation de la petite autorité qu'ils m'avaient accordée sur eux" (a confirmation of the little authority that they had given me over them; *Cleveland,* 252; *The Life,* 246), whereas for the local community, Angélique's pregnancy is read as a sign of Bridge's divine punishment. As the consistory deems,

> Qu'il n'était pas vraisemblable que de six jeunes gens qui eussent le même commerce avec de jeunes filles de leur âge, il n'y en eût qu'un qui fût devenu père. Effectivement, il y avait quelque chose de si extraordinaire dans cet événement, que j'étais embarrassé moi-même à l'expliquer. Je le regarde encore comme une preuve sans réplique de la réalité de quelque puissance maligne qui s'est comme emparée de mon sort, et *qui change le cours même de la nature pour assurer ma perte.* (*Cleveland,* 258; emphasis added)

> It was not plausible that out of six young men who frequented young women of their age, there was only one of them who became a father. This was indeed so peculiar a circumstance, that I could scarcely account for it, quite embarrassed as to explaining it. I view it as an irrefutable proof of the reality of a malignant power that has taken hold of my destiny, and *even changes the usual course of nature to make my destruction certain.* (*The Life,* 253; emphasis added)

In this example of a single-instance pregnancy, nature's exception is interpreted as a God-ordained diversion. At bottom, the inscrutability of the authorship of events reminds Prévostian characters of the limits of their agency, subject as they are to various origins and modalities of play ("jeux de la nature," divine Providence, and chance) whereby intentions and outcomes become disjointed. In spite of the characters' tendency to either misread, dismiss, or appropriate Providence for their own purposes, their recourse to chance has much to tell the modern reader about the way they understand chance as a possible social corrective to human injustice. Lots and play allow the Prévostian characters to reclaim their agency and impose their will even when disguising this, if necessary, as Providential fulfillment. In other words, they play with chance even while refusing to be *playthings* of chance. Des Grieux and Bridge evince a desire to test, and occasionally question, the arbitrary limits set by the social order that deprive individuals of their freedom. The colonial marriages by lottery described in *Manon Lescaut* and *Cleveland* serve as sharp cases in point. The play of *alea* (chance) is used to highlight the potential differences between the genuinely random and the arbitrary, the latter of which is often shown to be social in origin.

In this way, games of chance appear as a powerful instrument in denouncing the reign of the arbitrary.

NOTES

Unless noted otherwise, all translations are my own.

1. Pierre de Joncourt, *Quatre lettres sur les jeux de hazard, et une cinquième sur l'usage de se faire celer pour éviter une visite incommode* (The Hague: T. Johnson, 1713), 13.

2. Louis de Jaucourt, "Sort," in *Encyclopédie; ou Dictionnaire raisonné des sciences, des arts et des métiers*, 17 vols., ed. Denis Diderot and Jean le Rond d'Alembert (Paris: Briasson, 1751–1765), 15:376.

3. As Montesquieu notes, "Voting by *lot* is in the nature of democracy; voting by *choice* is in the nature of aristocracy;" emphasis in the original. See Montesquieu, *The Spirit of the Laws*, trans. Anne M. Cohler, Basia Carolyn Miller, and Harold Samuel Stone (Cambridge: Cambridge University Press, 1989), 13.

4. Jean Sgard, "Tricher," in *Le jeu au dix-huitième siècle* (Aix-en-Provence, France: Édisud, 1976), 252.

5. According to Robert Mauzi, "Écrivains et moralistes du XVIIIe siècle devant les jeux de hasard," *Revue des sciences humaines* 90 (1958): 222, the Sorbonne made a pronouncement defending games of chance in "Résolution sur le jeu de hasard" (1697). The police prohibitions published by Nicholas de La Mare in *Traité de la police* and by the Marquis d'Argenson show the Paris police's dogged efforts to regulate gambling activities. Ever popular, these activities were tolerated more than they were veritably banned. For a chronological list of laws prohibiting games of chance, see Daniel Jousse, *Traité de la justice criminelle en France*, vol. 3 (Paris: Debure, 1771), 555–56.

6. Jean Barbeyrac, *Traité du jeu, où l'on examine les principales questions de droit naturel et de morale qui ont du rapport à cette matière*, vol. 1 (Amsterdam: Pierre Humbert, 1709), 415.

7. Jean-Michel Rey, *Le temps du crédit* (Paris: Desclée de Brouwer, 2002), 87, observes, for instance, that John Law was often viewed in France above all as a great gambler and as liable to extend gambling to the financial administration of the whole country. Britain witnessed a similar culture shift during the financial revolution, when the stock market was transformed into an adult playground, leading Daniel Defoe to grumble, in *The Anatomy of Exchange-Alley; or A System of Stock-Jobbing* (London: E. Smith, 1719), 43–44, that "Stockjobbing is Play; a Box and Dice may be less dangerous, the Nature of them are alike, a Hazard, and if they venture at either what is not their own, the Knavery is the same."

8. Sara Maza has studied the involvement of servants in gambling and the social mixing of gambling parties in French towns such as Aix-en-Provence. She argues that servants were hybrid creatures who, through proximity with their masters, could navigate the codes of the well-bred while also finding themselves playing alongside peasants at card games. See Sara Maza, *Servants and Masters in Eighteenth-Century France: The Uses of Loyalty* (Princeton, NJ: Princeton University Press, 1983), 147–48.

9. Montesquieu, *Persian Letters*, trans. Margaret Mauldon, ed. Andrew Kahn (Oxford: Oxford University Press, 2008), 131.

10. Abbé Prévost, *Histoire du chevalier des Grieux et de Manon Lescaut*, ed. Frédéric Deloffre and Raymond Picard (Paris: Garnier, 1965), 50; the translation is Abbé Prévost, *The Story of the Chevalier des Grieux and Manon Lescaut*, trans. Angela Scholar (Oxford: Oxford University Press, 2004), 36. Hereafter, citations will appear parenthetically in the text; the page numbers from the French edition will appear first (as *Manon Lescaut*), followed by page numbers for the English translation (as *The Story*).

11. Prévost tends to capitalize the word *Fortune*, borrowing from the classical allegorical tradition that elevates it into a superhuman power. For example, Des Grieux laments,

"La Fortune ne me délivra d'un précipice que pour me faire tomber dans un autre." (Fortune delivered me from the brink of one precipice only to plunge me over another; *Manon Lescaut*, 75; *The Story*, 52.) Likewise, Des Grieux's love rhetoric tends to create a quasi-agentless self: "L'amour est un bon maître." (Love is a good teacher; *Manon Lescaut* 117; *The Story*, 83.)

12. Abbé Prévost, *Manuel lexique, ou Dictionnaire portatif des mots français dont la signification n'est pas familière à tout le monde*, vol. 1 (Paris: Chez Didot, 1750), 349. The linkage and tension between Fortune and chance are commonly posited and debated in the seventeenth century. See John Lyons, *The Phantom of Chance: From Fortune to Randomness in Seventeenth-Century French Literature* (Edinburgh: University of Edinburgh Press, 2011), 2–3. Prévost, writing in the early eighteenth century, is interested in how traditional metaphors and images such as Fortune can be mobilized to make sense of modern social realities.

13. Louis de Jaucourt, "Fortune," in Diderot and d'Alembert, eds., *Encyclopédie*, 7:206.

14. For other early eighteenth-century literary (most often picaresque) examples of schemers' references to "restitution," see Sgard, "Tricher," 254.

15. As George Matoré explains, "À partir du 16 avril 1722, les pouvoirs publics autorisèrent à Paris huit maisons de jeu moyennant un forfait de 200,000 livres à verser aux pauvres." (Starting in April 16, 1722, the public authorities authorized eight gambling dens in Paris on the condition that a lump sum of 200,000 pounds be paid to the poor.) Abbé Prévost, *Histoire du chevalier des Grieux et de Manon Lescaut*, ed. Georges Matoré (Geneva: Droz, 1953), 210n1438. In *Manon Lescaut*, the Hôtel de Transylvanie is described to be still held under police surveillance.

16. Francis Freundlich, *Le monde du jeu à Paris, 1715–1780* (Paris: Albin Michel, 1995), 37–38. Three charitable lotteries were officially recognized by Louis XV starting in 1726. See Marie-Laure Legay, *Les loteries royales dans l'Europe des Lumières, 1680–1815* (Villeneuve-d'Ascq, France: Presses universitaires du Septentrion, 2014), https://books .openedition.org/septentrion/1556. For the longer historical tradition of using lotteries for justice, see Barbara Goodwin, *Justice by Lottery* (Chicago: University of Chicago Press, 1992). A parliamentary law of 1750 posited that the funds and merchandises related to illegal lotteries and *jeux de hazard* would be seized and sold to benefit nearby hospices and Hôtels-Dieu. See Jousse, *Traité de la justice criminelle*, 3:556.

17. "Je pris un valet pour moi et une servante pour Manon." (I took a valet for myself and a maid for Manon; *Manon Lescaut*, 189; *The Story*, 135.)

18. The poem, *Le vice puni, ou Cartouche*, relays the following on the gambler-bandit: "Il avait l'œil à tout, ne reposait jamais: / Soutenant tout le poids de la cause commune." (He had his eye on everything, never rested. / Bearing all the weight of the common cause.) Nicolas Racot de Granval, *Le vice puni, ou Cartouche* (Paris: Pierre Prault, 1725), 2.

19. Denis Diderot, *Le neveu de Rameau*, in *Contes et romans*, ed. Michel Delon (Paris: Gallimard, 2004), 610, emphasis in the original. The similarity between *Manon Lescaut* and *Rameau's Nephew* has also been pointed out in Sgard, "Tricher," 254. The reference to the dancer, Guimard, is noteworthy. Marie-Madeleine Guimard was a ballet dancer at the *Comédie française* and the *Académie royale de musique* and a onetime mistress of the Prince de Soubise. She enjoyed a life of luxury thanks to her wealthy patrons but was also known for her generosity and care of the poor. The *hôtel* she had built on the rue Chaussée d'Antin by Nicolas Ledoux in the early 1770s was sold through a lottery. See Émile Campardon, *Les Comédiens du roi de la troupe française pendant les deux derniers siècles, documents inédits recueillis aux Archives nationales* (Geneva: Slatkine, 1970), 127, 136.

20. Denis Diderot, *Rameau's Nephew and First Satire*, ed. Nicholas Cronk, trans. Margaret Mauldon (Oxford: Oxford University Press, 2006), 30–31.

21. "Industrie," in *Dictionnaire de l'Académie française*, 4th ed., vol. 1 (Paris: Brunet, 1762), 926.

22. Deloffre and Picard, in their footnotes to *Manon Lescaut*, 51, point out the *gardes du corps'* debauched reputation as libertine gamblers; and, on Lescaut's activities as a gambler, see *Manon Lescaut*, 52.

23. Jean Sgard, "Introduction to Abbé Prévost," in *Manon Lescaut*, ed. Jean Sgard, trans. Leonard Tancock (London: Penguin, 1991), xxvi.

24. Naomi Segal, *The Unintended Reader: Feminism and Manon Lescaut* (Cambridge: Cambridge University Press, 1986), 22. Julia Costich, "Fortune in *Manon Lescaut*," *French Review* 49, no. 4 (1976): 525, also diagnoses addiction as the spring of Manon's behavior.

25. See Baron Marc de Villiers, "The History of the Foundation of New Orleans (1719–1799)," *Louisiana Historical Quarterly* 3, no. 2 (1920): 214–15.

26. The scarcity of women in colonial Louisiana led to the use of lots in deciding on marriages. See Dumont de Montigny, "Arrivée d'un vaisseau chargé de filles à l'Isle Dauphine," in Dumont de Montigny, Georges-Marie Butel-Dumont, and Jean-Baptiste Le Mascrier, *Mémoires historiques sur la Louisiane*, vol. 2 (Paris: Bauche, 1753), 30–31.

27. Pierre Ambroise François Choderlos de Laclos, *Les liaisons dangereuses*, ed. René Pomeau (Paris: Flammarion, 2006), 261. The anecdote about *filles laides* being married off by lots seems to have a basis in reality; see L.-H. Légier-Desgranges, "De la Salpêtrière au Mississippi," *Miroir de l'histoire* 29 (1952): 85.

28. "Nous ne laissions point échapper l'occasion de rendre service et de faire du bien à nos voisins. Cette disposition officieuse et la douceur de nos manières nous attirèrent la confiance et l'affection de toute la colonie." (We let no opportunity pass of doing some good turn or service to our neighbours. Our willingness to oblige, and our mild-mannered ways, won us the trust and affection of the entire colony; *Manon Lescaut*, 189; *The Story*, 135.)

29. The recruiter, Mme Eliot, explains to Bridge, "Elles [the women] y ont presque toutes une heureuse fécondité; mais elles ne mettent au monde que des filles. A peine nous est-il né un enfant de votre sexe pour quatre du mien, depuis l'espace de vingt ans." (Most of them are very prolific, but then they bring nothing but girls into the world. Within the past twenty years, there have been born four females to one male child.) Abbé Prevost, *Cleveland: Le philosophe anglais, ou Histoire de M. Cleveland, fils naturel de Cromwell*, ed. Jean Sgard and Philip Stewart (Paris, Desjonquères, 2006), 189; the English translations are adapted from Abbé Prevost, *The Life and Entertaining Adventures of Mr. Cleveland, Natural Son of Oliver Cromwell, Written by Himself*, 2nd ed., vol. 1 (London: T. Astley, 1741), 175. Hereafter, citations will appear parenthetically in the text and are from the Desjonquères edition; the page numbers from the French edition will appear first (as *Cleveland*), followed by page numbers for the English translation (as *The Life*).

30. In the preface to *Cleveland*, Prévost writes about the "caverne de Rumney-Hole": "J'ajouterai seulement qu'on trouve dans plusieurs autres provinces de cette île de pareils jeux de la nature. Darbyshire en est remplie. Hockey-hole, près de Wells, et Shedercliffs, sont des raretés en ce genre qui meritent l'attention des voyageurs." (I will just add that one can find similar plays of nature in several other provinces of this island. Darbyshire is full of them. Hockey-hole, near Wells, and Shedercliffs are rarities in this genre and deserve the attention of travelers.) Abbé Prévost, preface to *Cleveland*, in *Œuvres de Prévost*, vol. 2, ed. Jean Sgard (Grenoble: Presses universitaires de Grenoble, 1986), 11.

31. See Lorraine Daston, *Classical Probability in the Enlightenment* (Princeton, NJ: Princeton University Press, 1988), 152. For the relationship between the birth of a blind-folded Justice and secularization, see Frédéric Chauvaud, ed., *Le sanglot judiciaire: la désacralisation de la justice, VIIIe–XXe siècles: Séminaire de Royaumont (1993–1994)* (Grâne, France: Créaphis, 1999); and Adriano Prosperi, *Justice Blindfolded: The Historical Course of an Image* (Leiden: Brill, 2018). It is telling in *Cleveland* that the use of "blind" lots purports to be of divine nature when it, in fact, emanates from tyrannical rule.

32. See Denis Grélé, "Escape from Utopia: Love, Religion and the State in Prévost's *Le philosophe anglais, ou Histoire de Monsieur Cleveland*," *Journal of the Association for the*

Interdisciplinary Study of the Arts 12, no. 3 (2017): 121; Robert Mauzi, *L'idée du bonheur dans la littérature et la pensée françaises au XVIIIe siècle* (Paris: Armand Colin, 1960), 143; and Jean-Michel Racault, *L'utopie narrative en France et en Angleterre, 1675–1761* (Oxford: Voltaire Foundation, 1991), 607.

33. Several commentators have examined in detail the specious nature of equality in the utopian colony; see Philip Stewart, "Utopias That Self-Destruct," *Studies in Eighteenth Century Culture* 9 (1979): 16–18, and Grélé, "Escape from Utopia," 123–24. For the purposes of this essay, I restrict my focus to the linkage between lots and egalitarianism and nature's mocking of the community through play in the Protestant colony.

CHAPTER 5

Boundless Play and Infinite Pleasure in the Chevalier de Béthune's *Relation du monde de Mercure*

Erika Mandarino

In the *Relation du monde de Mercure* (1750), the Chevalier de Béthune peoples the planet Mercury with cherubic libertines who communicate with animals, play magical lotteries, and have short, renewable marriage contracts. Behind the flippant facade, however, there is much to learn from the Mercurian model. By placing his utopia off-world, Béthune evades the constraints of cultural prejudice to envision a society that is politically, technologically, and morally advanced. The Mercurians owe their happiness first to the nature of their world, which allows them to embrace the invaluable gifts of variety and change from the infinite universe; and second, to their ruler, the Sun King. This is not king Louis XIV of Earth, but a being who literally descends from the sun to protect their right to pursue pleasure. This essay will ponder some of the ways in which Béthune's frivolous utopia, like those of Lucian of Samosata, François Rabelais, and Savinien de Cyrano de Bergerac before it, combines playfulness and usefulness in portraying a "better world" based on two criteria: the acceptance of infinite variety as essential to human happiness, and a social order that both fosters and tempers the pursuit of pleasure.

Paul Hazard makes the important observation in *La crise de la conscience européenne* that the idea of duty (toward God and toward the sovereign) in the seventeenth century was transformed into the idea of right (of individual conscience, of critique, of reason, and of citizenship) in the eighteenth century.[1] This transformation resulted in the emergence of a psychological morality that drew inspiration from a number of ancient and contemporary sources.[2] It did not prescribe good or evil; nor did it demand deprivation of earthly pleasures. Rather, it regarded these pleasures as essential to the human experience. Energies were therefore redirected toward regulating the desires of the individual in order to avoid interference with the well-being of the group, and happiness was sought in the present instead of in the uncertain future of the afterlife.[3]

Despite a dearth of biographical records, references in the *Relation* situate its author within this period of psychological transformation. Science fiction writer Brian Stableford deduces in the introduction to his translation of the book that the most probable candidate for authorship is Marie-Henri de Béthune (who died in Paris on May 3, 1744), son of Henri de Béthune, Comte de Selles.[4] Whether the story is by Marie-Henri de Béthune or someone else, its cultural references—evoking, for instance, the construction of the Garden of Versailles or René Descartes's *tourbillons*—point to an author contemporary to the reign of Louis XIV.[5]

The first textual element of the *Relation* is an *avertissement* in which the author raises the possibility of intelligent life beyond Earth and the plurality of worlds being subsumed under God's design for variety in the universe. In writing the *Relation*, a hodgepodge of ideas, styles, tones, and genres, thus mirroring the universe's heterogeneity, the author of the world of Mercury therefore imitates the author of nature. "L'Auteur du monde de Mercure," Béthune writes in the *avertissement*, "ne s'est pas contenté de rendre sa fiction amusante, il a encore eu dessein de donner un léger crayon, et comme une espèce d'essai des variétés que la Nature est capable de répandre dans tous les globes qu'il suppose pouvoir être habités." (The author of the world of Mercury did not content himself to make his fiction amusing; he also wanted to provide a sample of the variety that Nature is able to spread through all the planets that he supposes could be inhabited; 1:xiv).

The preface that follows describes the events leading up to the narrator's account of the Mercurian utopia. He searches the sky for the little planet, to no avail, until suddenly a Rosicrucian sage materializes and offers him a "microscope philosophique" (philosophical microscope; 1:3). The narrator's soul then enters a myrtle plant to symbolize his initiation into the Rosicrucian order and into the make-believe world of Mercury. Referring to clans and brotherhoods such as the Rosicrucian order, Johan Huizinga acknowledges in *Homo Ludens* the difficulty "to draw the line between, on the one hand, permanent social groupings particularly in archaic cultures with their extremely important, solemn, indeed sacred customs—and the sphere of play on the other."[6] As with fraternal orders, play entails an initiation into a separate realm where ordinary reality is suspended and replaced by a virtual experience consisting of different conventions and behavioral norms. The virtual worlds in Béthune's story are multiplied with the introduction of the scientific instrument, whose functions the sage explains: "Ce que vous voyez est un microscope philosophique, dans lequel vous ne trouverez que des verres et rien de plus; mais il est construit avec un tel art, qu'il rend visibles les objets les plus éloignés, comme les plus proches, aussi bien que les plus sombres et les plus éclairés." (What you see here is a philosophical microscope, composed of only lenses and nothing more; but it is constructed with such art that it makes visible the farthest objects and the closest, as well as the darkest and the brightest; 1:3–4.) Like the story itself, this instrument is not unidirectional or limited to a single function; instead, it is a means for the imagination to embark on scientific discovery. It invites aimlessness, curiosity, and impartiality. If we take those characteristics resulting from the appreciation of the endless variety that exists in the universe as the author's intention, a new sort of utopia emerges that is at once more favorable to its inhabitants and more amenable to scientific innovation. Among the virtual worlds accessible by the instrument is that of Mercury, on which the inhabitants engage in various ludic activities to access virtual worlds of their own.

The emerging psychological morality as Hazard describes it established itself in utopian fiction of the early eighteenth century as writers sought to imagine a society in which rights take precedence over authority, and Béthune's utopia is especially fit to capture this sentiment. By considering the world in its entirety, especially as opposed to that of another planet, we are able to imagine how human conduct is shaped by the physical nature of the globe. On a local scale, weather systems and natural disasters overturn communities, while on a cosmic scale, the planets orbit the sun at dizzying speeds—to mention nothing of our individual bodies, which are also in constant flux. Authority is similarly considered in the *Relation* as subject to change: Béthune critiques Louis XIV (the Sun King) by limiting the rule of the emperor—an eternal being who is literally appointed by God to descend from the sun to serve the Mercurians—to a mere hundred years.[7] To live in harmony with nature, then, Mercurians and humans alike must be allowed to embrace change and variety, not only in their individual lives but also in those structures that govern society.

Béthune's story draws inspiration from atomist and materialist philosophers who saw the universe as physical matter forever rearranging on infinite worlds, the soul as mortal, and divine providence as an impossible notion.[8] It is also a descendant of Bernard le Bovier de Fontenelle's *Entretiens* and Cyrano's *L'autre monde*: each of these tales exploits the heterodox Copernican system to endorse a certain libertinage.[9] The Copernican system represents at once a break from the Aristotelian system adopted by Christianity to promote the idea of one perfect world, and a revelation of a more complex and variable system of multiple worlds. Like his predecessors, Béthune exemplifies some essential characteristics of the erudite libertine who places secular morality above religious dogma, and despite the frivolity of his fiction, he opts for reason over passion at every turn.[10] But, unlike Cyrano, whose scathing satire promotes a materialist philosophy, Béthune resembles Fontenelle in using religious language to convey his libertine ideals.[11]

Although Béthune weaves libertine ideals and materialist notions into his tale, we will see that he neither extricates the Mercurians from providential order nor denies them an immortal soul. Indeed, the cherubic Mercurians are enlightened thanks to their ability to recognize the infinite variation of the physical world at play within a grander metaphysical system.

While in Fontenelle's *Entretiens* the proximity to the sun makes the Mercurian people "fous à force de vivacité" (vivacious to the point of madness), in Béthune's *Relation*, the Mercurians benefit more directly from its light, heat, and graces; it is naturally and literally a more "enlightened" planet than Earth.[12] Furthermore, the harshness of nature on Earth produces moral obstacles of which Béthune's planet is wholly relieved: food is provided to the people by animals, for example, and clothing is distributed by the emperor. In this Mercurian playground where the habitual pains of earthlings are abolished, time and energy can be dedicated entirely to the pursuit of pleasure and the satisfaction of curiosity.

With this premise as their principal motivation, Béthune's Mercurians revel in lives of leisure. One of their communal activities is a lottery with free admission for all, the prizes of which include rare and unique talents, or wondrous items that resemble modern technologies. These objects improve quality of life in diverse ways, either by making information more accessible or simply by providing entertainment. Among the lottery winnings one finds

> machines surprenantes, des automates merveilleux, . . . des instruments propres à augmenter l'action de tous les sens: comme par exemple des verres qui font voir dans l'intérieur des métaux et des pierres les plus dures, de petites loupes qui font lire dans l'âme des hommes, des cornets qui font entendre de dix lieues les discours qui nous sont adressés, des trompettes propres à fortifier le son de la voix, mais faites avec un tel art, que les paroles ne sont entendues que de la personne à qui on les adresse.

> extraordinary machines, marvelous automatons, . . . instruments that can augment the senses: for example, glasses that let you see through metal and the hardest stones, little magnifying glasses that let you read into the human soul, cones that let you hear speech directed to you from ten leagues away, trumpets that fortify the sound of the voice, but made with such art that the words are only heard by the person to whom they are addressed. (1:215)

These "gifts of chance" last for only a few decades to maintain the vibrancy and dynamism of the lottery. But this is but one of many forms of gambling embraced by Mercurians to promote healthy competition. They also gamble, for instance, to appropriate desirable body parts left behind by deceased comrades (1:44–45).

With these lotteries, however, as with all pleasurable activities on Béthune's planet, moderation is key; the lottery is held once per day so as not to become ruinous. Players may therefore benefit from, but cannot become dependent on, random chance.

Chance, in lotteries and other games, may be disconcerting in that the outcome is chaotic and unpredictable. But rather than oppose a divine providential plan, chance in Béthune's tale exists within a grander order. Imagine a game of cards: the overarching rules and progression of the game are fixed, yet each game yields a novel result. Both the structure provided by the rules and the unpredictable outcomes of such card games are fundamental to play in general. In *Homo Ludens*, Huizinga studies how games and the creative element of play contribute to culture, and for him, the "fun" of playing resists logical analysis. He concludes that play is free (an act of freedom), voluntary, and superfluous; it is never imposed by physical necessity or moral duty; it is secluded from ordinary life and is limited in time as well as in space; it follows strict rules that are repeated in each iteration of a given game, thus creating order; it is tense and begs a solution; and finally, play "loves to surround itself with an air of secrecy."[13] To this last characteristic Roger Caillois objects; in his understanding, play demystifies.[14] He also points out that games of chance that wager goods or money do not factor into Huizinga's definition of play, to the detriment of that definition. Risk of loss, for Caillois, is central to such games, and pleasure cannot endure without it.[15] The game that promotes change might lead to either a favorable or unfavorable outcome, and it is precisely this variety from indeterminacy that makes pleasure possible.

Change—in scenery, in perspective, and in motivation—therefore lends itself to pleasure in moments of play where invented rules temporarily usurp those of ordinary life. Robert Mauzi underscores the necessity of variety for pleasure in his "Le mouvement et les plaisirs," where he outlines three conditions for pleasure: diversity, because pleasure is by its nature fleeting, and if prolonged, it becomes its opposite; moderation, because when pleasure becomes obsessive or extreme, one is desensitized to it; and internalization, because it is subjective in the sense that pleasure is derived from the individual's perception of the object of pleasure rather than from the object itself.[16]

From the mid-seventeenth century to the end of the eighteenth, the French, according to Thomas Kavanagh, were especially obsessed with gambling. Not surprisingly, this growing obsession with chance was coupled with "a systematic rethinking of the notions of social identity, of happiness, and of individual freedom."[17] Kavanagh argues that as the aristocracy lost its status as a class of warriors, it found its new battleground in the social arena. Eighteenth-century aristocrats were both libertines and gamblers, and their weapon was the bluff. When they employed it adroitly, they were able to manipulate the other players of the card game in the same way that they were able to manipulate their object of sexual desire. Therefore, libertinage, like the card game Brelan from Kava-nagh's example, was a game of seduction and domination in which feminine vir-tue and masculine honor were staked or bluffed.[18] Both "games" had the power to infuse any social gathering with desire and excitement by dangling its play-ers between paranoia and euphoria. In the game of seduction—and likewise in gambling for money, goods, and services—the risk of loss arouses intrigue and suspense.

Returning to Béthune's fiction, the Mercurian love of gambling raises the question of how pleasure can be realizable in a world without risk. We have seen in the example of the lottery that the Mercurians put nothing at stake, and the same can be said for how the game of love is represented in the novel. Marriages are contracted to last for two years, after which the contract can be renewed. New lovers have two days to engage in physical intimacy before getting married, and when they do, they have the full support of a social network in the form of coun-seling and in regulated, lawful adultery. Prostitution is legal on Béthune's planet, but it is scorned for the sole reason that sex should always be shared freely.[19] The great distinction between typical aristocratic libertines and their Mercurian counterparts is that for the latter, sexual encounters and gambling alike produce pleasure from conviviality and mutual growth rather than from deceit and domination.

Pleasure on Mercury is therefore the culmination of three factors. The first is the willingness to participate in the game (of marriage or the lottery). The sec-ond is change itself (the Mercurians are in perpetual pursuit of advancement, and the prize is only interesting in its unexpectedness, its novelty, and its vari-ety). The third is social interaction (because one wins as a group rather than indi-vidually against an opponent). In this case, the bluff is as needless in gambling as it is in sex; in the lottery, as in coupling, mystery is dispelled. These factors are similar to the conditions for pleasure outlined by Mauzi: subjective partici-pation corresponds to internalization, change to diversity, and social interaction to moderation in that one moderates personal interest to accommodate the needs of the group. Mercurian happiness comes from the pursuit of communal pro-gress, and pleasure results not from the risk of deprivation but from the recog-nition and embrace of the infinite diversity provided by the universe.

We have come a long way since the strict social control of Thomas More's homogeneous utopia where the inhabitants are stripped of their individuality. On Béthune's Mercury, uniformity and the risk of boredom are to be avoided not only as a contagious ailment but as a fatal one (1:32–45). Boredom is indeed the death of play; it is, rather, change within the order of the ritual that keeps the inhabitants engaged in the pursuit of perpetual happiness. In the make-believe world of Mercury, gambling creates desire, excitement, and suspense, and the only risk is to slow the momentum and limit the frequency of gifts of chance.

The same goes for the Mercurian economy. Since all necessities of life come gratis to the Mercurians, their money exists strictly for the purpose of luxury: one can buy and sell physical and moral traits, talents, or anything else that might "tenter la curiosité des hommes" (tempt one's curiosity; 1:99). Jean-Michel Racault notes that this constant exchange of goods and services beyond the confinements of the necessary liberates social energy in a frenetic exchange that is an end in itself.[20] The *Relation*'s discourse on this subject is thus reminiscent of Voltaire's praise of luxury in his poem *Le mondain*, and its proclivity to generate trade and stimulate economic growth. The poem encourages readers, moreover, to take advantage of the "treasures" of the earth and to seek the superfluous because, in abundance, desire grows in a continual process of fulfillment and renewal. Voltaire ranks his era of ease, luxury, and ornamentation above the Golden Age because, for him, our ancestors were not virtuous but ignorant; they had nothing, and so they had nothing to offer one another, nothing to gain, and thus they lived uneventful, reclusive lives. The flourishing economy of Voltaire's time—both social and commercial—inevitably elevates quality of life, and so he concludes his poem by stating that paradise exists in the present.[21] Béthune's *Relation* conveys the same message by representing beings who seek the superfluous pleasures provided by their world and the dynamic social exchange that ensues. Their capitalist approach to life is a source of pleasure because it inspires social interaction and creative innovation.

Atomists like Democritus and Epicurus believed that while individuals are limited by their composite bodies, nature eternally renews itself by recombining atoms in perpetuity.[22] To a certain extent, the *Relation* shares this understanding of the universe, since it features the possibility of infinite worlds. Béthune's story, however, does not advocate materialism, and certainly not the atheism often associated with that philosophy. In the universe surrounding Béthune's Mercury, as in an endless game of cards, variation exists within a greater providential order with humanity at its core. The Mercurian belief concerning the afterlife reflects this order.

As in gambling (for quality of life, for entertainment, and for partnership), the risk of loss in death is eliminated. The soul is eternal, but rather than leave the earth body to forever inhabit heaven or hell, it returns to innumerable bodies on other planets in an endless cycle of metempsychosis. This "grand Pèlerinage" (great pilgrimage; 1:188), as Béthune calls it, begins in the body of a lesser creature. After this creature's corporeal death, its soul proceeds to live out a new life in the body of a more noble creature, and so on and so forth, until it reaches the end of the pilgrimage, where it begins life in the body of a human being. The soul is not limited to life on one planet but journeys throughout the universe. Finally, during its human life, the soul faces judgment, since "il n'y a que les hommes, à qui [Dieu] laisse la liberté d'user bien ou mal des lumières naturelles qu'il leur accorde assez abondamment, pour qu'ils soient en état de n'en pas abuser"

(God only grants humans the liberty to use their natural intelligence well or poorly, which he bestows upon them in abundance so that they are equipped to avoid abuse; 1:195–196). If humans fail to live well by choosing personal gain over universal happiness, however, the punishment is not eternal damnation but infinite chances for improvement: they must recommence the great pilgrimage. And after this do-over, they must perform cosmic community service to aid humankind as a Salamander (a sort of genie). Only then may they join the inhabitants of the stars to regain all knowledge of their sequential lives.

Alternatively, if the first pilgrimage is successful, the soul reaches the sun directly. There it experiences endless happiness and might stay for hundreds of millions of years before deciding to set out on a new pilgrimage. In other words, the soul is completely free to play again and again, and each time the game promises to be different. Béthune thus maintains the Christian fundamentals of judgment and revelation in the afterlife within a regimented providential order. But in the infinite context of the cosmos, this process is also infinite, giving the soul an endless means to learn from mistakes and to pursue its inherent curiosity and desire for change.

To perfect the soul is to accumulate knowledge from a variety of sources, and in Béthune's allegory of the Great Pilgrimage, the soul acquires knowledge from having experienced several lives. Rather than reject Christian doctrine altogether, the author champions a natural religion in which God's presence can be understood through the advancements of science (hence the scientific instruments in the lottery and the context of the plurality of worlds), as well as through many other epistemological sources outside of Christian dogma (such as the Kabbalah and ancient Greek and Roman texts). Without the finality of death—whether conceived as a suspension of perfection in heaven or eternal despair in hell—life becomes a game, where to win is to enhance the collective human experience. By altering our conception of the eternal—from unchanging to ever-changing—Béthune turns the Christian afterlife into a playful pursuit: instead of entering directly into a state of eternal stagnation after one mere roll of dice, the deceased have the opportunity to play again and again ad infinitum.

When the narrator first peeks through the philosophical microscope, he sees not only the inhabitants of the planet Mercury but also the "Atomes d'Epicure" (atoms of Epicurus; 1:4). On the one hand, these atoms refer to the atomist theory that championed a secular physics in which all events are guided by chance. On the other hand, it is a nod to an epicurean lifestyle. Unlike the Brelan players in Kavanagh's study, who waver between paranoia (losing) and euphoria (winning), for Epicurus, "The aim of the human life . . . is 'eudaimonia,' in the form of tranquility (ataraxia), salvation from convictions and beliefs that cause feelings such as hope or fear."[23] Béthune's epicurean take on the Christian afterlife effectively rids one of the hope or fear one may experience when faced with the promise of eternal bliss or punishment. On Mercury, hope and fear are instead transformed into an appreciation for and a trust in God's intention for the eternal soul to make use of creation for recreation in a process of continual learning and renewal.

———

In an effort to educate the reader of a moral imperative of plurality and modera-tion, the first line of the *Relation*'s foreword reads as follows: "Tout le monde sait que le moyen le plus sûr d'instruire, est de déguiser les conseils de la raison sous le voile de l'allégorie." (Everybody knows that the surest way to instruct is to disguise the counsels of reason behind the veil of allegory; 1:i.) Béthune describes his story as a fable, which, according to Aurélia Gaillard, is a sacred story.[24] The *conte*, on the other hand, came along in the second half of the seventeenth century as allegory gave way to analogy.[25] Béthune wrote his novel in the midst of this pivotal moment; it retains the qualities of the fable by addressing the sacred sub-jects of the inner workings of the universe, good versus evil, and the destiny of the eternal soul, while also incorporating analogy and an appeal to reason and sensibility, especially within its scientific-astronomical theme. By underscoring the allegorical nature of his story, Béthune playfully challenges the reader to find the reason behind the veil, and to uncover the real in the make-believe. Simulta-neously, by drawing attention to it, Béthune removes the mystery he pretends to maintain—a fundamental element of play, according to Caillois.[26]

The narrator begs the Rosicrucian sage to include him in the game and to let him look through the philosophical microscope. In doing so he anticipates a sort of revelation, be it religious or secular.[27] The interaction between the narrator and the sage is depicted in an unsigned image at the beginning of the book (see fig. 5.1) that further intertwines the *fable* (allegory) and the *conte* (analogy). This image shows the narrator and the sage pointing up toward Mercury. The sun's rays are shining favorably in the direction of its closest celestial companion. Anti-quated clothing permits us to identify similarities between the sage and the biblical figure of Moses, and also between the sage and the Roman mythologi-cal figure of the god Mercury or his Greek counterpart, Hermes.

In the first case, we recognize Moses because of the sage's beard and rod. Moses delivered the Ten Commandments from atop Mount Sinai in order to dic-tate moral behavior.[28] He performed the miracle of turning his rod into a snake to prove to the Egyptians that he was sent by God. Yet the staff-like instrument also evokes the caduceus, or the staff of Mercury, the Roman messenger god.[29] Hermes/Mercury is more than a psychopomp associated with the crossing of boundaries; he is the god of play, commerce, and fertility; he is a persuasive trick-ster who not only guides souls but pulls them back and forth between the realms of the living and the dead. His caduceus allows him to put to, or rouse from, sleep, and in this story, in particular, the guide will "awaken" the narra-tor, lead him across the boundaries of human custom and understanding as they

Figure 5.1. Frontispiece from Le Chevalier de Béthune, *Relation du monde de Mercure*, 2 vols. (Geneva Barillot, 1750). © Bibliothèque nationale de France.

exist on Earth, and permit him to contemplate a world with different rules. The god of play takes many forms, and his fluctuating character produces the indeterminacy that makes pleasure possible. His pranks and tricks are indeed a source of pleasure, but when he takes the form of a moral leader like Moses, that playfulness sheds light on a moral principle. Disguised as Moses, his appeal to pleasure from variety becomes a moral imperative, and the pursuit of change a social obligation.

Moreover, the mythical Greek/Roman god can just as easily be identified as the semihistorical Hermes Trismegistus,[30] the priest, sorcerer and scientist considered to be the inventor of alchemy and a master of a "means of attaining to a knowledge that may be gnostic, eclectic, or transdisciplinary—or all of these at once," writes Antoine Faivre in *The Eternal Hermes*.[31] It is therefore curious to see him depicted in striking resemblance to the image in Béthune's story, and pointing to the sky he invites us to measure, on a late-sixteenth-century astrolabe featured in the Veneranda Biblioteca Ambrosiana (see fig. 5.2).

For the Rosicrucian sage of the *Relation*, we know from Béthune's description in the text that the rod or caduceus is in fact a scientific instrument. Like Moses's rod, this device also performs a sort of miracle, but the miracle in this case is one of science. The implication here, however, is not that one replaces the other but that both have analogous and overlapping functions. By reimagining the biblical or mythical staff as an instrument of science, Béthune, taking up the transdisciplinary mantle of the thrice-great Hermes, compares—and gives the same function to—its biblical, mythical, and scientific interpretations. The natural world as we understand it through science can therefore also deliver moral truths and, ultimately, reveal the existence of God. As he does in his depiction of the Mercurian afterlife, Béthune here again contributes to a prevalent literature that attempted to rationalize religion; the scientific world is infused with a sense of divine presence, a notion that appealed to "enlightened" Christians and moderate deists who believed in an intelligent creator of the universe, who maintains it, but is distinct from it.[32]

The interplay of biblical, mythical, and scientific symbols constitutes the veil of allegory behind which Béthune offers his counsels of reason. The ultimate message imparted to the reader is the value of multiple perspectives in uncovering new realities to improve our shared world. The new type of utopia that emerges from this melding of genres and symbols is one that embraces infinite possibility to tend evermore toward perfection, rather than exist within it. In this utopia, the only risk is to obstruct change.

———

As Mercury guides the soul to learn the happy ways of the Mercurians in this tale, Béthune guides the reader to embrace a playfulness energized by the infinite possibilities of the boundless universe. The Mercurians expose the flaws of

Figure 5.2. Late sixteenth-century astrolabe depicting Hermes pointing to the heavens. Above Hermes's head is written "Trismegistus." Along the circumference of the image, we read "Deus est sphaera intelligibilis cuius centrum est ubique et circunferentia nusquam." (God is an intelligible sphere whose center is everywhere and whose circumference is nowhere.) © Veneranda Biblioteca Ambrosiana / Mondadori Portfolio. The English translation is from Antoine Faivre, *The Eternal Hermes: From Greek God to Alchemical Magus*, trans. Joscelyn Godwin (Grand Rapids, MI: Phanes, 1995), 133.

the author's contemporaries, who draw pleasure from their own deceit, from gaining at the expense of another's loss, from intimidation, and from domination—instead of from communal progress and shared pleasure. The recalibration of our desires toward seeking endless new outcomes for communal benefit is the reason that is thinly veiled behind allegory in Béthune's story. The cosmic setting of Mercury as a planet beyond our own opens the field of the possible to the vast stretches of the universe but still keeps humanity at its center. In an infinite playground, opportunities for enrichment of the soul are endless, and so are the sources of pleasure. And like the boundless playground of the universe, the *Relation* itself has no conclusion, which leaves the book open to interpretation, adaptation, and innovation.

Nods to alchemy, the Kabbalah, and superstitious folklore, according to Racault, fortify the book's premise that "tout est possible" (anything is possible).[33] That premise is useful to us in the sense that it liberates creativity, permits us to play, and lets us seek pleasure in variety. "Play is superfluous," Huizinga remarks succinctly in *Homo Ludens*, "for the adult and responsible human being play is a function which he could equally well leave alone."[34] The *Relation du monde de Mercure* is an example of pure play in the early eighteenth century. It was not published during the author's lifetime and therefore did not hold any promise of recognition, let alone fame or fortune. If ever Béthune's writing seems rambling or inconsequential, so is his unfinished voyage. We could say that just like Mercury, he journeyed "for the sheer pleasure of it."[35]

NOTES

1. Paul Hazard, *La crise de la conscience européenne 1680–1715* (Paris: Fayard, 1961), 9.
2. Hazard, *La crise de la conscience*, 272.
3. Hazard, *La crise de la conscience*, 273, 277.
4. The Chevalier de Béthune, *The World of Mercury*, trans. Brian Stableford (Encino, CA: Black Coat, 2015), 5. In Le Chevalier de Béthune, *Relation du monde de Mercure*, 2 vols. (Geneva: Barillot, 1750), 2:145, Béthune cites "Allégorie I: Torticolis," whose author, Jean-Baptiste Rousseau, was accused of writing calumnious couplets about Voltaire in 1701 and 1710. In the *Relation*'s allegorical chapter on calumny, ugly interplanetary intruders disguised as Mercurians mingle with the crowd, spread gossip, and ruin friendships. If the author of the *Relation* was indeed Marie-Henri de Béthune, and if this chapter on calumny is indeed a nod to Voltaire and Jean-Baptiste Rousseau's relationship, then we can narrow the window of its conception to after the publication of Voltaire's *Épître sur la calomnie* in 1736 and before Marie-Henri de Béthune's death in 1744. For more on Voltaire and Jean-Baptiste Rousseau's relationship, see D. J. Fletcher, "Introduction to *Épître sur la calomnie*," in *Œuvres complètes de Voltaire*, ed. Theodore Besterman et al., vol. 9 (Oxford: Voltaire Foundation, 1999), 278–85. All translations from the *Relation du monde de Mercure* are my own, and I have updated the spelling to standard, modern French. Hereafter, citations from the Barillot edition will appear parenthetically in the text and will include volume and page numbers. I would like to express my appreciation to Brian Stableford and Black Coat Press for bringing many obscure early modern science fiction stories to the English-speaking world; for the purposes of this chapter, however, the Black Coat Press translation of Béthune's work does not serve as a sufficiently edited source text.
5. Regarding the court of Louis XIV or Descartes's *tourbillons*, see Béthune, *Relation*, 1:77; 1:126; 1:139; and 2:104.
6. Johan Huizinga, *Homo Ludens: A Study of the Play-Element in Culture*, trans. R. F. C. Hull (London: Routledge and Kegan Paul, 1949), 12.
7. In a chapter titled "D'une peinture qu'on voit chez l'Empereur," Béthune presents us with a portrait that is more like a modern-day electronic tablet than a painting: "Il ne faut que toucher les noms de ceux ou de celles qu'on a dessein de voir, et qui sont tous gravés sur la bordure; dans l'instant même la personne paraît admirablement bien peinte dans le moment le plus brillant de son Histoire." (One need only touch the names of those one wishes to see, and which are engraved in the frame; in that instant the person appears admi-

rably well painted in the most brilliant moment of their History; 2:128.) This marvelous display is not a static but a moving tableau (2:129). After having shown the emperor in all his glory as a heroic warrior in a brilliant moment of triumph, he is then represented in four more vignettes that expose Louis XIV as a human just like any other. First, the emperor is shown to be pompous and arrogant as his servants mock him behind his back. Second, his greed is depicted in a series where he is shown squabbling over coins and denying happiness to others while he locks away his gold. In the third vignette, the lust of the sovereign is demonstrated in a scene in which he flirts with a young, bashful woman. And finally, the fourth lens shows the emperor in defeat and disgrace. Béthune explains, however, that this unflattering revelation is not intended to humiliate the emperor; it is instead meant to remind us that change, even in politics, is something to be desired.

8. According to Democritus and Epicurus, the universe is made up of infinite atoms that assemble in various ways; the supernatural has no role in nature or human life; and the body, mind, and soul are mortal. See Steven J. Dick, *Plurality of Worlds: The Origins of the Extraterrestrial Life Debate from Democritus to Kant* (Cambridge: Cambridge University Press, 1982), 45. For a discussion of atomism in the early modern context, see Catherine Wilson, *Epicureanism at the Origins of Modernity* (Oxford: Oxford University Press, 2008).

9. Frédérique Aït-Touati, *Fictions of the Cosmos: Science and Literature in the Seventeenth Century*, trans. Susan Emanuel (Chicago: University of Chicago Press, 2011), 64, 69, shows how Cyrano's cosmological discourse serves his free-thinking agenda.

10. "Connaissons donc le vrai, écoutons la raison, la passion subsiste et les inconvénients disparaissent." (Let us know the truth, let us hear reason, passion will subsist and inconveniences disappear; 1:181.)

11. For more on Fontenelle's religious language and libertine ideals, see Simone Mazauric, *Fontenelle et l'invention de l'histoire des sciences à l'aube des Lumières* (Paris: Librairie Arthème Fayard, 2007), 172–73.

12. Bernard le Bovier de Fontenelle, *Entretiens sur la pluralité des mondes*, ed. Christophe Martin (Paris: Flammarion, 1998), 123; the English translation is from Bernard le Bovier de Fontenelle, *Conversations on the Plurality of Worlds*, trans. H. A. Hargreaves (Berkeley: University of California Press, 1990), 49.

13. Huizinga, *Homo Ludens*, 3–12.

14. Roger Caillois, *Man, Play and Games*, trans. Meyer Barash (Urbana: University of Illinois Press, 2001), 4.

15. As Caillois, *Man, Play and Games*, 7, notes, "Every game of skill, by definition, involves the risk for the player of missing his stroke, and the threat of defeat, without which the game would no longer be pleasing."

16. Robert Mauzi, *L'idée du bonheur dans la littérature et la pensée françaises au XVIIIe siècle* (Paris: Armand Colin, 1960), 390–395.

17. Thomas Kavanagh, *Dice, Cards, Wheels: A Different History of French Culture* (Philadelphia: University of Pennsylvania Press, 2005), 68.

18. Kavanagh, *Dice, Cards, Wheels*, 70.

19. "C'est aller directement contre les intentions de la nature, de trafiquer les dons précieux que nous tenons d'elle, et qu'elle nous a donnés *gratis*, à dessein que nous les donnions de même." (To traffic those precious gifts she has given us *gratis* with the expectation that we will do the same is to go directly against the intentions of nature; 1:64.)

20. Jean-Michel Racault, *L'utopie narrative en France et en Angleterre, 1675–1761* (Oxford: Voltaire Foundation, 1991), 264.

21. See Voltaire, *Le mondain*, in *Œuvres complètes de Voltaire*, vol. 16 (Oxford: Voltaire Foundation, 2003), 295–303.

22. Wilson, *Epicureanism at the Origins of Modernity*, 5.

23. Kavanagh, *Dice, Cards, Wheels*, 77; Panos Eliopoulos, "Epicurus and Lucretius on the Creation of the Cosmos," *Philosophy and Cosmology* 14 (2015): 250.

24. Aurélia Gaillard, "La clé et le puits: À propos du déchiffrement des contes et des fables," *Féeries* 7 (2010): 190.

25. Magali Fourgnaud, *Le conte à visée morale et philosophique: De Fénelon à Voltaire* (Paris: Classiques Garnier, 2016), 9. See also Gaillard, "La clé et le puits," 190.

26. As Caillois, *Man, Play and Games*, 4, observes, "Without doubt, secrecy, mystery, and even travesty can be transformed into play activity, but it must be immediately pointed out that this transformation is necessarily to the detriment of the secret and mysterious, which play exposes, publishes, and somehow expends. In a word, play tends to remove the very nature of the mysterious."

27. On the subject of religious versus secular revelation, see Florence Boulerie, "Enquête sur la démarche cognitive des voyageurs philosophes dans les voyages imaginaires au temps de l'*Encyclopédie*," in *Le philosophe romanesque: L'image du philosophe dans le roman des Lumières*, ed. Pierre Hartmann and Florence Lotterie (Strasbourg, France: Presses universitaires de Strasbourg, 2007), 176.

28. As we read in the *Relation du monde de Mercure*, "C'est sur [la grande Montagne] qu'habitent les sages de Mercure, qui se distribuent dans tout l'univers. . . . Ils y règlent les affaires de la société." (The Mercurian sages, who distribute themselves throughout the entire universe, live atop the Great Mountain. There they regulate all of society's affairs; 1:147–48.)

29. See "Caduceus," in *The Hutchinson Unabridged Encyclopedia with Atlas and Weather Guide* (Oxford: Credo Reference, 2016); and Luke Roman and Monica Roman, "Hermes," in *Encyclopedia of Greek and Roman Mythology* (New York: Facts on File, 2010), 220.

30. Antoine Faivre, "Renaissance Hermeticism and the Concept of Western Esotericism," in *Gnosis and Hermeticism from Antiquity to Modern Times*, ed. Roelof van den Broek and Wouter J. Hanegraaff (Albany: State University of New York Press, 1998), 113.

31. Antoine Faivre, *The Eternal Hermes: From Greek God to Alchemical Magus*, trans. Joscelyn Godwin (Grand Rapids, MI: Phanes, 1995), 14.

32. Jonathan Israel, *Radical Enlightenment: Philosophy and the Making of Modernity, 1650–1750* (Oxford: Oxford University Press, 2001), 473.

33. Racault, *L'utopie narrative*, 265.

34. Huizinga, *Homo Ludens*, 8.

35. Faivre, *The Eternal Hermes*, 13.

CHAPTER 6

The Politics of Orientalist Fantasy in French Opera

Katharine Hargrave

In 1745 a masked ball took place in the Hall of Mirrors at Versailles. The event celebrated the marriage of Louis XV's son, the dauphin, with the Infanta of Spain, Maria Teresa Rafaela. While this costume party is now commonly referred to as the Yew Tree Ball, because the king and several of his attendants were disguised as topiaries, many of the guests dressed in Chinese and Turkish costumes.[1] Charles Nicolas Cochin's ink and watercolor depiction of the event shows guests wearing grossly oversize turbans and pagoda-shaped hats. This party exemplifies a widespread fascination in eighteenth-century France with both the exotic and masked balls, the fun of which was to hide one's real identity to the fullest extent possible and to bend the rules of formal court behavior without repercussions.[2]

Playing with transgressive identities manifests itself in a variety of art forms during this period—notably, the fashion known as *turquerie*. From portraits of western Europeans dressed in Turkish costumes to Ottoman-themed rooms, there is abundant evidence that all things Turkish were in vogue. Playwrights and composers caught on to this craze, and the public was treated to a certain number of highly popular onstage productions set in the Middle East, such as Wolfgang Amadeus Mozart and Gottlieb Stephanie's *The Abduction from the Seraglio*, a 1782 opera set in Turkey.[3] Five years later, Antonio Salieri and Pierre-Augustin Caron de Beaumarchais staged the successful opera *Tarare*, which is set in nearby Persia. Following its premiere in 1787, one critic wrote,

> *Tarare! Tarare! Tarare!* mon cher ami; l'on ne parle plus ici que de *Tarare*: et la marquise, et la grisette, et le prince et le financier ne prononcent plus que *Tarare*. Voilà le refrain chéri: Avez-vous vu *Tarare*? Connaissez-vous *Tarare*? Savez-vous les airs de *Tarare*? Quel est donc, me direz-vous, cet ouvrage tant vanté? Est-ce un chef-d'œuvre de l'art? Est-ce un chef-d'œuvre du génie? Le

grand Corneille est-il ressuscité? Ou enfin son ombre errante parmi vous, se plairait-elle encore à faire éclore des œuvres qui étonnent l'esprit humain? *Tarare*, mon ami, *Tarare*! nous ne connaissons plus que ce joli mot-là!

Tarare! Tarare! Tarare! my dear friend; all anyone can talk about here is *Tarare*: the marquise, the working girl, the prince, and the financier only speak of *Tarare*. The popular refrain is: Have you seen *Tarare*? Do you know *Tarare*? Do you know the airs from *Tarare*? What, you might ask, is this renowned work? Is it a masterpiece? Is it a work of genius? Has [Pierre] Corneille been revived? If his wandering spirit were among you, would it find pleasure in discovering works that surprise the human mind? *Tarare*, my dear friend, *Tarare*! This is the only word we know right now.[4]

Tarare was so popular with audiences in Paris that fashion designers took inspiration from the opera for their own clothing and accessories. A 1787 women's fashion magazine shows a large, green, feathered hat deemed the latest trend in Paris. Named the Tarare, it is specified as being directly inspired by Salieri and Beaumarchais's opera.[5] This example illustrates the popularizing effect of exoticism that, like the masked ball, encourages the public to play dress-up and explore a new public image inspired by the fantastic imaginings of Asian dress. This craze led certain critics at the time to denounce this type of vision of foreign cultures as superficial. As Denis Diderot noted in his 1767 critique of artist Jean-Baptiste Le Prince's depictions of Russia, "Si un Tartare, un Cosaque, un Russe voyait cela, il dirait à l'artiste: Tu as pillé toutes nos gardes-robes; mais tu n'as pas connu une de nos passions." (If a Tartar, Cossack, or Russian saw this, he'd say to the artist: You've pillaged our wardrobes, but haven't a clue about our feelings.)[6] In today's terms, one could say that Diderot criticizes artists for favoring cultural appropriation over cultural appreciation.

In this chapter, I examine how two eighteenth-century French operas, Jean-Philippe Rameau and Louis de Cahusac's *Zoroastre* (1756) and Salieri and Beaumarchais's *Tarare* (1787), demonstrate the way in which artists capitalized on the public's fascination with the exotic to popularize their productions and endear themselves to audiences.[7] While the inaccurate depictions of Middle Eastern cultures may give the illusion of being superficial and trite, I suggest that these operas also play with Orientalist fantasy as a smoke screen to convey transgressive sociopolitical ideologies. This misrepresentation of other cultures to criticize one's own is not unique to the stage and encompasses a general tendency of exoticism in pre-Revolutionary France. In his examination of the phenomenon of *turquerie*, Haydn Williams argues that this fashion is "more a reflection of the cultural milieu that conceived it than a representation of the supposed subject. . . . While primarily a means of providing amusement and delight, it was sometimes charged with a more symbolic role, to emphasize status and magnificence, or even used to cover criticism of the establishment."[8] Montesquieu is a notable example of an author who toys with this dual role of exoticism both to amuse and instruct the public. Roger Caillois acknowledges Montesquieu's influence on defining the sociology of play in dedicating his book *Man, Play, and Games* to the author with the words "Secundum Secundatum." This translates to "according to the rules of Secondat" in reference to Montesquieu's full name, Charles-Louis de Secondat, Baron de la Brède et de Montesquieu. Although this is the only mention of Montesquieu in Caillois's book, there is much to say about the ludic function of exoticism, whether it is in Montesquieu's *Persian Letters* or the operas *Zoroastre* and *Tarare*. In *Man, Play, and Games*, Caillois divides play into four fundamental categories, one of which is mimicry. He notes that, in mimicry, the player temporarily imagines "that he is someone else, and he invents an imaginary universe."[9]

While mimicry may shed light on the playful process of imagining a universe such as that of the *Persian Letters*, *Zoroastre*, or *Tarare*, it also underscores how spectators are encouraged to play along by decoding the signs and symbols of this new make-believe setting. As Caillois observes, "secrecy, mystery, and even travesty can be transformed into play activity, but it must be immediately pointed out that this transformation is necessarily to the detriment of the secret and mysterious, which play exposes, publishes, and somehow expends."[10] The function of play through the lens of mimicry is to decipher and reveal the hidden meaning behind the mysterious—or, in this case, the exotic. The exotic therefore works as a veil that enchants and entertains the public for the duration of the performance, but it is ultimately cast aside when it ends.

The exotic settings in *Zoroastre* and *Tarare* employ mimicry as a means of pulling in spectators, who may then discern clues from the text and its performance to decode the author's message. Both operas use the perspective of an outsider's gaze in order to induce criticism of the French state. Srivinas Aravamudan refers to this body of fiction that uses social observation and an imaginative Orientalism to interrogate domestic society as "Enlightenment Orientalism." He argues that these works have a doubling nature: they can be at once "inside and outside the nation, self-critical and also xenotropic, philosophical and also fantasmatic."[11] While exoticism had quantifiable entertainment value and promised an increase in ticket sales, I maintain that it also served a ludic function according to which discerning ambiguities eventually lead to a moment of self-examination. In *Zoroastre* and *Tarare*, the use of exoticism on the operatic stage exemplifies a form of play that encourages the public to entertain fanciful ideas, explore new identities, and push conventional boundaries. While Caillois suggests that one of the formal qualities of play is that it is necessarily unproductive, I argue that these works show that it can also be productive in terms of offering intellectual value. If these operas were allowed on the lyric stage, it is because they appear insignificant on the surface. Yet, using Orientalist fantasy as a ruse, the authors of these works encourage audience participation by turning the performance into a deciphering game from which the reader/spectator emerges having gained a serious and important outlook on France's political situation.

EXPLORING NEW HORIZONS

When first performed in 1749, *Zoroastre* received mixed reviews.[12] The composer, Jean-Philippe Rameau, and his librettist, Louis de Cahusac, subsequently made considerable revisions to both the musical score and the libretto, resulting in a second version of the work that was completed and staged in 1756. The revised edition was an immediate success with the public. Fourteen years later, *Zoroastre* was still considered a sure crowd-pleaser, and it was chosen for the inaugural performance of the Salle du Palais-Royal in 1770.[13] The popularity of Rameau's 1756 *Zoroastre* raises an important question: What aspect(s) of this lyric tragedy led to its enduring success in France throughout the High Enlightenment?

Unlike the traditional *tragédie en musique*, this opera focuses on a theme that is derived from Persian religious sources and myths rather than classical mythology.[14] It takes place in Bactria, one of the possible birth places of Zoroastrianism.[15] Zoroastre is the protagonist of the opera and represents Orosmade, the god of light. Zoroastre is opposed by Abramane, who serves Ariman, the spirit of darkness. After the death of the king of Bactria, Abramane devises a plan to steal the throne from the rightful heiress, Amélite. Her sister, Érinice, joins forces with Abramane since she is jealous that the man she loves, Zoroastre, is in love with her sister and is defending her right to the throne. The fighting comes to an end in the final act of the opera when the heavens intervene to bestow the throne upon Amélite and Zoroastre. Meanwhile, Abramane and Érinice are swallowed whole by the earth, never to be seen again. In an operatic game of thrones, good ultimately triumphs over evil.[16]

While the conflict between hero and villain may be prototypical of operas in the ancien régime, Rameau and Cahusac's choice of exotic setting and characters is unique to the genre. For Sylvie Bouissou, Cahusac most likely made the decision to situate the opera in Bactria because it allowed him to construct a fantasy world in which to stage the wise prophet, Zoroastre, as a combatant of evil.[17] This analysis of the opera is in keeping with Graham Sadler's interpretation of the thematic content, which he understands as a testament to Masonic ideology.[18] He explains that Zoroastrianism is important to Freemasons because it insists on the same founding dichotomies of good versus evil and enlightenment versus ignorance. Therefore, presenting the story of Zoroastre on the French stage was a way for the librettist, himself a Freemason, to promote values such as friendship, virtue, innocence, and peace.[19]

Given the political risks associated with Freemasonry in mid-eighteenth-century France, the Masonic values are not explicit in the opera but instead disguised in a fictitious universe that effectively gives the audience the opportunity to freely contemplate these beliefs. This is achieved, in part, through the setting and set designs as described in the libretto. *Zoroastre* opens to the gardens of the kings of Bactria, which are badly damaged from a thunderstorm that has just passed—a thunderstorm the audience is led to believe was caused by the wrath of the gods (*Zoroastre*, 33). This ravaged backdrop is in keeping with Cahusac's own *Encyclopédie* article on decoration at the opera, in which he notes that a good set design should allow the spectator's imagination to run free rather than limit it to a known and well-defined space: "La *décoration* commence l'illusion; elle doit par sa vérité, par sa magnificence, et l'ensemble de sa composition, représenter le lieu de la scène et arracher le spectateur d'un local réel, pour le transporter dans un local feint." (*Set design* is the starting point for the illusion. Its verisimilitude, magnificence, and overall composition should capture the setting of the scene and pull spectators out of a real place in order to transport them to one that is imaginary.)[20] From the beginning of *Zoroastre*, spectators are plunged into a fictionalized space with no discernible point of departure, effectively encouraging them to embark on a journey in an unknown land, free from French sociocultural expectations.

This *as if* is maintained throughout the opera while sound and visual effects are used routinely to maximize spectator engagement. After agreeing to usurp her sister from the throne, Érinice goes to Amélite with the demand that she leave the kingdom or face the consequences. Her appearance on the darkening stage is preceded with what sounds like the rumblings of an earthquake (*Zoroastre*, 43). This is in stark contrast to the types of effects used to accompany Zoroastre's presence and actions on stage, which are often accompanied by great flashes of light. When Orosmade tasks Zoroastre with freeing Amélite and restoring her to the throne, the hero is enveloped in a celestial radiance that will guide him to the completion of his duty. Blinded by a cloud of light and surrounded by Spirits of the Elements, Zoroastre cries out in bewilderment and awe,

> Où suis-je? Un nouveau jour m'éclaire.
> Quels parfums enchanteurs! Quels sons mélodieux!
> Des secrets éternels je perce le mystère.
> Mon âme vole dans les cieux.

> Where am I? A new light illuminates me.
> What enchanting scents! What melodious sounds!
> I grasp the mystery of the eternal secrets.
> My soul flies in the heavens. (*Zoroastre*, 51)

Zoroastre is depicted as the enlightened savior who has come to illuminate the people and bring back peace and justice following the havoc that has ravaged the country as the result of impulsive and impassioned behavior.

This passage serves as an example of how the spectator, like Zoroastre, is inspired to participate in the discovery of this new world by imagining its perfumed scent, hearing its celestial music, and seeing its incredible light. Through a combination of imagined and visible clues, the spectator joins Zoroastre in an adventure that seeks to defeat tyranny and restore order and peace. According to Susan Bennett's theorization of the audience at the theater, experience during a performance is comprised of outer and inner frames. The outer frame is a cultural construct that guides the audience's expectations for and definitions of the performance at hand. The inner frame, on the other hand, defines the spectator's experience, which is created through "production strategies, ideological overcoding, and the material conditions of performance." Bennett explains that it is the coming together of these two frames that defines a spectator's experience and understanding.[21]

Through this process of overcoding, the audience member becomes an active participant in the live production. While any performance seeks to engage the public and capture its attention, accounts from the eighteenth century suggest that few operas were fully able to do so. People regularly talked throughout performances, but this was not the case for *Zoroastre*. Even during its first run in 1749, critics commented on the exceptional silence of the public enraptured by this "[o]uvrage singulier" (singular work).[22] *Zoroastre* distinguishes itself from other operas of the time, at least in part, due to its subject matter that does not draw on well-known stories from classical mythology. This new and unexpected story line is peppered with hints throughout the performance in the form of recognizable iconography in costumes and set designs, or even lyric clues, that turn the spectacle into a decoding game from which meaning is gleaned.

In the case of *Zoroastre*, the spectator is encouraged to engage actively with the production not only through the visual and codified presentation of the story on stage but also through the published lyrics, which audience members could purchase at the door to read during the performance. Throughout the opera, the onstage chorus offers hints as to who is playing for what side while, at times, almost giving away who will eventually win. In act 1, scene 3, Amélite laments being separated from her lover, Zoroastre, and fears she may never see him again. In response to her cries of woe, the chorus repeatedly answers,

Rassurez-vous, tendre Amélite,
Voyez nos jeux, écoutez-nous.
Que le trouble qui vous agite
Cède à l'espoir le plus doux.

Take comfort, tender Amélite,
Watch our sport, listen to us;
May the distress that troubles you
Yield to the sweetest hope. (*Zoroastre*, 41)

While Amélite is focused on her current plight, the chorus warns her not to lose herself to irrational passions, but instead to focus on the game at hand—a game they foresee her winning.

The chorus's seeming ability to foresee the future underscores an element of the supernatural that is present throughout the opera. For example, when Abramane and Érinice agree to work together, Abramane breaks his magic wand in two and gives one half to Érinice to seal the deal (*Zoroastre*, 39). In another example, when, at the end of the opera, Zoroastre is on the verge of losing the battle against Abramane, the divine god Orosmade interferes to turn the fates in his favor (*Zoroastre*, 109). The importance of this dichotomy of reality versus illusion, natural versus magical, is foregrounded in Cahusac's article in the *Encyclopédie* on enchantment. According to Cahusac, opera is a theater of illusion in which marvels occur thanks to the intervention of gods, fairies, and magic. He is careful to note, however, that these illusions should not be abused by authors but instead used with parsimony to increase the audience's pleasure at key moments. If the supernatural powers on stage appear to have no grounding in reality, he argues, spectators will never believe what they are seeing and the desired effect will be diminished.[23]

Cahusac's observations on enchantment may be compared to Caillois's definition of mimicry, according to which a game of role-play is only effective inasmuch as all the participants fully acquiesce to the proposed illusion. If even one individual denounces the absurdity of the game at hand, the spell is broken and the illusion fails.[24] Maintaining this illusion is arguably essential in *Zoroastre* given that the plot of the opera, depicting the overthrow of a despotic ruler, could be read as a critique of the divine right of kings. Paul Tillit suggests that the original 1749 version of *Zoroastre* was initially intended to praise Louis XV, the ruling monarch at that time. He explains, however, that as the king's popularity waned following the Seven Years War, the utopian kingdom delineated by Cahusac unintentionally attained new meaning as promoting governmental reform:

> Ce que Cahusac a négligé de prévoir en exprimant cette utopie, c'est que le roi populaire qu'il songeait à flatter pouvait, avec le temps, devenir impopulaire. C'est donc postérieurement, et malgré son auteur, que l'on peut voir dans la réplique de Zoroastre une contestation de l'absolutisme de la fin de l'Ancien Régime.

> In his depiction of this utopia, Cahusac failed to predict that the popular king he sought to flatter could, with time, become unpopular. It is therefore in hindsight, and despite the author, that the reader can see in Zoroastre's response a challenge to absolutism at the end of the ancien régime.[25]

While, as Tillit notes, the opera appears to advocate for a constitutional monarchy with no absolute ruler, the exotic setting allows the author to transmit this

Masonic objective without openly appearing to critique the French state. I dispute the idea that Cahusac did not purposefully attack the monarchy in his libretto when it was first written and published in 1749. Given the author's intentional use of Orientalism within the opera, I see the creation of a fantastical world as serving as a buffer to protect the librettist from the contentious ideologies he was promulgating.

By camouflaging his critique of the government in an exotic setting, Cahusac invites the audience to play along by attempting to decipher the message hidden in this foreign landscape. Play, in this context, aligns with Brian Edwards's definition of the term in *Theories of Play and Postmodern Fiction*, in which he describes play as a state of mind coupled with actions that promise "freedom and possibility against restriction, resignation and closure, thus blurring distinctions between observation and participation, and between spectators and collaborators."[26] This translates to opera in the sense that spectators are not passive observers; their active engagement with the performance dictates whether it will fail or succeed. An exotic setting may initially pique the curiosity of spectators, but the story must be realistic enough to hold their attention and encourage them to play along without their dismissing it as nonsensical. Cahusac therefore creates a fictional space based on rules of logic where spectators can imagine themselves in a new world, free to play the role of explorers discovering a new sociopolitical reality.

Taking Control of Destiny

Nearly forty years later, in 1787, another opera appeared on the stage of the Académie royale de musique that also featured a setting in the Orient, as well as a similar message promoting the idea of a revised monarchy. From the beginning, Salieri and Beaumarchais's *Tarare* presents itself as a game of chance in which man is not responsible for the cards he is dealt in life, but he can still decide how he wants to play his hand. The opera begins with a prologue depicting the birth of all the performance's characters at the hands of Nature and the God of Fire. In defiance of the notion that kings are expressly chosen by God, *Tarare* opens by suggesting that royal birth is a question of chance rather than of divine right. The character Nature looks at two shadows without names and randomly selects one to become a tyrannical despot (Atar) and the other a pure-hearted soldier (Tarare). The libretto stipulates that while both men are born equal, society will soon distance them from one another according to their assigned social rank:

> Enfants, embrassez-vous: égaux par la nature,
> Que vous en serez loin dans la société!
> De la grandeur altière à l'humble pauvreté,

Cet intervalle immense est désormais le vôtre;
À moins que de Brama la puissante bonté,
    Par un décret prémédité,
    Ne vous rapproche l'un de l'autre,
Pour l'exemple des rois et de l'humanité.

Children, embrace one another: equal by nature,
You will be far from it in society!
From haughty grandeur to humble poverty,
This great divide is now yours;
Unless Brahma the almighty,
    By premeditated decree,
    Brings you together,
For the instruction of kings and all humanity.[27]

This warning not to heed society's arbitrary judgments about personal worth based on social class is not dissimilar from Figaro's famous monologue in another of Beaumarchais's dramatic works, *The Marriage of Figaro* (1778). In act 5, scene 3, Figaro laments, "Parce ce que vous êtes un grand seigneur, vous vous croyez un grand génie! . . . [N]oblesse, fortune, un rang, des places; tout cela rend si fier! Qu'avez-vous fait pour tant de biens? vous vous êtes donné la peine de naître, et rien de plus." (Because you are a great nobleman, you think you are a great genius! . . . Nobility, fortune, rank, position! How proud they make a man feel! What have you done to deserve such advantages? Put yourself to the trouble of being born—nothing more.)[28] There is a common theme in both *The Marriage of Figaro* and *Tarare* that speaks to the arbitrary nature of social class and the subsequent unfairness of any judgments brought against an individual for something out of her control.

This notion opposing fate to free will is exemplified in *Tarare* through the character of Atar, who abuses his power as king to wage a personal vendetta against one of his subjects. The first act of *Tarare* takes place decades after the prologue and shows that Atar is frustrated with the people's love for the common soldier, Tarare. He therefore steals Tarare's wife in an attempt to destroy his character and popularity. His plan backfires, and Tarare successfully wins back his wife to the applause of the people who demand that he become the new ruling monarch. The humiliated king subsequently commits suicide. Following his death, the people plead with Tarare to take the crown. He reticently accepts, stating,

Enfants, vous m'y forcez, je garderai ces fers:
Ils seront à jamais ma royale ceinture.
De tous mes ornements devenus les plus chers,

Puissent-ils attester à la race future
Que, du grand nom de roi si j'acceptai l'éclat,
Ce fut pour m'enchaîner au bonheur de l'État!

Children, you force me to keep these irons:
From now on, they will be my royal belt.
Of all the possessions that are dear to me,
Let this be a testament to future generations
That, if I took on the name of king and accepted this recognition,
It was only to chain myself to the happiness of the state! (*Tarare*, 588)

Tarare, who is chosen by the people, is not an absolute monarch but rather an elected official.

Tearing down one monarchy to build a new one raises doubts as to whether any progress has been made, or if one demagogue has simply been replaced by another with no assurance of success and possibly to the detriment of future progress. This in turn suggests that, if true societal advancement is to take place, the people must overtake the monarchy and run it by and for themselves on the merits of their good character and sense of moral decency. Otherwise, if one monarchy is simply overturned for another, nothing has changed. Corruption begets further corruption, and the threat of tyranny remains ever present. Considering this message along with the brazen onstage demonstration of the suicide of a monarch and the subsequent meteoric rise of a soldier who takes his place, it is not negligible to consider if this opera would have been allowed on stage had it not taken place in an Oriental setting.

Using a scene added to *Tarare* years later entitled "Le couronnement de Tarare" (1790) that is blatant in its Revolutionary underpinnings, Thomas Betzwieser argues that Beaumarchais could only explore such politically contentious subjects before the French Revolution by setting his opera in the Orient and hiding behind an "exotic masque." Betzwieser concludes that, after the storming of the Bastille, Beaumarchais was free to express his political opinions without having to worry about the repercussions.[29] To prove his point, Betzwieser cites Beaumarchais's preface to the 1790 edition of *Tarare*:

Ô citoyens! souvenez-vous du temps où vos penseurs inquiétés, forcés de voiler leurs idées, s'enveloppaient d'allégories et labouraient péniblement le champ de la Révolution. Après quelques autres essais, je jetai dans la terre, à mes risques et périls, ce germe d'un chêne civique au sol brûlé de l'Opéra.... L'œuvre a reçu son complément dans le "Couronnement de Tarare," l'an premier de la liberté; nous vous l'offrons pour son anniversaire. Ce 14 juillet 1790.

Citizens! Remember the time when your disquieted thinkers, forced to disguise their ideas, clothed themselves in allegories, laboriously preparing the field for the Revolution. After various other attempts I cast down—at my own risk and peril—this seed of a civic oak upon the scorched earth of the Opéra. . . . The work has reached its completion in *The Crowning of Tarare* in the first year of liberty; we offer it to you on its anniversary. 14 July 1790.[30]

Unlike Betzwieser, and despite what Beaumarchais cites as his reasons for extensively revising his libretto, I am reticent to celebrate Beaumarchais as the paradigm of the liberated artist who previously tricked censors into thinking that his opera was little more than a lyric fantasy set in a faraway place.

Beaumarchais was a coy businessman who knew how to toy with convention while—both literally and figuratively—keeping his head. His own explanations of his writings should therefore be treated with some degree of caution, because they change depending on the political climate. For example, in his 1787 preface, "Aux abonnés de l'Opéra qui voudraient aimer l'opéra," Beaumarchais implies that an exotic setting opens up creative possibilities in which to represent a violent society in decline due to its pension for unbridled passion and unwavering tradition.[31] He further explains that setting the opera in Hormuz is a means of more clearly elucidating the dangers of irrational behavior:

> Je penserais donc qu'on doit prendre un milieu entre le merveilleux et le genre historique. J'ai cru m'apercevoir aussi que les mœurs très civilisées étaient trop méthodiques pour y paraître théâtrales. Les mœurs orientales, plus disparates et moins connues, laissent à l'esprit un champ plus libre et me semblent très propres à remplir cet objet.

> I thought that a place should be chosen between the fantastic and the historical. I also believed that very civilized mores would be too methodical to appear theatrical. Oriental mores are more disparate and less well-known, giving the mind a vision that is freer, which seemed to me more appropriate in order to attain my objective. (*Tarare*, 503)

Beaumarchais stipulates earlier in his preface that this "objective" is to create an energetic and clear storyline that piques the audience's curiosity (*Tarare*, 502). Yet he uses the kingdom of Persia not only to excite spectators and encourage wide attendance at performances of his opera but also to allow himself the freedom to communicate ideas too radical to express openly. Like *Zoroastre*, *Tarare* invites the spectator to participate in a game of hermeneutical deciphering in a fictionalized foreign land.

Beaumarchais insists on the importance of this exotic setting on more than one occasion, citing its ability to inspire spectators to action. In a letter sent to the censor responsible for editing and approving *Tarare* before its first performance, Beaumarchais begins by referring to his *étrange opéra* (foreign opera): "Je vous envoie, brave censeur, mon étrange opéra pour l'approuver. Je vous demande en grâce qu'il ne sorte pas de vos mains." (I am sending you, brave censor, my *étrange opéra* to approve. I would ask that you please not let it leave your hands.) By referring to his opera as *étrange*, Beaumarchais insists, first and foremost, on the work's foreignness. He then insinuates that this setting, and the exaggerated passions of the exotic characters, will mask his intended message that could otherwise be read by his adversaries as foolhardy conceit:

> Si j'avais mis le véritable titre, il s'appellerait *Le Libre Arbitre*, ou *Le Pouvoir de la Vertu*; mais on m'eût accusé d'une prétention ridicule.
>
> Sous cet aspect pourtant, j'espère que les choses fortes, sortant de caractères tranchants, trouveront grâce devant vous.

> If I had put my desired title, it would be called *Free Will*, or *The Power of Virtue*; but I would have been accused of ridiculous pretension.
>
> Even from this point of view, I hope that the strong elements, coming from the bluntness of the characters, will appeal to you.[32]

If Beaumarchais mentions the title he would have liked to have given his opera, he does so in order to underscore the serious moralizing lesson at play in this production. In fact, later in the same letter he expresses hope that audience members will comprehend and appreciate his portrayal of justice as a virtue that is earned rather than inherited. According to Beaumarchais, the important message to take away from this performance is that men, no matter what their position in society, can recognize the error of their ways by realizing that purity of character is the most important quality an individual can possess. For this reason, he points out the lyric passage at the end of *Tarare* that speaks most closely to his desired moralizing message:

> Mortel, qui que tu sois, brame, prince ou soldat.
> Homme! ta grandeur sur la terre
> N'appartient point à ton état:
> Elle est toute à ton caractère.

> You are mortal, whether you are a brahmin, a prince, or a soldier.
> Man! Your greatness on earth
> Is not beholden to your status:
> It has everything to do with your character.[33]

In other words, the worth of any individual should be based on the deliberate decisions he makes in life rather than on the arbitrary social status into which he is born.

The efficacy of this message is debated by critics because of the seemingly lighthearted genre in which it occurs. At times, even Beaumarchais himself appears self-deprecating. As Daren Hodson notes, "in the *Avertissement de l'auteur* from 1787, [Beaumarchais] admits that his 'preliminary discourse' (i.e., the preface) may have been 'un peu badin' [somewhat playful]."[34] Given that this preface argues, in part, for a rethinking of opera as serious literature and not simply a childish pastime, it raises the question of whether Beaumarchais is dismissing his own production as nothing more than meaningless entertainment. To this point, some scholars do consider *Tarare* an unfortunate and worthless work in Beaumarchais's corpus. According to William D. Howarth, "the libretto, shorn of its musical accompaniment, makes sorry reading for those of today's students who are determined to explore the totality of Beaumarchais's dramatic output." He concludes that *Tarare* is nothing more than a stereotypical portrait of a despot fighting against the virtues of a unified and selfless people—a platitude Howarth finds too "cliché."[35] René Pomeau criticizes Beaumarchais not so much for his subject matter, but rather for the decision to convey the message in the form of an opera. "Un contexte différent l'eût [l'idée du caractère] sans doute mieux mise en valeur" (a different context would have valorized [the idea of morality] more), Pomeau notes, adding, "On déplore surtout que l'indigence de sa versification la réduise à n'être plus qu'une platitude cacophonique." (It is a shame that the penury of versification diminishes the worth [of the message] and reduces it to a cacophonous platitude.)[36]

These biting critiques draw upon a centuries-old debate about the political engagement of opera that continues to this day. For example, historian R. J. Arnold suggests that opera and the debates it engendered in pre-Revolutionary France did not concern politics, but only music. As he argues, "it strains credulity to suppose that the vast range of participants in the various musical *querelles* could have been employing mutually comprehensible illicit idiolect which escaped detection not only by the contemporary authorities but by posterity."[37] Conversely, musicologist Olivia Bloechl supports the idea that opera had a distinct political agenda that changed over the course of the eighteenth century. She concludes that while opera under Louis XIV reflected the monarch's absolute reign and supremacy, content evolved during the eighteenth century to underscore composers' changing views of the royal family and a gradual liberalization of politics.[38]

Opera is an entertainment genre whose potential for seriousness is often met with skepticism. Throughout the seventeenth and eighteenth centuries, opera was publicly ridiculed by some for being immoral and poorly written literature, while others took this as an indication of the levity with which the genre should be treated. In either case, the conclusion is that operas are lighthearted entertainment incapable of engaging in serious topics, let alone of encouraging social or political change. A comical example of this viewpoint, and its persistence even into the late eighteenth century, is a periodical published between 1785 and 1789 entitled the *Courier lyrique et amusant, ou Passe-temps des toilettes.* This biweekly publication focused principally on the latest lyric productions by providing a variety of reviews, anecdotes, and satirical songs.[39] Much like today's tabloids, the *Courier lyrique* marketed itself as a mindless way to pass the time.

Given the success of *Tarare*, it is not surprising that a satirical song about the opera was published in the *Courier lyrique*. Sung to the air of "Jardinier, ne vois-tu pas," the vaudeville begins with the following biting critique:

Le jeune homme est trop léger,
Le vieillard trop avare:
Vouloir tous deux les changer,
Prétendre les corriger;
Tarare! Tarare! Tarare!

The young man is too lighthearted,
The old man too avaricious:
To want to change them both,
To pretend to correct them;
Tarare! Tarare! Tarare![40]

The vaudeville continues by criticizing Beaumarchais for appearing to villain-ize the nobility for their attempts to gain royal favors when, in the end, he con-tends that authors are doing the same by ingratiating themselves to their audiences. Overall, this vaudeville chides Beaumarchais for taking his work too seriously, as if his silly opera could cure the wrongs of society:

Chacun prend avec fureur,
Dans ce siècle barbare,
Les titres pour le bonheur,
L'honnêteté pour le bonheur:
Tarare! Tarare! Tarare!

Everybody gets angry,
In this barbaric century,
With titles for happiness,
Honor for happiness:
Tarare! Tarare! Tarare![41]

Beaumarchais is depicted as a hypocrite, hiding behind his opera to preach morality to the masses when he himself is guilty of the same improprieties. After all, the word *tarare*, according to the *Dictionnaire de l'Académie française*, is a mocking rejoinder that essentially means "nonsense."[42] By naming his opera *Tarare*, it is almost as if Beaumarchais is challenging his audience to a game of Truth or Dare. Does the spectator choose to see this opera as fictional entertain-ment, or does she dare to consider a more real, and perhaps even dangerous, condemnation of French society? In this sense, Beaumarchais, like Cahusac, confronts one of the key definitions of play: that it ought to be unproductive. According to Caillois, play "creat[es] neither goods, nor wealth, nor new elements of any kind."[43] Yet while *Tarare* or *Zoroastre* may not benefit spectators materially, they do provide them with a transformative experience. These performances offer audience members the chance to participate in a game of deciphering, which yields benefits in the form of new ideas that challenge long-standing preconceptions.

Primary sources indicate that the public was aware of Beaumarchais's hidden political message and took it seriously. In September 1790 the *Journal encyclopédique* published an open letter from the secretary for the Académie royale de musique to Beaumarchais addressing the public uproar the reprise of *Tarare* had incited during a recent performance and expressing the opera committee's concern:

> Le comité me charge de vous observer que le bruit qui s'est fait hier au spectacle ne peut venir que de l'erreur où sont tombées plusieurs personnes sur vos intentions. Ne pourriez-vous pas, Monsieur, mettre quelque chose dans les journaux, qui expliquât ce que l'on n'a ni lu ni écouté? Vous obligeriez infiniment le comité de l'Opéra, qui n'est pas accoutumé à voir de pareilles rumeurs à son spectacle.

> The committee has tasked me with bringing to your attention the controversy caused by a performance of your work yesterday, which can only be the result of misconceptions by people who do not understand your intentions. Could you please, sir, publish something in the newspapers to explain what was clearly neither read nor heard? The Opera Committee would be immensely grateful, because they are not accustomed to hearing such rumors circulate after a performance.[44]

While the committee abstains from expressing any opinion on the matter, preferring instead to feign polite ignorance, Beaumarchais's response explicitly underscores his intended political message at the time. He stands by his presentation of a constitutional monarchy, writing that, after much reflection, he defends the line in *Tarare* suggesting that the reigning king deserves the people's respect and that his power should not be usurped:

> Moi, j'ai dit ce que je pensais, ce que je pense encore *sur le respect dû à nos rois*; et j'y ai beaucoup réfléchi. Permis aux chroniqueurs de me prêter de lâches intentions, en reportant au jour d'hier une maxime très ancienne, consacrée de tout temps dans le cœur des Français.

> As for myself, I said what I thought and what I still think *about the respect our kings deserve*, and I have thought about this a lot. Let critics speak ill of my intentions, by publishing an age-old maxim that has been instilled within the French since time immemorial.[45]

Beaumarchais's response is unapologetic. Rather than negating the perceived political underpinnings of his opera, he defends them. While the prologue of

Tarare sets the scene for a game of *alea* (chance) in which destiny decides the fate of humankind, the ending shows the underprivileged breaking from the binds of social prejudice to take control of the future. Like the character of Tarare, Beaumarchais assumes ownership of the monster he has created and consequently casts light on opera as a genre that has agency on both the theatrical and political stages.

A STAGE FOR CHANGE

In *Les caractères* (1688), Jean de La Bruyère suggests that the marvelous, or *le merveilleux*, is the sole purpose of opera. He writes, "Il ne faut point de vols, ni de chars, ni de changements aux *Bérénices* et à *Pénélope*, il en faut aux *Opéras*, et le propre de ce spectacle est de tenir les esprits, les yeux et les oreilles dans un égal enchantement." (Flights, chariots, and transformations are not necessary in the *Berenices* or in *Penelope*. You need them in *Opera* in order to keep the mind, eyes, and ears in an equal state of enchantment.)[46] The implication is that while dramatic theater has quality text and therefore little need for special effects, opera requires them to keep the audience entertained. For La Bruyère, opera relies on dazzling set designs, costume changes, and machinery to entertain the public because of its substandard literary content. This idea that opera's only goal is to blindly entertain the public is perpetuated throughout the seventeenth and eighteenth centuries. Opera and the opera house acquire a reputation for exciting passion in spectators using visual trickery and music to the detriment of both reason and morality. But the stereotype that opera is first and foremost an arena of play that is necessarily distinct from the real world and the worries of daily life is reductive and untenable. Any performance, regardless of the fantasy world it depicts, is anchored in reality. As Jacques Ehrmann argues, "play cannot be defined by isolating it on the basis of its relationship to an *a priori* reality and culture. To define play is *at the same time* and *in the same movement* to define reality and to define culture."[47] Play—in this case, operatic play—allows the audience to see the status quo as a rigged and unfair game while concomitantly providing the opportunity to contemplate different and fairer codes of conduct.

Envisioning change, political or otherwise, is a risk that requires the player to bet on a future that may or may not be better than the present. Both *Zoroastre* and *Tarare* encourage spectators to embark on a journey of hermeneutical possibilities that could lead down a path toward self-revelation and/or collective change. Orientalist fantasies such as *turquerie*, however frivolous and trite they may have appeared on the surface, were at times serious. Playing dress-up, creating fictionalized exotic realms, and engaging in mimicry are not just escapist ploys used in operas to entertain mindlessly. Cahusac and Beaumarchais both took the calculated risk of using these settings to entice audience members to play along in imagining a fictional universe that, once decoded, offered them new insights and perspectives. Exoticism in these performances subsequently becomes a deciphering game that invites willing participants to expend the illusion of make-believe to unveil a serious message at the end of the game that encourages radical new approaches to governing.

NOTES

Unless noted otherwise, all translations are my own.

1. For a visual portrayal, see Charles Nicolas Cochin, *Decoration for a Masked Ball at Versailles, on the Occasion of the Marriage of Louis, Dauphin of France, and Maria Theresa, Infanta of Spain (Bal masqué donné par le roi, dans la grande galerie de Versailles, pour le mariage de Louis dauphin de France avec Marie-Thérèse infante d'Espagne, 1745)*, etching, 1760, Metropolitan Museum of Art, New York, https://www.metmuseum.org/toah/works -of-art/30.22-34_34/.

2. Jacques Bonnet, *Histoire générale de la danse sacrée et profane* (Paris: d'Houry, 1724), 149.

3. Larry Wolff, *The Singing Turk: Ottoman Power and Operatic Emotions on the European Stage from the Siege of Vienna to the Age of Napoleon* (Stanford, CA: Stanford University Press, 2016), 1.

4. *Analyse critique de Tarare* (Hormuz and Paris, 1787), 3.

5. *Magasin des modes nouvelles, françaises et anglaises* 27 (1787): 209.

6. Denis Diderot, *Salon de 1767*, in *Œuvres complètes*, vol. 16, ed. Herbert Dieckmann, Jean Fabre, Jacques Proust, and Jean Varloot (Paris: Hermann, 1975), 313. The English translation is from *Diderot on Art*, vol. 2, *The Salon of 1767*, trans. John Goodman (New Haven, CT: Yale University Press, 1995), 182.

7. *Zoroastre* was performed for the first time in 1749. As explained later in the chapter, I have chosen to focus on the revised 1756 version.

8. Haydn Williams, *Turquerie: An Eighteenth-Century European Fantasy* (New York: Thames and Hudson, 2014), 7.

9. Roger Caillois, *Man, Play and Games*, trans. Meyer Barash (Urbana: University of Illinois Press, 2001), 44.

10. Caillois, *Man, Play and Games*, 4.

11. Srinivas Aravamudan, *Enlightenment Orientalism: Resisting the Rise of the Novel* (Chicago: University of Chicago Press, 2012), 8.

12. Graham Sadler, "Avant-propos," in *Opera omnia Rameau*, ser. 4, vol. 19, *Zoroastre*, ed. Graham Sadler (Paris: G. Billaudot, 1999), xxv.

13. Paul Tillit, "*Zoroastre* (1749) de Rameau: Droit et utopies dans un opéra franc-maçon du siècle des Lumières," *Droit et cultures* 52 (2006), http://journals.openedition.org /droitcultures/631.

14. Cynthia Verba, *Dramatic Expression in Rameau's* Tragédie en Musique: *Between Tradition and Enlightenment* (Cambridge: Cambridge University Press, 2013), 133.

15. Jenny Rose, *Zoroastrianism: An Introduction* (London: I. B. Tauris, 2010), 10.

16. Louis de Cahusac, *Zoroastre*, trans. Adrian Shaw, accompanying booklet to *Rameau: Zoroastre*, orchestra and choir dir. William Christie, with Les Arts Florissants, Warner Classics/Erato 0927 43182-2, 2002, compact disc, 33. Hereafter, page numbers will be cited parenthetically in the text as (*Zoroastre*).

17. Sylvie Bouissou, *Jean-Philippe Rameau: Musicien des Lumières* (Paris: Fayard, 2014), 714.

18. Sadler, "Avant-propos," xxix.

19. Bouissou, *Jean-Philippe Rameau*, 712.

20. Louis de Cahusac, s.v. "Décoration (Opera)," in *Encyclopédie; ou Dictionnaire raisonné des sciences, des arts et des métiers*, 17 vols., ed. Denis Diderot and Jean le Rond d'Alembert (Paris: Briasson, 1751–1765), 4:701, emphasis in the original.

21. Susan Bennett, *Theatre Audiences: A Theory of Production and Reception*, 2nd ed. (New York: Routledge, 1997), 1–2.

22. Sadler, "Avant-propos," xxiv.

23. Louis de Cahusac, s.v. "Enchantement, (Belles-Lettres)" in Diderot and d'Alembert, eds., *Encyclopédie*, 5:619.

24. Caillois, *Man, Play and Games*, 19.

25. Tillit, "*Zoroastre* (1749) de Rameau."

26. Brian Edwards, *Theories of Play and Postmodern Fiction* (New York: Garland, 1998), 17.

27. Pierre-Augustin Caron de Beaumarchais, *Tarare*, in *Œuvres*, ed. Pierre Larthomas and Jacqueline Larthomas (Paris: Gallimard, 1988), 520. Hereafter, page numbers will be cited parenthetically in the text as (*Tarare*).

28. Beaumarchais, *Le mariage de Figaro* in *Œuvres*, 469. The English translation is from *The Barber of Seville and the Marriage of Figaro*, trans. John Wood (Harmondsworth, UK: Penguin, 1964), 199.

29. Thomas Betzwieser, "Exoticism and Politics: Beaumarchais' and Salieri's *Le couronnement de Tarare* (1790)," *Cambridge Opera Journal* 6, no. 2 (1994): 93.

30. Pierre-Augustin Caron de Beaumarchais, "Notes et variantes," in *Œuvres*, 1458, quoted and translated in Betzwieser, "Exoticism and Politics," 93.

31. Betzwieser, "Exoticism and Politics," 91.

32. Pierre-Augustin Caron de Beaumarchais, "Lettre à Bret," in *Œuvres*, 1452.

33. Beaumarchais, "Lettre à Bret," 1452.

34. Daren Hodson, "Beaumarchais' *Tarare*: Courtly Art and Radical Enlightenment," in *Opera Libretti of the Eighteenth Century: Essays on the Libretto as Enlightenment Text*, ed. Pamela Gay-White (Lewiston, NY: Edwin Mellen, 2014), 123.

35. William D. Howarth, *Beaumarchais and the Theatre* (London: Routledge, 1995), 196, 204.

36. René Pomeau, *Beaumarchais ou La bizarre destinée* (Paris: Presses universitaires de France, 1987), 176.

37. R. J. Arnold, *Musical Debate and Political Culture in France* (Woodbridge, UK: Boydell, 2017), 8.

38. Olivia Bloechl, *Opera and the Political Imaginary in Old Regime France* (Chicago: University of Chicago Press, 2017), 20–21.

39. According to the prospectus printed at the beginning of each issue, the *Courier lyrique* was an "ouvrage périodique, composé d'ariettes nouvelles, de romances, de vaudevilles, de contredanses et d'anecdotes curieuses" (periodical composed of new ariettas, romances, vaudevilles, contra dances, and curious anecdotes). See *Courier lyrique et amusant, ou Passe-temps des toilettes*, ed. Adélaïde-Gillette Dufrénoy (Paris: Knapen et fils, 1787).

40. François Guillaume Ducray-Duminil, "Tarare, Vaudeville," in Dufrénoy, ed., *Courier lyrique et amusant*, 118.

41. Ducray-Duminil, "Tarare, Vaudeville," 119.

42. "Tarare," in *Dictionnaire de l'Académie française*, 4th ed., vol. 2 (Paris: Brunet, 1762), 801.

43. Caillois, *Man, Play and Games*, 10.

44. "Lettre du comité de l'opéra à l'auteur de *Tarare*," *Journal encyclopédique ou universel* 6 (1790): 462.

45. Pierre-Augustin Caron de Beaumarchais, "Extrait de la Réponse de l'auteur de *Tarare* au comité de l'opéra," *Journal encyclopédique ou universel* 6 (1790): 463, emphasis in the original.

46. Jean de La Bruyère, *Les caractères*, ed. Emmanuel Bury (Paris: Librairie Générale Française, 1995), 143–44, emphasis in the original.

47. Jacques Ehrmann, "Homo Ludens Revisited," trans. Cathy and Phil Lewis, in *Game, Play, Literature*, ed. Jacques Ehrmann (Boston: Beacon, 1971), 55, emphasis in the original.

CHAPTER 7

Playing at Theater

MODES OF PLAY IN *THÉÂTRE DE SOCIÉTÉ*

Maria Teodora Comsa

Among the myriad meanings of the word *play*, theater is one of the most delight-ful, and in the eighteenth century—the age of *la théâtromanie*—the dramatic practice that perhaps best showcases the intricacies and theatrical functions of play is *le théâtre de société*, or society theater.[1] Performed by high society and common people alike, society theater was a private activity intended as a play-ful *divertissement* in which amateur actors rehearsed and "played" for—and with—their select *société*. These shows entailed the staging of oneself and the acting out of situations and events often drawn from the daily life of a given society—situations that were all the more amusing to the group in that the per-formances mirrored its own behavior. The performance was also a game that could facilitate seduction, personal advancement, social and political maneuver-ing, and power plays and manipulation. Its participants' diverse motivations and multiplicity of interactions, as well as its specific settings and texts, made society theater distinct from other forms of eighteenth-century theater. In a milieu in which playacting and social intrigue were closely intertwined, the stakes usually associated with this private theatrical performance were particu-larly high. As with any game resulting in winners and losers, society players put themselves at risk, making society theater a dangerously ludic production.

Society theater was a genre in its own right, and it gradually became a social phenomenon during the second half of the eighteenth century. By the 1770s the vogue was so prevalent that it seemed as if everyone had joined in the fray of "playing at theater":

> On comptait plus de deux cents théâtres bourgeois existant dans la capitale; il y
> en avait dans tous les quartiers, dans toutes les rues, dans toutes les maisons. . . .
> On jouait la comédie dans les boutiques des marchands de vin, dans les cafés,

dans les caves, dans les greniers, dans les écuries, sous des hangars. La fureur du théâtre s'était emparée de toutes les petites classes de la société, cela se gagnait, c'était épidémique, une influenza, une grippe, un choléra dramatique!

One could count more than two hundred bourgeois theaters in the capital; there was one in every neighborhood, on every street, in every house.... Comedy was played in wine merchants' shops, in cafés, in cellars, in attics, in stables, under sheds. The theater furor had taken all the smaller classes of society; it was spreading, it was an epidemic, an influenza, a flu, a dramatic cholera![2]

Though this account by Nicholas Brazier is somewhat hyperbolic, it expresses the extraordinary popularity of society theater and amateur acting and shows that its attraction went well beyond members of high society who may have been inspired directly by performances at the royal court. In fact, society shows varied widely: they could go from very simple to highly elaborate, just as the performance space could range from bare-bones, improvised stages to semiprofessional efforts. The types of texts performed varied as much as the theaters: they could be private celebrations (*fêtes privées*) or performances of a mix of *parade*,[3] dramatic proverbs, farce, or comedy. A great majority of shows were comedic and involved parody or caricature of the mainstream, official theater (i.e., the content presented at the Comédie française).[4] While the repertoire of society theater reflects its ostensible purpose of amusing the participants, its function was more complex than simple entertainment.

Ancien régime society was highly theatrical; what began as the royal court etiquette established in the seventeenth century by Louis XIV became a normal form of social spectacle that the beau monde of the subsequent century performed at all times.[5] One had to act in a certain way in order to be accepted at court or even into its outer circles. Performing one's role in society, or "social acting," amounted to following a specific script dictated by rank, title, or wealth, and the constant role-play could be tiresome and alienating. Owing to the success of society theater, one could momentarily exchange this social acting for playacting—that is, acting for fun in a society play.

Commissioning playwrights to compose plays, and staging them for the amusement of an intimate group, was not only prime entertainment but also the ultimate show of influence and status. Numerous society texts were accompanied by paratexts (songs, poems, compliments, etc.) in praise of their author's sponsor or *commanditaire*,[6] similar to the *dédicaces* intended for the king. Emulation of royal court practices did not stop at commissioning and staging plays; many members of high society found great pleasure in appearing on stage and acting (just like the king and his immediate entourage), either among their peers or sometimes in the company of professional actors who were invited to perform or to coach the amateurs in the craft of playacting. The ludic nature of this form of theater is contained in the French verb for acting, *jouer*, which doubles as "to play." But was playacting truly an escape for all participants? A discussion of society theater's functioning as described by Giacomo Casanova will shed some light on the implications of playacting and reveal some of its risks and alienating side effects. Analysis of a *proverbe dramatique* (dramatic proverb) by Louis Carrogis Carmontelle will further explore how play arises in society theater, why it is amusing, and how it unifies the *société* through laughter. As society theater mirrors daily events and behaviors on the private stage, its texts incorporate a documentary value and subversively hint at the cruelty of a game of mockery that is seemingly intrinsic to society performances.

More direct than regular plays (which were intended for the public theaters), and using normal everyday language that would have been easier for amateurs to memorize and recite, society plays offer insight as to the way people spoke and interacted with others, and even about what they found amusing or compelling. These short plays (usually one or two acts, or simply a series of scenes) were often based on anecdotes that only the closed society would know and delight in revisiting. The dramatic genres varied widely, but the subject was often society itself, represented through small vignettes that reflected attitudes and reactions to life. The following two descriptions of the functioning of society theater are only a quick introduction to a vast and complex subject. The excerpt from Casanova's memoirs shows how society theater fits within real life, and the proverb by Carmontelle reveals how real life is represented on the society stage.

CASANOVA AND SOCIETY THEATER

Society theater was an amateur practice,[7] yet it had broad appeal—first, because of the amusement participants derived from it and, second, because it allowed members of high society to escape their daily duties of social acting. As Jean de La Bruyère famously explained, courtiers laughed with one eye and cried with the other, always carefully presenting a public persona while concealing their true deeper character.[8] The vogue of society theater can be interpreted as a response to the obligation to act in a controlled, appropriate manner. In taking a part in a society play, participants could, on the one hand, escape their obligatory day-to-day social acting and, on the other, gain some reprieve from the reality of their public *and* private personae. Yet society theater performances often led to a blurring of lines between social acting, or acting for "duty," and playacting, or acting for "play." This was most evident in the case of prominent public figures, such as the Duke of Orléans,[9] who enjoyed playing theatrical roles before a private audience. But his choice of roles could lead to speculation as to the message he wished to send. Because of his social standing and his position as *commanditaire*, there was no escape from his social acting role. His playacting was intertwined with social acting and could be interpreted as subversive— namely, by playing a part contrary to his everyday social role, the duke was perhaps able to signal that he did not take his social persona too seriously. His case (similar to that of *commanditaires* of court society theaters) stood out because his position in society was established and well respected. But, unlike the duke, less important members of high society could lose their social standing or reputation by choosing the wrong type of acting. In other words, not all participants in society theater could afford to blur the line between play and duty because, for some, playacting could be more alienating than the reality they were trying to escape. An excellent example of such alienation is provided by Giacomo Casanova, one of the most famous libertines and a practitioner of society theater.[10]

Son of the successful Venetian actress Zanetta Farussi, Giacomo Casanova was, one might say, born to perform. His first years were spent in the back of the San Samuele Theater in Venice, but his mother made sure that he would follow a different profession from hers. His ascent from the lowest to the highest levels of European society, however, would not have been possible without his remarkable instinct for performance. At an early age, Casanova found a talent for knowing what to say and how to act in society so as to entertain and make people seek out his company. This innate affability was enhanced by his polished education, and it matured into his two secret "superpowers": his great ability to study human nature and his instinct for taking on the most appropriate social role in each circumstance.

Given his inherent ease with social acting, society theater was second nature to Casanova, and his memoirs underline the utility of this practice in the pursuit of love affairs and in cultivating social ties. He also mocks those who are not as deft as he in shifting between modes of acting. One particular episode—an amorous adventure in Switzerland—illustrates how Casanova turned society theater and the mixing of play and social acting into the ultimate game.

Casanova recounts that in 1760 in Zurich, where he had entertained the idea of becoming a monk in order to "finir d'être le jouet de la fortune" ([escape] once and for all from the sway of fortune),[11] he noticed a young woman dressed "*en ce qu'on appelait amazone*" (*en amazone* as the expression went; *Histoire*, 286; *History*, 96). The young woman—with whom Casanova was instantly besotted—attracted his attention because she was not dressed like a regular lady of her station, but rather was wearing a costume worthy of the best theaters:

> Cette jeune brune avec des yeux noirs très fendus à fleur de tête sous deux sourcils intrépides à teint de lis, et joues de rose coiffée par un bonnet de satin bleu d'où pendait une houppe d'argent qui lui tombait sur l'oreille est un talisman qui me rend stupide. Je mets ma poitrine sur la hauteur d'appui de la fenêtre pour gagner dix pouces, et elle lève sa charmante tête comme si je l'avais appelée. Ma position extraordinaire la force à me regarder avec attention une demi-minute: c'est trop pour une femme modeste. (*Histoire*, 286)

A young brunette, with very large, black, prominent eyes under two fearless brows, with a lily complexion and cheeks of roses, wearing a blue satin bonnet from which dangled a silver tassel which hung over one ear—she is a talisman which stupefies me. I lean over the window sill to gain ten inches, and she raises her charming head as if I had called to her. My strange posture makes her look at me attentively for half a minute—too much for a modest woman. (*History*, 97)

Though not yet society theater, the first act of this adventure functions in the manner of a dramatic text, complete with exposition, intrigue, and action. After they first spotted each other from a distance, the two future "lovers" briefly met in the inn's hallway, where they inquired about one another's identity. Casanova carefully instructed his servant not to reveal who he was, a precaution worthy of the best theatrical intrigue. Learning that the Amazon's party would be dining in their chamber, he determined the only approach: to go in as a waiter. The prospect of playacting delighted him, and his pleasure began with the preparations for his role: "J'arrange mes cheveux en catogan, je me décollette, je mets le tablier par-dessus une veste d'écarlate galonnée d'or à système, je me regarde au miroir, et je me trouve l'air ignoble et faux modeste du personnage que je devais représenter. Je nage dans la joie." (I put the apron over a scarlet waistcoat laced with gold, I examine myself in the mirror, and I find I have the look of baseness and false modesty demanded by the part I am to play. I am in raptures; *Histoire*, 288; *History*, 99.) Careful to assume the "air" and countenance of the type of man he would play, Casanova was certain that his identity would not be discovered by the three women accompanying the Amazon. Once in costume, he performed his role perfectly. Only his intended lover suspected the ruse, and she played along. To make the game more enticing, the Amazon pointed out his lace cuff when he served at the table, threatening to unmask him. But Casanova was quick to invent an explanation, delivering a line worthy of the stage:

Le jabot sortant un peu de l'ouverture, elle l'aperçoit et me dit: Attendez, attendez.—Que souhaitez-vous madame?—Laissez-moi voir donc. Voilà des dentelles superbes.—Oui madame, on me l'a dit; mais elles sont vieilles. C'est un seigneur italien qui a logé ici qui m'en a fait présent. (*Histoire*, 89)

The frill beginning to show a little at the opening, she said to me:
   "Wait, wait."
   "What do you wish, Madame?"
   "Let me look. This is magnificent lace."
   "Yes, Madame, so I have been told; but it is old. An Italian nobleman who stopped here gave it to me." (*History*, 100)

The woman's recognition and tacit acceptance of the Venetian's improvised masquerade marks the beginning of a delightful conspiracy, while the rest of the company is left unaware of the overlap of social acting and playacting. Realizing that his game was succeeding, Casanova rejoiced in the pleasure of acting against social norms and gaining favor through his performance. To add to his delight, he discovered in the mysterious Amazon a worthy fellow thespian who took on her role naturally, enjoying it as much as the seducer yet maintaining the appropriate coldness toward the supposed waiter. Their interaction is a subtle example of social acting turned playacting, and the scene climaxes with the Amazon granting Casanova the distinct pleasure of removing her boots.

The second act of the adventure builds into a complicated amorous intrigue. After learning that the Amazon was a Mme de =, from Soleure, Casanova uses his social connections from Paris to gain an introduction to the French ambassador to Switzerland, M. de Chavigni. Reminding the reader that all social interactions are a game of sorts, Casanova presents the encounter with the ambassador as another theatrical endeavor: "Je me proposais de jouer un personnage fait pour en imposer." (I intended to play the role of an important personage; *Histoire*, 295; *History*, 108). Again he succeeds in the role he undertakes, charming the Frenchman to such an extent that, when the Amazon's companions warn him that Casanova is an impostor, the ambassador refuses to believe them, turning instead to Casanova for the truth. When Casanova reveals to him that he had indeed played the role of a waiter so as to approach Mme de =, Chavigni is charmed. Reminded of similar escapades from his own youth, he immediately decides to aid the seducer in pursuing his love affair. To dissipate any suspicion, Chavigni invites M. and Mme de = to a dinner and, to the great delight of the entire company, Casanova is introduced as the waiter from Zurich. To mislead the husband of his love interest, Casanova takes on another role, feigning interest in the most unattractive among the companions of Mme de =, a woman referred to as Mme F. . . . His choice is not arbitrary: Mme F . . . is the one who had denounced Casanova as an impostor (a waiter). Casanova uses her as cover for his love affair with Mme de = even as he plots revenge for her attempt to have him excluded from the ambassador's *société*.

This episode of social acting is a perfect example of the manipulative games that took place in the high society of the time. The people with the most wit and ability for playacting and improvisation, like Casanova, were desirable company because their manipulation of others was amusing to the entire group and broke the monotony of social interactions dictated by etiquette. This is why the ambassador took such a liking to the Venetian seducer and was ready to join the improvisation and help his new friend. Just like Casanova, he is eager to blur the lines between social acting and playacting. Knowing the usefulness of society theater in love pursuits, and confident that Mme de = will not dare refuse a dignitary of his social rank, Chavigni asks her to reprise her role in a society theater show that she has recently performed in:

L'ambassadeur ... la pria de jouer une autre fois *l'Écossaise*.[12] ... Elle lui répondit que deux acteurs manquaient; il s'offrit alors à jouer le lord Monrose, et j'ai dans l'instant dit que je jouerais Murrai. Ma voisine F ... fâchée de cet arrangement parce qu'elle devait jouer l'odieux rôle de Miladi Alton me lâcha un lardon. Pourquoi me dit-elle, n'y a-t-il pas dans la pièce un rôle de sommelier! Vous le joueriez à merveille.—Mais vous m'instruirez, lui répondis-je, à jouer encore mieux celui de Murrai. (*Histoire*, 300)

The ambassador ... asked her to play the heroine in *L'Écossaise* again. ... She replied that there were two actors missing; he offered to play Lord Monrose and I instantly said I would play Murray. The arrangement infuriating my table companion F., for it left her to play the hateful role of Lady Alton, she let fly a shaft at me.

"Why isn't there a waiter's part in the play?" she said. "You would act it wonderfully well."

"But you," I replied, "will teach me to act the part of Murray still better." (*History*, 113)

Staging a society show for amusement is a natural step in the group's attempt to bypass social norms. In line with social acting rules, the ambassador flatters M. de = by publicly praising his wife's theatrical skills and honoring her with the main role in his private show. But what seems to the public like an innocent request is in fact a manipulative act. He arranges for Casanova and Mme de = to have time together for rehearsals and performances. As Mme F ... recalls the waiter incident and threatens to spoil the fun (indirectly showing that she is aware of the manipulation), she is deftly humiliated and reminded of her role as cover for the real love affair. She fails at swiftly mixing social acting and playacting, becoming the victim of those who outmatch her in the game.

No other game could advance love affairs more quickly than society theater. In a matter of days, and under the pretext of the upcoming society play, Casanova is able to publicly proclaim his love for Mme de = without attracting suspicion from her husband or the ambassador's entourage. He describes the society performance and a script perfectly adapted to his amorous quest:

Notre première représentation eut pour spectateurs tous les gens comme il faut de la ville. ... Mais mon sang se glaça lorsqu'à la troisième scène du cinquième acte Lindane me dit: *Quoi? Vous! Vous osez m'aimer?* Elle prononça ces cinq mots si singulièrement, d'un ton de mépris si marqué, sortant même de l'esprit de son rôle, que tous les spectateurs applaudirent à outrance. Cet applaudissement me piqua, et me mit hors de contenance, car il me parut que le jeu avait empiété sur mon honneur. Lorsqu'on se tut, et que, comme mon rôle le voulait, j'ai dû lui répondre: *Oui, je vous adore, et je le dois,* j'ai

prononcé ces mots d'un ton si touchant que les applaudissements furent doubles: le *bis* de quatre cents voix me forcèrent à les répliquer. (*Histoire*, 301)

Our first performance was attended by all the best people in the city. . . . But
my blood froze when in the third scene of the fifth act Lindane said to me:
"What! You! You dare to love me!" She uttered the seven words so strangely,
in a tone of such deliberate scorn, even stepping momentarily out of her part,
that the whole audience applauded wildly. The applause nettled and disconcerted me, for I thought the manner had trespassed on my honor. When silence
was restored and I, as my role prescribed, had to answer her with, "Yes, I adore
you, and I must," I brought out the words in a tone so moving that the applause
redoubled: *Bis, bis* from four hundred voices forced me to repeat them. (*History*, 114–15)

To the seducer's delight, the text matches his situation perfectly and allows him
to "hide" his true intentions from all except those who are aware of his strata-
gem. For the latter, the playacting is much more amusing because they are privy
to the show's purpose. Casanova's analysis of love declarations exchanged with
Mme de = illustrates just how subtle and complicated the distinction between
social acting and playacting could be. That he takes offense at her "stepping
momentarily out of her part" and showing "deliberate scorn," as any honest wife
should have done, indicates that he is clearly more concerned with how her acting will affect his honor in the eyes of those who know or suspect the secret love
affair. His response is more in line with his desires and personality rather than
with any notion of social obligation, showing again just how convenient the practice of society theater could be for furthering one's personal interests.

Though the first performance of *L'Écossaise* is quite successful, the ambassador
continues his manipulation and requests a full day of rehearsals at his country
estate, providing Casanova further opportunities for seduction. While the third
act of the adventure does not end happily for the Venetian, it is nevertheless quite
theatrical and on a par with similar scenes from Pierre Choderlos de Laclos's
Les liaisons dangereuses. After Casanova is assured of Mme de ='s shared love,
he arranges to consummate the affair. As both Mme de = and Mme F . . . are
staying at his country house, he attempts to visit Mme de =, but in the dark, by
the treachery of Mme F . . . , he mistakenly spends his time with her instead. The
next morning, he discovers, to his dismay, that Mme F . . . had learned of the plan
and taken the younger woman's place. To add insult to injury, Casanova realizes
that he has been not only deceived but also given a venereal disease. In a letter,
Mme F . . . explains that her actions were her revenge for all the public humili-
ations inflicted on her by Casanova's and Mme de ='s playacting:

Je suis sortie, monsieur, de votre maison assez satisfaite, non pas d'avoir passé
deux heures avec vous, car vous n'êtes pas différent des autres hommes, et

mon caprice d'ailleurs ne m'a servi qu'à me faire rire; mais de m'être vengée
des marques publiques de mépris que vous m'avez données, car je vous ai par-
donné les particulières. Je me suis vengée de votre politique en démasquant vos
desseins, et de l'hypocrisie de la =, qui ne pourra plus me regarder à l'avenir
de l'air de supériorité qu'elle empruntait de sa fausse vertu. (*Histoire*, 329)

I left your house, Monsieur, sufficiently content, not because I had spent two
hours with you, for you are not different from other men and in any case my
whim was only something to amuse me, but because I have avenged myself
for the public marks of contempt which you have shown me, for I have for-
given you the private ones. I have avenged myself on your scheming by
unmasking your designs and the hypocrisy of your . . . , who in future can no
longer look down on me with the show of superiority which she borrowed
from her pretended virtue. (*History*, 150)

As this letter illustrates, social games entail many risks, and the victim of collective mockery can in turn punish her tormenter. The most alienating aspect
of losing in this game is the public humiliation at being shown inferior. Mme
F . . . identifies it as "public marks of contempt" or "looking down" on someone.
At this point she seems to have won and is ready to unmask and humiliate not
only Casanova but also his paramour. Yet, in his innately witty manner, the
seducer finds the perfect way to punish her instead: as he discovers that his valet
has just come down with a venereal disease, he informs Mme F . . . that she did
not spend the night with him, but with his servant, and that she owes the poor
fellow money for his (medical) treatment. This concludes the adventure in a
favorable way for the seducer and saves the reputation of Mme de =, whom he
(supposedly) never managed to possess. One cannot fail to notice the similarity
between Mme F . . . and Laclos's Mme de Merteuil from *Les liaisons dangereuses*. Similar to Laclos's characters, Casanova's entourage is aware of his love
intrigues, but they play along, refusing the risk of unmasking the seducer who
is backed by the French ambassador. Society theater thus serves its twofold purpose: it advances the seducer's personal interests and provides entertainment for
the *société*. The "winners" of this episode prevail because for them social acting
is not an alienating burden but rather an opportunity to manipulate and out-
play their peers. While Casanova's example might seem shocking by today's standards, during his time it was not exceptional. In fact, rakes and seducers were
not the only ones to use society theater to pursue romance or seduction. Numerous society theater texts show that both men and women were equally eager to
use a good (theatrical or social) performance to facilitate their amorous quests,
social advancement, revenge, or simply to have fun at another's expense. The
texts of Louis Carrogis Carmontelle, a well-known dramatist and author of multiple volumes of *Proverbes dramatiques*, document numerous examples of such
play and its risks.

CARMONTELLE'S *PROVERBE XI: LA SORTIE DE LA COMÉDIE FRANÇAISE*

Situations similar to the adventure described by Casanova abound in Carmontelle's *Proverbes dramatiques*, suggesting that manipulation and public humiliation of others were common modes of social acting. Dramatic proverbs were short plays that illustrated an aphorism or a morality—*le mot* (the key)—that the audience was expected to guess at the end of the performance.[13] Numerous volumes of these short plays attest to the genre's popularity, and Carmontelle was one of its most prolific and representative authors; his texts were widely appreciated and often staged in society. Through light but realistic dialogue, Carmontelle's *Proverbes* re-created on the private stage the preoccupations and attitudes of the people who performed in them. Fashioned to please the amateur actors for whom they were written, and to amuse the friendly audience, these texts also hinted at a more sinister side of a society that was quick to laugh at the expense of others. *Proverbe XI: La sortie de la Comédie française* is the society theater counterpart to the real-life episode of social acting and playacting described by Casanova.[14] Set on the stairway of the Comédie française (a most unusual setting for a society play), this proverb constitutes a musing on the "polite" interaction between *gens du monde* after a show at France's most famous public theater house. Organized in a single short act (or, rather, a series of brief scenes), the proverb presents two women who encounter various acquaintances as they exit the theater. Because they take the risk of publicly exhibiting their "friendship" with these individuals, the two ladies (and their partners) are publicly humiliated. They endure their embarrassment in front of everyone as their acquaintances congratulate themselves for the mortifications they have just imparted. The key of the proverb is "La moitié du monde se moque de l'autre." (Half of the world is mocking the other [half]; *Proverbe XI*, 378.) Its plot imitates real life and illustrates how the overlap of social acting and playacting negatively affects some of the less astute players.

The two women in *La sortie de la Comédie française* are Mme de Vermont and Mme de Mirville. We learn that Mme de Vermont is in a relationship with a chevalier, and Mme de Mirville with a count. As they await their gentlemen, the two friends notice a certain "monsieur Le Duc" who is not keen on seeing them. Eager to attract his attention and show that she is his friend, Mme de Mirville calls out to him reproachfully and forces him to stop:

> MME DE MIRVILLE: C'est lui-même; il ne veut pas nous voir. Monsieur le duc! monsieur le duc! C'est fort joli de passer comme cela devant les gens sans les regarder.
>
> LE DUC: Ah, madame, je me prosterne! Je suis furieux de ne vous avoir pas aperçue; c'est que je regardais si je verrais mon coureur. Est-on allé appeler vos gens?

MME DE MIRVILLE: It is him indeed; he does not want to see us. Monsieur
le duc! monsieur le duc! It is not nice to pass people without looking at
them.

LE DUC: Ah, madam, I bow before you! I'm furious to not have noticed you;
it is because I was watching to see if I could find my servant. Have they
gone to call your people? (*Proverbe XI*, 123)

This first exchange hints at the intricacies of social acting in the public setting;
even if the duke would rather avoid the two women, they call to him in such a
loud and noticeable manner that the codes of politeness obligate him to respond.
His overplayed reaction leads to immediate *comique de situation*. The exchange
must have resonated with many society theater amateurs who knew that social
acting rules required maintaining a polite demeanor even against one's contrary
inner truth. Such situations contained a certain discomfort or awkwardness that,
when revealed in performance, elicited laughter. By choosing to stage this dis-
crepancy between inner sentiment and outer display through society plays, the
participants reenacted and denounced the duplicity and ridicule of their daily
social interactions. The burden of this type of social acting is clear in the duke's
subsequent replies, where his tone is increasingly false and patronizing:

MME DE MIRVILLE: Oui, oui. Restez avec nous jusqu'à ce qu'on nous
avertisse.

LE DUC: Comment, si j'y resterai? Assurément: je suis comblé, enchanté de
cette rencontre: c'est une bonne fortune pour moi; il y a mille ans que je
n'ai eu l'honneur de vous aller chercher; j'y suis pourtant allé un de ces
jours; je ne sais si on vous l'aura dit; je serai encore assez malheureux pour
qu'on m'ait oublié.

MME DE MIRVILLE: Yes, yes. Stay with us until we are called upon.

LE DUC: What do you mean, shall I stay? I am certainly overjoyed and
delighted by this meeting: how fortunate for me; it has been a thousand
years since I had the honor of your company; however, I did call on you
recently; I do not know if you were told; I will have again had the misfortune of being forgotten. (*Proverbe XI*, 123–24)

Mme de Mirville insists that the duke stay with them, using an imperative and
hinting at a close past relationship. Clearly she desires to be publicly seen in the
company of this man who might not otherwise associate with her. His response,
though polite, is filled with antiphrasis and hyperbole, indicating his disdain and
aloofness toward the lady. The *comique de langage* reinforces the *comique de situation* as the duke's acting contradicts his words. His being "delighted" and
"overjoyed" at seeing the two ladies should be understood as the deep displeasure and misfortune of running into the exact people he did not want to see. As
he slips and starts to explain why he has not called on Mme de Mirville in ages,

he realizes that he should not justify himself and quickly changes course, adding yet further antiphrasis: "I will have again had the misfortune of being forgotten"—meaning, in fact, "Oh how happy would I be if I had been forgotten." This comical situation underlines the difficulty of navigating one's social role when it goes against personal preferences. Because of that slight embarrassment, the duke neglects to acknowledge Mme de Vermont's presence, which the lady is prompt to point out in an accusatory manner: "Vous ne me dites rien, à moi, monsieur le duc?" (And to me, monsieur le duc, you say nothing?) and "Vous me délaissez aussi un peu, monsieur le duc" (You seem to neglect me, monsieur le duc; *Proverbe XI*, 124.) This accusation of neglect further hints at another close past relationship, as the lady insists on "à moi," and she chooses the verb "délaisser," which means to abandon something one formerly possessed. To escape this recrimination, the duke protests, but goes much further than a simple denial and flaunts his own importance:

> LE DUC: Non, je vous assure, ce n'est pas cela; mais c'est que je suis toujours à Versailles, à Choisy, à Saint-Hubert.... Tout mon temps se passe sur les chemins. Je regrette bien celui où ... mais je ne veux pas perdre cet instant; je ne vous quitterai point, je vous en réponds, que vous ne partiez d'ici.

> LE DUC: No, I assure you, it is not that, but I am always at Versailles, at Choisy, at Saint Hubert.... All my time is spent on the road. I miss the time when ... but I do not want to waste this moment; I will not leave you, I promise, until you leave here yourself. (*Proverbe XI*, 124)

After emphasizing his influence and rank—he goes to Versailles, supposedly to be present at court—and claiming to spend all his time on the road, the duke reluctantly promises to make up for his past neglect and stay with the women until their carriage arrives. But the moment his carriage is announced, he leaves them, offering more vain promises of paying them a visit the following day. Evidently he does not intend to keep his word, but for the sake of social acting, he lies: "Sûrement. Je ferai l'impossible pour ne pas y manquer." (Certainly. I will do whatever it takes to be there; *Proverbe XI*, 125). Privately he may despise or hate the two women, but publicly he does his utmost to be polite and follow the norms of social acting. The exaggerated tone, which betrays disdain and sarcasm, indicates that for the duke social acting doubles as playacting. In other words, he knows that everyone but the two ladies is in on his duplicity. Everyone knows that he is openly mocking them. The audience for Carmontelle's *Proverbe* would have been only too familiar with such scenes, and would doubtless have been amused by the ladies' conclusion:

> MME DE MIRVILLE: Eh bien, madame, comment trouvez-vous cela? N'avez-vous pas cru qu'il allait rester avec nous?
> MME DE VERMONT: Bon! voilà comme sont à présent tous les hommes.

MME DE MIRVILLE: Well then, madame, what do you think of this? Did
you not think he would stay with us?

MME DE VERMONT: Oh well! that is how all men are nowadays. (*Proverbe
XI*, 125)

The two women must accept that the duke is merely playing his social role and
politely deflecting from the truth—that he would rather avoid interacting with
them. Their exchange is reminiscent of that between Mme F . . . and Casanova:
the two women are publicly humiliated and must pretend not to notice this in
order to save face. They have taken a risk and lost their social gamble, so they
conclude by blaming all men (the male half of the world). Carmontelle's audience would recognize many of their acquaintances in these characters, and some
perhaps would even recognize themselves as players in the cruel social game that
advances one party at another's expense.

The two friends' woes are far from over, as the next interactions submit them
to further humiliation. When the chevalier rejoins Mme de Vermont, she quickly
accuses him of abandoning her, but he explains that he ran into a man who would
help him gain a place in a regiment, hinting that the theater was his opportunity to pursue social advancement. In the public space of social acting, important people would be less likely to refuse speaking to those they wanted to avoid,
just as the duke could not avoid the two ladies. By reenacting such interactions
on a private stage, the amateurs of society theater made fun not only of their
own awkward positions when called on publicly by others but also mocked those
who annoyed them—which raises the question as to the role of spectacle during
this period. Was going to the theater an act of public duty (i.e., social acting), or
one of private enjoyment? Carmontelle seems to suggest that even if they accept
the duty of social acting, the characters cross over into playacting and seek to
punish those who force them to perform their social role when they would rather
enjoy themselves.

Having been snubbed by the duke, the two lady friends must confront another
harsh reality of their time: the duplicity of men. Joined by the chevalier, they
inquire about a "pretty" young woman they see descending the stairs. The chevalier responds that she is "ce que nous avons de mieux" (the best we have got;
Proverbe XI, 126), hinting that she is an actress. The use of "nous" as possessor
of the actress has a double meaning: first, it can refer to the collective theater
audience, which includes the two ladies; second, it points to the men who pursue actresses. Immediately, the two women retort that the girl is "hideous." Their
contempt comes from jealousy spurred by the knowledge that they are in direct
competition with these "filles." As they observe and discuss the ridiculous posture of men pursuing actresses or dancers, Mme de Mirville summarizes male
duplicity by describing a certain baron whom all three of them know: "il don-
nerait la main droite à une femme de qualité, et l'autre à une danseuse en même

temps; cela ne lui fait rien du tout; il vous quitte, vous revient dans l'instant comme il lui plaît; cela lui est égal" (he would give his right hand to a lady, and the other to a dancer at the very same time; it does not bother him at all; he leaves you, he comes back in an instant as he pleases; it is all the same to him; *Proverbe XI*, 127). Unperturbed, the chevalier defends the man: "On le connaît sur ce ton là, on ne lui en veut point de mal." (He is known for it, so we do not hold it against him; *Proverbe XI*, 127.) Such a defense would have been quite amusing for male spectators of society theater as many of them resembled the baron in this regard and were devoted to the same "filles." The exchange also reveals the prevalence of malicious gossip in the societies that are mirrored in the proverb. As in the episode from Casanova's memoirs, this proverb shows how society texts match reality while highlighting the risks involved. Indeed, some society players had to play the victims of mockery, even if such a role carried over into their real lives. The final scenes in Carmontelle's proverb underline that cruel and risky side of playacting.

As the company still waits for Mme de Mirville's partner, the count, a marquis arrives. He plays with her, like a cat with a battered mouse, and completes her humiliation. He begins by complimenting her profusely, and she ungraciously welcomes his praise. Her tactless acceptance of compliments turns comical, as the marquis negates each statement as soon as she agrees with him:

> LE MARQUIS: Savez-vous que vous êtes éblouissante!
> MME DE MIRVILLE: Oui, on me trouve assez bien mise.
> LE MARQUIS: Mais c'est de votre santé que je parle.
> MME DE MIRVILLE: Il est vrai que depuis quelques jours je me porte assez bien.
> LE MARQUIS: Mais je dis, on n'a jamais été comme cela. Y a-t-il longtemps que vous attendez? Vous êtes bien mal là.

> LE MARQUIS: Did you know that you look stunning!
> MME DE MIRVILLE: Yes, people tell me that I am fairly well-dressed.
> THE MARQUIS: But it is your health that I'm talking about.
> MME DE MIRVILLE: It is true that for the past few days I have been feeling fairly well.
> THE MARQUIS: I would say, we have never been like this. Have you been waiting here long? You seem uncomfortable. (*Proverbe XI*, 127)

The marquis cruelly points out her discomfort in waiting for her lover and her carriage. As his social acting turns into playacting, he is toying with her, taunting, teasing, and demeaning her, all with the tone of a polite social exchange. Just like the duke, he flaunts his adroitness at playing the game of mockery and unsettles Mme de Mirville to the point that she has to change the subject. Impatiently awaiting her lover (the count), she asks the marquis if he knows the two women who have delayed him. She falls directly into the marquis' trap: the latter tells her that the Comte is in love with one of those ladies. Visibly pleased at her expression of shock, he assures her that he has learned this from people in the know, and that the information is reliable. As Mme de Mirville is left to regain her composure, the marquis quickly brags to his newly arrived friend, the viscount:

> LE MARQUIS: Je viens de faire une bonne tracasserie. Tu sais que madame de Mirville a Versin? . . . Qu'elle est très jalouse? . . . Elle vient de me demander ce qu'il faisait là-bas avec ces deux femmes. Je lui ai dit que c'est qu'il est amoureux fou de madame de Préval; que c'était une affaire arrangée: et elle le croit.
>
> LE VICOMTE: Ah, c'est très-bon! Tu es un homme charmant! Veux-tu que je te ramène?
>
> LE MARQUIS: I just performed some good mischief. You know that Mme de Mirville is with Versin? . . . That she is jealous? . . . She just asked me what he was doing there with those two ladies. I told her that he is madly in love with Mme de Préval; that it was a done deal: and she believes it.
>
> LE VICOMTE: Ah, that is very good! You are a charming man! Do you want a lift? (*Proverbe XI*, 128)

The audience recognizes that the marquis intended to humiliate Mme de Mirville from the onset. Yet the viscount is only slightly amused at the trick his friend has played, suggesting that this type of manipulative and malicious behavior was common and no cause for surprise. In fact, the viscount has his own trick to play on the chevalier, Mme de Vermont's partner. Making sure that Mme de Vermont overhears, he asks the chevalier whether he would dine at the Nouvelle-France—a "maison close" where men could enjoy the company of actresses and dancers. As the chevalier scrambles to defend himself, claiming he has not been there in ages and never will again, the viscount jokingly points out, "Ah, ce n'est pas à moi qu'il faut dire cela." (Oh, it is not to me that you should explain this; *Proverbe XI*, 129.) The viscount scores his own points in the social humiliation game that the marquis had initiated, and he makes sure to draw attention to his prank: "Tu as entendu? Je me suis diverti, et voilà le chevalier qui est querellé à présent." (Did you hear? I had my fun, and now it is the chevalier who is in trouble; *Proverbe XI*, 129.) The two tricksters watch amusedly as Mme de Mirville scolds her lover over the marquis' lie, and the chevalier hastily leaves with the now suspicious Mme de Vermont. Both couples have been toyed with, divided, and publicly humiliated, to the viscount's and the marquis' delight. The latter concludes with a self-congratulatory observation: "Eh bien, cela n'a pas mal réussi, comme tu vois." (Well then, that worked quite well, as you can see; *Proverbe XI*, 130.) Their final "success" indicates that social acting can double as playacting, especially when the victim of the joke is as unaware as the two ladies in Carmontelle's proverb. As Carmontelle puts it in one of his comedies, *Les acteurs de société*, "kind people" like the viscount and the marquis are in fact vile manipulators, but nobody dares tell them so because they are powerful and feared. Just like any other social game, society theater had specific rules, and those rules could often be cruel to those less apt at wit and manipulation.

In this context, society theater can have a cathartic effect: participants pretend to make fun of others but they are also making fun of themselves. The moral clue given in the proverb key (one half of society mocks the other) illuminates the functioning of society theater: the audience is laughing at the actors, while the actors are laughing at the characters whom they also recognize in the audience and in themselves. But there is also another possible interpretation: the half that is part of the group mocks the half that aspires to belong to it. This interpretation brings us to another important function of society theater: it unifies the society that performs it.

———

The success of society plays also reflects on the audience that enjoyed such playacting. Merrymaking and laughter represented important ways of uniting the people who practiced society theater. Unlike in official venues, where the audience was relegated to the role of spectators, society theater embraced its audience in both the dramatic performance and social amusement. The intimacy of the society stage allowed members of the audience to interact more readily with the actors. This interplay not only heightened the amusement but also reinforced the cohesion of the group. At the end of a performance, the *société* felt a complicity in play that would be unattainable at a public theater.

The subject matter of the plays served to catalyze the fusion of each *société* in other ways. Often the texts were inspired by day-to-day events, anecdotes, or mishaps that the entire company knew and found amusing. Indeed, the scenes from *La sortie de la Comédie française* would have been normal occurrences at the exit of the Comédie française. Firsthand knowledge and understanding of the content further increased the ties within a group that felt privileged to be in on the joke. This complicity also excluded those who were not fully integrated or who were not aware of the play's meaning, in every sense. Mme F . . . in Casanova's *Histoire de ma vie* and the two women in Carmontelle's *La sortie de la comédie française* are examples of individuals marked for exclusion from the group to which they desperately strive to belong. They must observe the rules of social acting (i.e., to accept being humiliated by the playacting of the rest of the group) or risk being eliminated from the group altogether. Casanova (in a real-life episode) and Carmontelle (in a play) point out a key rule of the acting game: participants have to perform within overlapping modes of acting to avoid humiliation and exclusion. Ultimately, only those who were able to swiftly move from one to the other and enjoy social acting by turning it into playacting are desirable company for the *société*; the others are simply characters to be mocked both socially and on the private stage of society theater. As Marie-Emmanuelle Plagnol Diéval points out, society theater plays "représentent par mimétisme ou caricaturent" (represent [society] through mimesis or caricature it). The ultimate aim, she adds, is to transform "une réalité dont ils connaissent les usages, les interdits et les rouages, ce qui les autorise à la sublimer en une fête quasi permanente, mi-improvisée, mi-élaborée, dans laquelle le groupe se perd et se retrouve" (a reality whose manners, prohibitions and workings [the participants] know, and that allows them to sublimate [society theater] into a quasi-permanent, half-improvised, half-elaborate celebration in which the group loses and finds itself).[15] By re-creating the social exchange typically observed after attending a public show of the Comédie française, the *société* would laugh and sublimate itself, losing and finding itself again—literally—on the private stage.

Carmontelle's proverbs reveal yet another function of society theater. They were intended also as moralizing pieces: the audience was supposed to have a moment of revelation when they discovered the key—that is, the proverb—in each play. In *La sortie de la comédie française*, where half of the world mocks the other half, the play is a pretext for society to mirror, admire, and ridicule itself on stage. The actors play at playing themselves. They escape the routine of social acting by recognizing, staging, and laughing at its absurdity. Through this form of amusement, they also prove how self-absorbed they are, at once celebrating and chastising their own duplicities. Self-reflexive texts abound in the society theater repertoire, suggesting that these *sociétés* loved putting on plays about themselves putting on a play. As they performed, they caricatured social acting through playacting. Strikingly, in many of these plays the characters were less often shining role models than flawed individuals whose difficulties seemed amusing on stage, however difficult they might be in real life. Because of their moralizing dimension, the *Proverbes dramatiques* can be interpreted as an attempt to change society from within through laughter, in keeping with the intent traditionally attributed to comedy. But, in light of the examples discussed here, this approach appears insufficient. Both Casanova's and Carmontelle's texts suggest a feeling of shared complicity in society performances, between the author and the *commanditaire*, among the players as they prepare to perform, and between the actors and the audience. The latter is key in its function as the second party to share the joke. Just as in *La sortie de la comédie française*, where the marquis cannot fully enjoy his prank without sharing it with the viscount, the actors were most able to enjoy their game when its target was clearly recognized by the audience. Sadly, perhaps, the moral of both stories is that playful mockery (a common game and a constant risk) and playing along with it were ultimately preferable to the threat of defeat and real social humiliation.

NOTES

Unless noted otherwise, all translations are my own.

1. *Théâtromanie* is a term coined after an eponymous 1783 play by Pierre de La Montagne, a short comedy largely inspired from Alexis Piron's widely popular *La métromanie*, a 1738 play mocking people's passion for writing poetry. For the most complete overview of *théâtre de société*, see Marie-Emmanuelle Plagnol-Diéval, *Le théâtre de société: Un autre théâtre?* (Paris: Honoré Champion, 2003). See also Jean-Claude Yon and Nathalie Le Gonidec, *Tréteaux et paravents: Le théâtre de société au XIXe siècle* (Paris: Créaphis, 2012).

2. Nicholas Brazier, *Chroniques des petits théâtres de Paris: Depuis leur création jusqu'à ce jour*, vol. 2 (Paris: Allardin, 1837), 284–85.

3. For a detailed explanation of parade and its poetics, see Jennifer Ruimi, *La parade de société au XVIIIe siècle: Une forme dramatique oubliée* (Paris: Honoré Champion, 2015).

4. For a discussion of the distinction between official and nonofficial theater, see David Alfred Trott, *Théâtre du XVIIIe siècle: Jeux, écritures, regards: Essai sur les spectacles en France de 1700 à 1790* (Montpellier, France: Éditions Espaces 34, 2000).

5. For more on the theatrics of royal court etiquette during the ancien régime, see Norbert Elias, *La société de cour* (Paris: Flammarion, 1985).

6. Marie-Emmanuelle Plagnol-Diéval coined the term *commanditaire* to designate the person who commissions and/or stages a society play. See Plagnol-Diéval, *Le théâtre de société*, 18–19.

7. Plagnol-Diéval, *Le théâtre de société*, 11, defines society theater as "un théâtre amateur, discontinu et non lucratif (sauf exceptions ponctuelles), distinct des autres théâtres amateurs" (an intermittent, amateur and nonlucrative form of theater (with some specific exceptions), distinct from other forms of amateur theater).

8. Jean de La Bruyère, *Les caractères*, ed. Emmanuel Bury (Paris: Librairie Générale Française, 1995), 331–32.

9. Louis Philippe I, Duke of Orléans, was an avid practitioner of society theater.

10. For more on the life of Casanova, see J. Rives Childs, *Casanova, a New Perspective* (New York: Paragon House Publishers, 1988) and Marie-Françoise Luna, *Casanova mémorialiste* (Paris: Honoré Champion, 1998).

11. Giacomo Casanova, *Histoire de ma vie*, vol. 2, ed. Gérard Lahouati and Marie-Françoise Luna (Paris: Gallimard, 2015), 283; the English translation is from Giacomo Casanova, *History of My Life*, vol. 6, trans. Willard R. Trask (New York: Harcourt, Brace and World, 1966), 83. Hereafter, page numbers will appear parenthetically in the text, first in the French (as *Histoire*), then followed by the translation (as *History*).

12. See Voltaire, *L'Écossaise*, in *Oeuvres complètes*, vol. 5 (Paris: Garnier, 1877), 397–479.

13. Clarence D. Brenner, *Le développement du proverbe dramatique en France et sa vogue au XVIIIe siècle* (Berkeley: University of California Press, 1937), 2.

14. Louis Carrogis Carmontelle, *Proverbe XI: La sortie de la Comédie française*, in *Proverbes dramatiques de Carmontelle: Précédés de la vie de Carmontelle, d'une dissertation historique et morale sur les proverbes et suivis d'une table explicative de l'origine des proverbes*, vol. 1 (Paris: Delongchamps, 1822). Hereafter, page numbers will appear parenthetically in the text (as *Proverbe XI*).

15. Plagnol-Diéval, *Le théâtre de société*, 280–281.

CHAPTER 8

Between Play and Ritual

PROFANE MASQUERADE IN THE FRENCH REVOLUTION

Annelle Curulla

Iconoclastic acts loom large in the popular imagination of the Terror, from the battering of sacred statues with sticks, to the burning of the Pope's effigy, to the desecration of religious objects and clothing in mock processionals. Scholars from a range of disciplines have increasingly approached scripted and unscripted acts of profanation not just as indexes of anti-Catholic sentiment but as forms of cultural expression that reveal diverse attitudes toward futurity, authority, and religiosity itself.[1] This chapter focuses on one aspect of iconoclasm: *profane masquerade*, a term I use to describe groups of nonecclesiastics performing in Roman Catholic vestments. Accounts of profane masquerade in visual culture, drama, chronicles, and official records are well documented, but its meanings and functions remain undertheorized. In keeping with the aims of this volume, therefore, I view profane masquerade as a form of play, with three main objectives in mind: to draw attention to play's importance within the cultural practices that emerged in Revolutionary political culture; to show how play can provide an alternative analytical framework to the less useful binaries of popular versus elite, official versus unofficial, and hegemonic versus counterhegemonic; and to show how the playful strategies of profane masquerade differed from the civic festivals that took shape during the same period. As I argue, the concept of play and its potentials can shed more light on the complicated relationship between the sacred and the profane in the Revolutionary period.

In the past two decades, a current of work in intellectual history has increasingly questioned one of the Enlightenment's prime narratives—that of the separation of religious and secular categories into separate spheres over time. In the French context, scholars including Jeffrey Burson, Charly Coleman, Sanja Perovic, and Dale Van Kley have explored the various ways in which eighteenth-century notions of the sacred and the profane were flexible, changing, and interpenetrating.[2] This work has implications for our understanding of secularization and, by extension, of Revolutionary iconoclasm. Official discourses of Revolutionary politicians and authorities described iconoclasm as a process of expunging superstitious belief from the people, an effort to expose liturgical objects and relics as nothing more than metal, wood, or a bit of cloth. Indeed, the parliamentary archives from the height of France's dechristianization campaign in the fall and winter of 1793 contain commonplace references to religious objects as trifles or toys: "les hochets de la superstition," and "hochets du fanatisme."[3] Joe Moshenska, in his fascinating work on play and iconoclasm, charts a similar effort in the English Reformation to align sacred objects as playthings. He notes that iconoclasm would appear to be, on the surface, the very clearest example of secularization as "disenchantment," a desire to destroy playthings and abolish childish play from modern life. Yet, Moshenska argues, "if there is one lesson that the history of iconoclasm teaches repeatedly, it is that the disappearance or destruction of an object is often less decisive than it appears."[4] Sacred objects do not vanish; they can be broken, mended, or put to new uses. They can fall from use or revert to old uses just as easily.

Such nonlinear trajectories are found in the origins of profane masquerade. Originally, pseudoreligious processionals involving laypeople and domestic animals were closely tied to the festivals of Carnival, an important Catholic practice that preceded the celebration of Lent. Mikhail Bakhtin's profoundly influential work on official culture and Carnival has shown how this period of license and feasting was a momentary suspension whose beginning and end were regulated by the liturgical calendar.[5] Even in 1786, only a few years before Carnival was banned by the French Revolutionary government, one visitor to Paris recounted that "some thousands were in masks, men in the dress of women, and women in the dress of men, all assuming characters, and many sustaining those characters with spirit. Popes, cardinals, monks, devils, courtiers, harlequins, and players all mingled in one promiscuous crowd."[6] The promiscuity made possible by the suspension of norms is central to the concept of masquerade since, as Terry Castle has shown, disguising one's social identity implicitly creates a common ground for commingling, blending, and potentially subverting hierarchies and norms related to gender, race and ethnicity, or social class.[7] After 1789, however, this practice was not necessarily controlled by the Church. Profane masquerade—the kind invented in Revolutionary political culture—can be considered as distinct from the masquerade practices of Carnival or even the Bakhtinian "carnivalesque." As Richard Clay has noted, Carnival practices relied on homemade or ephemeral copies of Catholic objects, while dechristianizing processions generally focused on actual Catholic signs that were used to oppose Catholicism and "signified permanent disrespect that warranted the objects' imminent destructions."[8] Moshenska's more supple understanding of an object's endlessly changing functions can push Clay's insights further by suggesting that dechristianizing processions were not merely a means of denigrating religious beliefs associated with the objects: they also created new uses for once-sacred objects.

Even after the Revolutionary government's interdiction of Carnival in 1790, customary forms of play such as the burning of effigies, masquerade, and the charivari continued. The French government began enacting a series of sweeping religious reforms, the most radical of which took shape following the 1792 declaration of the first French Republic, when the National Convention set about replacing Christian imagery and practices with a new secular and patriotic iconography. The Gregorian calendar was replaced with a new Republican calendar based on the metric system. Its feasts celebrated the virtues of French heroes and patriots, as well as the seasonal cycles of growth and renewal. In 1793, following the abdication of thousands of priests, the closure of churches, and the suspension of public masses, the government instated civic festivals meant to take the place of Catholic worship. Profane masquerade appeared in earnest at this time. In November 1793, as dechristianization reached its height in Paris, citizens began organizing mock processionals as a means of presenting the Church's riches seized from decommissioned churches.

Profane masquerade occupies an ambiguous place in the historiography of the French Revolution. François-Alphonse Aulard describes profane masquerade as a popular practice associated with the Hébertistes, as well as the politically active *sans culottes*.[9] Other accounts have nuanced earlier views of profane masquerade as belonging to a more spontaneous, authentic culture of the people, one that was opposed to the staid and highly orchestrated rituals of the Revolutionary festival. While acknowledging the *longue durée* of folk practices that were incorporated into profane masquerade, Michel Vovelle has convincingly shown that these practices did not necessarily emanate from the people but could be appropriated by groups of citizens or by authorities. Moreover, he writes, these practices could be considered as a supplement to the scripted, carefully stage-managed civic rituals put into place by the government, such as the Festival of the Supreme Being. For Vovelle, "La mascarade, comme l'auto-da-fé, ne sont pas fêtes en eux-mêmes, mais plutôt l'une des formes d'expression de la fête, liturgies nouvelles si l'on veut, inventées dans le feu de l'action." (Both the masquerade and the *auto-da-fé* [ritual burnings] were not festivals in themselves: they were rather just one of the ways in which the festival expressed itself, new types of liturgy, created in the heat of the action.)[10] Mona Ozouf, in her important work on the Revolutionary festival, notes that profane masquerades were not necessarily motivated by religious causes. She points to spikes in profane masquerades during the traditional Carnival season, or during political situations in which the masquerade's symbolic violence and intimidation lent to the Republic's wartime identity. Like Vovelle, Ozouf also doubts the intrinsically popular nature of the masquerade, instead ascribing it a more ambivalent place in the new forms of Revolutionary festival, a kind of *anti-fête* whose unruliness and potential for violence menaced the "transfer of sacrality" at the heart of the Revolutionary festival.[11]

One reason for profane masquerade's ambiguous place in Revolutionary historiography, as Vovelle and Ozouf suggest, is that the practice does not readily fit into binaries such as popular versus elite, spontaneous versus contrived, or play versus ritual. Theories of play can enrich this historical issue. The following sections consider the concept of profanation and play as developed by Giorgio Agamben, whose work can be productively applied to the study of profane masquerade in the French Revolution. From there, the chapter proceeds by considering masquerade first as a form of play and then as a form of ritual. In some cases, the same profane masquerade could be described either as a ritual or as a form of play. It is important to consider what these contrasting representations imply for our understanding of profane masquerade's perceived purposes and potentials.

Play and Ritual

The relationship between play and profanation is a key feature of Agamben's multifaceted thinking on the sacred, most explicitly articulated in a short essay, "In Praise of Profanation." Agamben's thinking on profanation and secularization as opposing concepts can illuminate the considerable differences between the performance practice and the official system of national festivals put into place by the Revolutionary government. For Agamben, secularization does not annihilate the sacred insofar as it effects a "transfer," to borrow Ozouf's signal concept. For Agamben, too, secularization "leaves intact the forces it deals with by simply moving them from one place to another. Thus the political secularization of theological concepts (the transcendence of God as a paradigm of sovereign power) does nothing but displace the heavenly monarchy onto an earthly monarchy, leaving its power intact." Profanation, in contrast, effects a kind of deactivation of the sacred. When a sacred thing is misused, neglected, or otherwise contaminated, that action enables its return to common use. Thus, Agamben argues, "both are political operations: the first [secularization] guarantees the exercise of power by carrying it back to a sacred model: the second [profanation] deactivates the apparatuses of power and returns to common use the spaces that power had seized." For Agamben, "negligence" is a form of profanation, since it neglects norms or ritual acts that are required for an object to maintain its status as separate and unavailable to the ordinary world.[12] We see, then, the proximity between play and profanation insofar as profanation ignores, crosses, or otherwise toys with the threshold that guarantees the separation of the sacred from the profane. New games invent new uses for objects, and profanation does too.

According to Agamben, the child is a prime figure of play and a master of profanation. This is because the child, like a philosopher, does not take social norms as a given. Both can create novel approaches to things that are normally taken seriously or treated reverentially. As Agamben observes, "this [profanation], however, does not mean neglect (no kind of attention can compare to that of a child at play) but a new dimension of use, which children and philosophers give to humanity." Children and philosophers are creatively capable of inventing new possibilities because of their willingness or imaginative ability to ignore the relationship between means and ends—that is, to envision a means without ends. It is only through moving outside the legitimating power of ritual that we can open "a gateway to a new happiness." Play is the process of discovering this new gateway, of transforming a sacred object into a toy, or a sacred word into a novel context. In such an account, ritual and play are opposing behaviors: "Play breaks up this unity [between word and myth]; as *ludus*, or physical play, it drops the myth and preserves the rite; as *iocus*, or wordplay, it effaces the rite and allows the myth to survive."[13] Thus, through its careful practices for observing the proper use of the sacred, ritual is a process compatible with that of secularization. Play, in contrast, neglects the sacred, threatening to render it inoperative through refusing the legitimizing power of ritual.

Turning back to profane masquerade, we see Agamben's concept of neglect illustrated in masquerade's appropriation of the clothing worn by the clergy to designate their identity, authority, and separation from the secular world. Such vestment is central to the celebration of the Eucharist, as well as official forms of processional such as the Feast of Corpus Christi and other important celebrations. When worn as costume, however, consecrated clothing and liturgical objects lose their aura and take on a function different from that of their ritual use. Laypeople who donned ecclesiastical vestment or paraded with objects did not do so in order to disguise their identity, as in more traditional forms of masquerade. Instead their faces were unmasked, and their own bodies were on display as they danced in holy robes, burned effigies of the Pope, and generally played with liturgical objects with impunity.

Agamben's account of profanation helps us to better view the apparent contradiction presented by profane masquerade in the historical record. This practice would appear to belong to a "new liturgy" of customs that were integrated into the Revolutionary festival. Yet as an *anti-fête* of riotous, unpredictable behavior, the profane masquerade threatened the Revolutionary festival's legitimating functions. The following sections reframe this issue by focusing less on the Revolutionary crowd than on the objects included in performances. By so doing, two of masquerade's distinct and opposing potentials will become visible. On the one hand, profane masquerade could function as a form of play, a mistreatment of sacred objects that resulted in the creation of new practices and uses for those objects. On the other hand, when those same objects were presented to the Republic, profane masquerade could be folded into rituals of secularization, becoming part of Revolutionary dechristianization and serving as an adjunct to it.

MASQUERADE AS PROFANE PLAY

Roger Caillois's four categories of play help define the strategies and functions of profane masquerade. *Agôn* thrives on conflict and competition; *mimesis* requires players to imitate the actions or identities of others; *alea* engages chance and randomness; *ilinx* or vertigo-inducing games deliberately alter a player's perception.[14] Of these four, *mimesis* is the prime category to which masquerade belongs. As noted, profane masquerade's promiscuity and commingling did not derive from masked identity; rather, it was the conjunction or juxtaposition between the player and the clothing that was worn that generated profane masquerade's many meanings. As the examples herein demonstrate, the less perfect or convincing mimicries were, the more effectively profane the masquerades proved. Players could pair a Phrygian bonnet with a priest's liturgical raiment, they could show their inability in ceremony by awkwardly manipulating a monstrance, or an obscene gesture could replace one of blessing.

Louis-Sébastien Mercier illustrates the creative tendency of play as collective discovery and reinvention in one passage of his highly subjective chronicle of Revolutionary life in *Le nouveau Paris*. He emphasizes the spontaneity of mimicry and play's potential to suspend norms and create new and surprising uses for objects once held as sacred. Mercier represents the November 1793 procession organized by the Section de l'Unité in the following terms:

> Les acteurs qui y figurèrent étaient encore ivres de l'eau-de-vie qu'ils avaient bue dans les calices, après avoir mangé des maquereaux sur les patènes. Montés à califourchon sur des ânes dont des chasubles couvraient le derrière, ils les guidaient avec des étoles; ils tenaient empoignés de la même main, burettes et Saint-Sacrement. Ils s'arrêtaient aux portes des tabagies, tendaient les ciboires, et les cabaretiers, la pinte à la main, les remplissaient trois fois.

> The actors who participated were still inebriated from *eau-de-vie* that they had drunk from chalices, after having eaten mackerels off of patens. Mounted astride donkeys whose hind flanks were draped with chasubles, [the riders] guided them with stoles, as they grasped Holy Sacrament and vessels in the same hand. They stopped at the door of tobacconists, holding out their ciboria, which the shopkeepers, pint in hand, filled three times.

To be sure, Mercier's account compels its readers to feel shock and surprise through the contrasts it presents. He emphasizes, "On ne procédait pas à ces destructions avec la fureur du fanatisme, mais bien avec une dérision, une ironie, une gaieté saturnale, bien propre à étonner l'observateur." (These destructions were not carried out with the furor of fanaticism, but with a derisiveness, an irony, a saturnalian gaiety quite astonishing to the observer.)[15] The passage works through a series of contrasts and substitutions of the sacred with the profane: the blood of Christ is substituted with liquor; the body of Christ is replaced with mackerels; priest's stoles are used as a lead rope for a donkey whose shanks are covered by priestly raiment. Besides the bemused indignation of its author, this passage evokes the new and unexpected uses of objects that profanation makes possible. Here we see play's episodic rhythm, its collective nature, and the boundary testing of the players involved.

Turning from narrative to visual representation, artist Etienne Béricourt's depictions of profane masquerade underscore the choppy, imperfect, nonlinear way in which new relationships between animals, objects, and humans coalesce and break apart in the process of play. Béricourt's subject matter was that of genre painting: scenes from streets and public gardens, garrisons and battlefields. Four of the artist's thirty watercolors housed by the Bibliothèque nationale de France depict various forms of profane masquerade or *processions burlesques*.[16] These works depict in exquisite detail scenes from profane masquerades that took place in Paris in 1793. Regardless of their historical accuracy or inaccuracy, these works are valuable for what they tell us about play's proximity to profanation. For example, one watercolor depicts a profane version of the Eucharistic procession of Corpus Christi: There are thurifers, candle bearers, and boat bearers, as well as celebrants who address the crowd. The form of a Corpus Christi procession is imitated outwardly, but the content of that ceremony is emptied out by the improper use of sacred objects and vestments that are normally treated with reverence. The boat includes a statue of the Virgin Mary, who is wearing a Phrygian cap. The three celebrants' profane mimicry is made all the more apparent through their imperfect performances and their secular clothing, which shows from underneath their ecclesiastical garb. One drinks greedily from the ciborium, another jokingly displays the monstrance, and a third anoints the crowd with holy water.

Play's open, episodic nature is further underscored in the movements of children in Béricourt's burlesque processions. Children are at once observers and imitators of adults. As they weave in and out of the forward-moving procession, they show salient details that unfold on the margins. Children's gesturing toward these details helps to point out the many jokes embedded in the scene (see fig. 8.1), thereby providing the viewer with an alternate, nonlinear path for analyzing Béricourt's image. On the far right of the image, a little boy notices a wheelbarrow full of male and female saints that have been turned to face each other in a sexually provocative manner. In their new context, the statues in the cart move as if they are magically animated. On the far left of the image, a little boy and girl notice an elderly woman from whose skirt hangs a rosary. The woman, unable

Figure 8.1. Étienne Béricourt, *Procession burlesque de révolutionnaires chargés d'objets de culte: dessin.* © Bibliothèque nationale de France.

to watch the profanation before her, turns her back and weeps into her apron as a dog bites at the hem of her skirt. This trio of dog, children, and old woman thematizes mimicry's reliance on observation: the woman refuses participation by hiding her eyes; the children and the dog witness and mock the old woman's resistance; and the Republican soldier observes the behaviors of all from over his shoulder. Mimicry's doubling and redoubling is also evident in children's play itself. Unlike the little girls who are generally relegated to the role of onlookers, little boys have the privilege to imitate what they have observed. At the center of the painting, a group of little boys tries to proceed with a black shroud they have painted with skulls and crossbones, its funereal connotations contrasting with the liveliness of the children. Mimicry and invention show us the importance of children, especially boys, as privileged vehicles in the transmission of play: they imitate adults' embodied practices, and in the process, create their own versions.

Another of Béricourt's watercolors offers a prime example of the charivari implicitly described by Mercier in the passage quoted earlier. The charivari had diverse functions in the early modern period, but this ritual often involved an individual who was made to ride through town backward on a donkey. Present in Europe since medieval times, the practice was revived in the mock processionals of 1793. In the charivari scene described by Mercier, the individual riding backwards on the donkey is defined only as a player who transforms religious vestment into riding tack. In Béricourt's image, both the rider—riding

Figure 8.2. Étienne Béricourt, *Procession burlesque de révolutionnaires chargés d'objets de culte, l'un d'eux monté sur un âne, portant la crosse et la mitre épiscopales: dessin.* © Bibliothèque nationale de France.

forwards—and the donkey become objects of spectacle. The rider is more readily identified as an object of spectacle and the butt of a joke (see fig. 8.2). This scene of ritual humiliation is a form of extreme mimicry that requires the donkey's rider to turn his body into a plaything, as his identity flickers between himself and the other whom he mocks. The rider wears a crozier and a miter, but his mimicry is imperfectly performed. The rider leaves his cassock open to expose his bare legs and genitalia, even as he raises two fingers that show the universal sign for a cuckold's horns. Indeed, the exposure of the rider's genitals performs a function similar to ecclesiastical-themed erotica published before, during, and even after the French Revolution. Exposing what was hidden beneath priestly or monastic robes draws attention to the body and appetites that celibacy and spiritual practice seek to eradicate. Adding to the mechanics of debasement in this scene, the donkey, too, performs badly, braying, defecating, and refusing to budge. A young girl turns her back to this, plugging her nose and laughing. In contrast to the elderly woman who hides her face in her apron and weeps in the aforementioned watercolor, this young woman directs our attention to the vignette and invites our laughter and complicity.

The theater offers another prime site for considering Revolutionary masquerade's profane potential as a form of play.[17] As new political imperatives weighed on the theater establishment in year II of the Republican calendar, dramatized scenes of profane masquerade were performed and sometimes encouraged by cultural authorities who viewed profanation as an expurgation of superstition.

La feuille du salut public asked, "Quels progrès rapides devrait faire l'esprit public, si tous nos spectacles n'offraient aux citoyens que la destruction des préjugés?" (What rapid progress public opinion would make, if all of our theaters were to only offer to citizens the destruction of prejudices?)[18] Not all anticlerical plays were emphatically didactic in nature, however. For example, in 1793, three competing vaudevilles treated the medieval legend of Pope Joan, the wise woman who allegedly served as pontiff for several years until becoming pregnant and giving birth.[19] In Charles-Auguste de Fauconpret's vaudeville, Joan happens upon the desire to become the Pope only after playfully trying on the papal tiara and seeing herself in the mirror. Mimicry creates the desire for more mimicry, and Joan petulantly convinces the cardinal Maffeo to elect her, refusing him any affection until her wish is granted. The conclavists concede, and in a lengthy song and dance number, they place Joan on the Pope's throne, crown her with the tiara, and kiss her ring with reverence. Her coronation is ruined, however, when an untimely fall causes her to give birth on the steps of the Basilica of St. John Lateran.

Like the donkey's rider in Béricourt's image, the holy father who becomes a mother in this vaudeville relies on the exposure of what lies hidden beneath sacred robes. The heroine's inability to hide her infidelity and to stop the physical process of childbirth offers a gender-inflected example of how imperfect mimicry adds to the repertoire of profane performance. Moreover, even in the space of play, we can also see Republican gender ideology at work in this vaudeville, for although Joan's actions and behaviors show that she can wield power in ways that grant her authority, her reproductive powers invalidate her claims and prevent her from seizing this authority. Indeed, Joan's lover chides her not for pretending to pass as a pontiff but for trying to pass for a man. He sings,

AIR: *La Béquille du père Barnabas*
DIS-MOI: quel désespoir,
Quel horrible scandale,
Si l'on allait savoir,
O douleur sans égale,
Que le saint père est fille,
Et qu'il ne jouit pas
Du droit de la béquille
Du père Barnabas.

AIR: *Saint Barnabas's Cane*
Tell me: what despair,
What horrible scandal,
If it were discovered,
O pain without equal,

That the holy father is a girl,
And does not enjoy
The right to the cane
Of Father Barnabas.

It is worth dwelling briefly on the air to which this vaudeville is sung, since it is taken from a satirical song that was wildly popular before the French Revolution. *La béquille du père Barnabas* derived from an anecdote of a priest who returned to his monastery without the cane he needed to walk, having left it behind in a brothel. Père Barnabas's cane took on obvious metonymic meanings that were exploited to no end in eighteenth-century song culture, revealing again the endless permutations that exist for words and objects that enter the realm of play.[20]

While Père Barnabas's sexuality transforms his *béquille* into a detachable object of play, the female Pope's sexuality remains stubbornly fixed to her body, leading to labor instead of pleasure. Fauconpret's *La papesse Jeanne* transforms a papal coronation into a profane masquerade that culminates in the birth of a baby boy. This scene is kept offstage and related only in song:

AIR: *Annette à l'age de quinze ans (Annette et Lubin)*
Le pape gémit et se plaint,
Chacun pour lui frémit et craint,
On le secourt, mais que voit-on? . . .
Que le saint père
Venait de faire . . .
Un gros garçon.

AIR: *Annette at fifteen (Annette and Lubin)*
The pope hollers and moans,
All quiver and fear for him,
We come to his aid, but what do we see? . . .
The holy father
Has just had . . .
A big boy.[21]

The miniature masquerade in Fauconpret's play relies not on the liturgical calendar as a natural start and stop to transgression; instead it is Joan's body itself that brings about the end of masquerade. As with the other narrative and visual representations of masquerade glimpsed at herein, play does not so much destroy the sacred as it forestalls or deactivates its power by means of mimicry. Playing with sacred objects allows for their creative reuse or recontextualization, which unfolds through a series of episodes or moments that resist any overarching narrative. Remembering Caillois's characterization of play as "pure form, activity that is an end in itself, rules that are respected for their own sake," it seems inaccurate or simplistic to view all representations of profane masquerade as mere reflections of Revolutionary propaganda or as iconoclasm in the sense of a destruction or expurgation of the sacred.[22] Indeed, this much seems clear when we contrast examples of masquerade above with forms of political ceremonial that took place at the National Convention.

Masquerade as Profane Ritual

Early in 1793 the Jacobin politician Léonard Bourdon called for a festival for all of Paris's forty-eight sections involving representatives and the people alike, "où les citoyens, revêtus et chargés de toutes les bagatelles qui servaient à entretenir les erreurs du peuple, aillent en procession déposer toutes ces riches futilités à la Convention nationale" (where citizens went, dressed and carrying all of the playthings once used to keep the people in error, and in procession surrendered all of these rich futilities to the National Convention).[23] The politician, who was already falling out of favor with Maximilien de Robespierre, quickly retracted the proposition when a council member observed that the people's procession would be "une mascarade proprement dite; [et] que de pareils procédés ne seraient pas propres à donner une idée avantageuse de la dignité et de la circonspection qui conviennent aux magistrats du peuple" (a masquerade, strictly speaking; [and] that such acts would not be suitable for giving a favorable idea of the dignity and circumspection befitting the magistrates of the people).[24] Regardless of the council's mistrust of masquerade, it nevertheless tolerated a series of delegations from Paris's sections to appear within the National Convention in November 1793. We have seen that some artists and chroniclers depicted profane masquerades—perhaps the same events—as primarily playful occasions, but the Archives parlementaires and press accounts tell another story, one of unity, cohesion, and deference to the Republic.

Despite the variation of their forms, the official accounts of profane masquerades enacted in the fall of 1793 generally share the overarching theme of transformation from superstition to reason. Citizens cast off childish ignorance in favor of new political identities made possible by the Republic. This theme was expressed repeatedly through a simple gesture: the removal of liturgical vestment. To be sure, the trope of uncovering or unmasking was dominant in Revolutionary discourse. Unmasking took on different meanings and associations throughout the 1790s, but one key meaning in the period of dechristianization concerned priestly abdications that were encouraged by the government in early November 1793. Priests could receive a kind of severance provided that they removed their religious garb, ceased their priestly functions, and agreed to marry.[25] Casting off religious clothing is also a supremely theatrical act, and so it is no surprise that this symbolic gesture was performed ceaselessly in the theatrical productions of the Revolutionary period.

One such example is found in a drama by Philippe-Aristide-Louis-Pierre Plancher de Valcour, cowritten with other playwrights, including Pierre-Louis Moline and Léonard Bourdon, the politician who had proposed enacting masquerades in all forty-eight sections of Paris. Their *Le tombeau des imposteurs et l'inauguration du temple de la vérité* incorporated festival forms into a series of dramatic tableaux of dechristianization, including a Pope's abdication:

Et renonçant au nom de pontife chrétien,
J'adopte avec transport celui de citoyen! . . .
Mais à l'obscurité je consacre ma vie;
Je dois au dernier rang défendre ma patrie.
Je dis la vérité. . . . pour la première fois!
. . . .
Sachez mettre à profit cet exemple terrible,
Eloignez du brasier le souffre combustible,
Et réfléchissez bien, si vous voulez la paix.
Qu'un membre gangrené, ne se guérit jamais.
(*Il se dépouille de ses habits pontificaux, ainsi que ceux de sa suite et brûle
    sur l'autel ses lettres de prêtrise*).

By renouncing the name of Christian pontiff,
I adopt with transport that of citizen! . . .
But I must defend my country
From the obscurity to which I consecrated my life.
I speak the truth . . . for the first time!
. . . .
Learn from this terrible example,
Remove the brimstone from the fire,
And remember, if you want peace,
That a gangrened limb never heals.
(*He removes his pontifical vestments, as well as those of his followers,
    and burns his ordination letters*).[26]

As we have seen with the charivari figure in Béricourt, and Pope Joan in Fauconpret's play, looking underneath religious vestment has to do with the pleasure of seeing what is hidden, challenging taboos, and playing with the differences between *être* and *paraître*. In contrast, unmasking or defrocking is a more aggressive act that involves dispelling error and transforming identity. Unmasking is more closely aligned to profane masquerade's ritual functions rather than to its playful ones, since unmasking unifies word and deed in order to support a coherent narrative.

The ritualized notion of unmasking was a prominent feature of a profane masquerade that was organized by the Gravilliers section on November 12, 1793.

The *Moniteur universel* describes the careful choreography that took place before the National Convention:

> On apporte des bannières, des croix, et, à l'instant où le dais entre, on joue l'air: *Ah! le bel oiseau*. Tous les citoyens de cette section se dépouillent à la fois et, de dessous les travestissements du fanatisme, on voit sortir des défenseurs de la patrie, couverts de l'uniforme national. Chacun jette le vêtement qu'il vient d'ôter, et l'on voit sauter en l'air les étoles, les mitres, les chasubles, les dalmatiques, au bruit des instruments et aux cris répétés de *Vive la liberté! Vive la République!*

> They carried in banners, crosses, and, when the dais entered, the tune *Ah! le bel oiseau (Ah! the Beautiful Bird*) was played. All of the citizens of this section simultaneously removed their vestments and, from underneath the travesties of fanaticism, the defenders of the country appeared wearing the national uniform. The people threw away the priestly robes they had just removed, and one saw flying in the air, stoles, miters, chasubles, dalmatic capes, to the sound of instruments and the repeated cries of *Long live liberty! Long live the Republic!*[27]

The false costume of priests is replaced with the true "uniforme national," which corresponds to its wearers' political identities. Masquerades like this one were performed all around France in the autumn of 1793. Although there are many parallels in the objects, music, dancing, and clothing of masquerade, its ritualized, didactic functions were not play, but evoked instead what Vovelle calls "la vocation de la cérémonie iconoclaste, démonstration pédagogique à usage populaire" (the vocation of the iconoclastic ceremony—an educational demonstration in popular use).[28] In the ritual of unmasking performed in the Gravilliers' masquerade, the sight of so many sumptuous pieces of fabric thrown in the air was like the flight of birds set free. Unlike the lowly donkey associated with charivari and other earthy antics of the street, birds are noble creatures associated with the realm of immaterial spirits. Indeed, birds feature prominently in the script written for the Festival of Unity in August 1793. Its author imagined their quasi-sacred function in proposing that thousands be released all at once: "des milliers d'oiseaux rendus à la liberté, portant à leurs cols de légères banderoles, prendront leurs vols rapides dans les airs, et porteront au ciel le témoignage de la liberté rendue à la terre" (thousands of birds returned to freedom, wearing inscribed bands on their necks, rapidly took flight in the air, carrying to heaven the testament of freedom returned to the earth).[29] Another procession, similar to that of the Gravilliers, was performed by the Section de l'Unité only a few weeks later. This procession also offered an allegory of liberation and adoration of the Republic:

> On apporte ensuite sur des brancards des calices, des ciboires, des soleils, des chandeliers, des plats d'or et d'argent, une châsse superbe, une croix de pierreries, et mille autres ustensiles de pratiques superstitieuses. Ce cortège

entre dans la salle aux acclamations des spectateurs, aux cris de *vive la liberté, la république, la Montagne!* aux fanfares des instruments guerriers. Un drap noir, porté au bruit de l'air *Malborough* [sic] *est mort et enterré*, figure la destruction du fanatisme. La musique exécute ensuite l'hymne révolutionnaire: on voit tous les citoyens revêtus d'habits sacerdotaux danser au bruit de l'air *Ça ira, la Carmagnole, Veillons au salut de l'empire*, etc. L'enthousiasme universel se manifeste par des acclamations prolongées.

Next they brought out chalices, ciboriums, monstrances, chandeliers, plates of gold and silver, a superb shrine, a cross of precious stones, and a thousand other tools of superstitious practices. This cortege entered the room to the acclamations of spectators, to the cries of *long live the republic, the Mountain!* to the fanfare of warlike instruments. A black flag, carried to the tune of *Malborough* [sic] *est mort et enterré*, represented the destruction of fanaticism. The musicians next played a revolutionary hymn: we saw all of the citizens dressed in priestly habits dance to the sound of *Ça ira, La Carmagnole*, and *Veillons au salut de l'empire*, etc. Universal enthusiasm was expressed by prolonged applause.[30]

Just as Béricourt's watercolors show profane masquerade in the street as taking the outward form of a Corpus Christi processional, the Section de l'Unité's masquerade borrows the ritual form of a funeral procession to mark the symbolic death of "fanaticism." In the place of prayer is substituted joyful Revolutionary "hymns" that reinforce shared bonds of community and dedication to country.

Did rituals such as this try to capture some of play's power, even as it maintained a concept of the sacred that buttressed the legitimacy of the state? Or were masquerades finally rejected by the Revolutionary government because, despite their ideological coherence and didactic potential, there was something inescapably playful that remained? Georges Danton demanded that masquerades organized by the Revolutionary sections of Paris be ended:

> Que les individus qui voudront déposer sur l'autel de la patrie les dépouilles des églises ne s'en fassent plus un jeu ni un trophée. Notre mission n'est pas de recevoir sans cesse des députations qui répètent toujours les mêmes mots. Il est un terme à tout, même aux félicitations. Je demande qu'on pose la barrière.

> Let the individuals who wish to surrender church goods on the altar of the country make it no more a game or a trophy. Our mission is not to endlessly receive deputations who constantly repeat the same words. There is an end to everything, even to celebrations. I ask that the barrier be raised.[31]

Danton and other like-minded politicians trivialized profane masquerade as a form of play that threatened the seriousness of the Republic and its work. And

yet, as I have suggested in this chapter, the fact that we find contrasting representations of profane masquerade points to at least two distinct functions of play
that took shape in the context of dechristianization. First, play could serve a
secularizing function. Profane masquerades performed in the context of Revolutionary festivals or in the halls of government served to legitimate a new source
of authority—the Republic—and to valorize a new set of shared values. Second,
play could serve a profane function, in Agamben's sense. The forms of play found
in Fauconpret's *La papesse Jeanne* and street processionals represented by Mercier and Béricourt did not support some new source of authority; rather, these
profane masquerades deactivate or ignored power and authority altogether.
Alongside the official debates and competing political forces that accompanied
the process of dechristianization, play offers an additional means for observing
how Revolutionaries attempted to reconfigure the symbolic and political functions of the sacred in public life.

NOTES

Unless noted otherwise, all translations are my own.

1. See Richard Clay, *Iconoclasm in Revolutionary Paris: The Transformation of Signs, 1789–
1795* (Oxford: Voltaire Foundation, 2012); Nina Dubin, *Futures and Ruins: Eighteenth-
Century Paris and the Art of Hubert Robert* (Los Angeles: Getty Research Institute, 2012);
Dario Gamboni, *The Destruction of Art: Iconoclasm and Vandalism since the French Revolution* (New Haven, CT: Yale University Press, 1997); Michael Kelly, *Iconoclasm in Aesthetics* (Cambridge: Cambridge University Press, 2003); Joe Moshenska, *Iconoclasm as Child's
Play* (Stanford, CA: Stanford University Press, 2019); and Elizabeth Williamson, *The Materiality of Religion in Early Modern English Drama* (Burlington, VT: Ashgate, 2009).

2. See Jeffrey D. Burson, *The Culture of Enlightening: Abbé Claude Yvon and the Entangled Emergence of the Enlightenment* (Notre Dame, IN: University of Notre Dame Press,
2019); Charly Coleman, *The Virtues of Abandon: An Anti-Individualist History of the French
Enlightenment* (Stanford, CA: Stanford University Press, 2014); Sanja Perovic, ed., *Sacred
and Secular Agency in Early Modern France: Fragments of Religion* (London: Continuum,
2012); Dale Van Kley, *The Religious Origins of the French Revolution: From Calvin to the
Civil Constitution, 1560–1791* (New Haven, CT: Yale University Press, 1996). See also Knox
Peden, "The Politics of Disenchantment: Marcel Gauchet and the French Struggle with Secularization," *Intellectual History Review* 27, no. 1 (2017): 135–150, and Anton M. Matytsin
and Dan Edelstein, eds., *Let There Be Enlightenment: The Religious and Mystical Sources of
Rationality* (Baltimore: Johns Hopkins University Press, 2018).

3. Michel Vovelle, *La Révolution contre l'Église: De la Raison à l'Être Suprême* (Paris: Éditions Complexe, 1988), 90.

4. Moshenska, *Iconoclasm as Child's Play*, 2–3, 145. Moshenska's book appeared as I was
completing the later drafts of this chapter; I am indebted to his linking secularization narratives to iconoclasm.

5. Mikhail Bakhtin, *Rabelais and His World*, trans. Hélène Iswolsky (Bloomington: Indiana University Press, 1984).

6. Joseph Townsend, *A Journey through Spain in the Years 1786 and 1787: With Particular Attention to the Agriculture, Manufactures, Commerce, Population, Taxes, and Revenue of That Country; and Remarks in Passing through a Part of France; in Three Volumes*,
vol. 1 (London: C. Dilly, 1791), quoted in Peter Burke, *Popular Culture in Early Modern
Europe* (Aldershot, UK: Ashgate, 1994), 183.

7. Terry Castle, *Masquerade and Civilization: The Carnivalesque in Eighteenth-Century English Culture and Fiction* (Stanford, CA: Stanford University Press, 1986).

8. Clay, *Iconoclasm in Revolutionary Paris*, 252–53.

9. François-Alphonse Aulard, *Le culte de la Raison et le culte de l'Être Suprême (1793–1794): Essai historique* (Paris: F. Alcan, 1892); see also Daniel Guérin, *La lutte de classes sous la première République: Bourgeois et "bras nus," 1793–1797*, vol. 1 (Paris: Gallimard, 1946), 276.

10. Michel Vovelle, *La Révolution contre l'Église*, 166, 170; the English translation is from Michel Vovelle, *The Revolution against the Church: From Reason to the Supreme Being*, trans. Alan José (Columbus: Ohio State University Press, 1991), 108. See also Michel Vovelle, *Les métamorphoses de la fête en Provence de 1750–1820* (Paris: Aubier-Flammarion, 1976), 124–29; and Serge Bianchi, "La déchristianisation de l'an II: Essai d'interprétation," *Annales historiques de la Révolution française* 50, no. 233 (July–September 1978): 341–71.

11. On anticlerical mascarades and transfer of sacrality, see Mona Ozouf, *La fête révolutionnaire, 1789–1799* (Paris: Gallimard, 1976), 150–57, 462–67; Mona Ozouf, *Festivals and the French Revolution*, trans. Alan Sheridan (Cambridge, MA: Harvard University Press, 1988), 92–97, 275–78.

12. Giorgio Agamben, "In Praise of Profanation," in *Profanations*, trans. Jeff Fort (New York: Zone Books, 2007), 77, 75.

13. Agamben, "In Praise of Profanation," 74, 76.

14. Roger Caillois, *Man, Play, and Games*, trans. Meyer Barash (Urbana: University of Illinois Press, 2001), 12.

15. Louis-Sébastien Mercier, *Le nouveau Paris*, ed. Jean-Claude Bonnet, Anne Le Fur, and Jean Sellier (Paris: Mercure de France, 1994), 554.

16. These watercolors are part of the Collection Michel Hennin and are accessible on the Bibliothèque nationale de France's Gallica website, https://catalogue.bnf.fr/rechercher.do?index=AUT3&numNotice=14952579.

17. I have written on this and related phenomena; see Annelle Curulla, *Gender and Religious Life in French Revolutionary Drama* (Liverpool, UK: Liverpool University Press, 2018).

18. *La feuille du salut public*, no. 127 (15 brumaire, an II [November 5, 1793]).

19. For a history of the various legends of Pope Joan, see Alain Bourreau, *La papesse Jeanne* (Paris: Aubier, 1988). There are two extant copies of Pope Joan plays from the French Revolution: Charles-Auguste de Fauconpret, *La papesse Jeanne, opéra bouffon en vaudevilles, en trois actes* (Paris: Veuve Hérissant, 1793); and François-Pierre-Auguste Léger, *La papesse Jeanne* (Paris: Cailleau, 1793).

20. Fauconpret, *La papesse Jeanne*, 36, 68–69.

21. Fauconpret, *La papesse Jeanne*, 68–69.

22. Roger Caillois, *Man and the Sacred*, trans. Meyer Barash (Urbana: University of Illinois Press, 2001), 155.

23. *Journal de la Montagne* no. 16, (20 brumaire, an II [November 3, 1793]). For a biography of Léonard Bourdon, see Michael J. Sydenham, *Léonard Bourdon: The Career of a Revolutionary, 1754–1807* (Waterloo, ON: Wilfrid Laurier University Press, 1999).

24. *Journal de la Montagne* no. 16.

25. Joseph F. Byrnes, *Priests of the French Revolution: Saints and Renegades in a New Political Era* (University Park: Pennsylvania State University Press, 2014), 142.

26. Léonard Bourdon, Philippe-Aristide-Louis-Pierre Plancher de Valcour and Pierre-Louis Moline, *Le tombeau des imposteurs et l'inauguration du temple de la vérité, sanculottide dramatique mêlée de musique*, in Suzanne J. Bérard, *Le théâtre révolutionnaire de 1789–1794: La déchristianisation sur les planches* (Paris: Presses universitaires de Paris Ouest, 2009), 416.

27. Léonard-Charles-André-Gustave Gallois, ed., *Réimpression de l'ancien Moniteur, seule histoire authentique et inaltérée de la Révolution française, depuis la réunion des États-Généraux jusqu'au Consulat (mai 1789–novembre 1799)*, vol. 18 (Paris: Plon, 1847), 420.

28. Vovelle, *La Révolution contre l'Église*, 96; Vovelle, *The Revolution against the Church*, 58.

29. *Ordre et marche de la Fête de l'Unité et de l'Indivisibilité de la République, qui aura lieu le 10 août, décrété par la Convention nationale* (Paris: Gourdin, 1793), 6.

30. Réimpression du *Moniteur universel* no. 62 (duodi 2 frimaire, an II [November 22, 1793]), 479.

31. *Archives parlementaires*, vol. 80 (November 26, 1793), 164.

CHAPTER 9

The Return of Play, or the End
of Revolutionary Theater

Yann Robert

When teaching a course on the theater of the French Revolution, I often conclude with Victor Hugo's *Hernani* (1830), a play that postdates Revolutionary drama but shares with it the dubious distinction of being known today less for its content than for the tumultuous events it occasioned. Yet the famed *bataille d'Hernani* scarcely resembles the dramatic conflicts of the Revolutionary era. Although Hugo tried, by equating romanticism and liberalism in his preface, to politicize the quarrel, its focus was almost entirely aesthetic in nature. Hugo's provocative use of enjambments brought tempers to a boil, not the obvious political readings supported by a play with a reckless, immoral king (Carlos, at a time when a Charles ruled over France) who turns benevolent the instant he becomes an emperor (a boost to Bonapartists). I ask my students to imagine how differently such a play might have been received during the Terror, a time when many deemed it downright criminal to treat the theater as a space of aesthetic reflection and enjoyment cut off from current events. Criminal was Louis-Benoît Picard's lighthearted, apolitical play, *La moitié du chemin*, since "distraire de la chose publique est justiciable du Tribunal Révolutionnaire" (to distract from public affairs is prosecutable by the Revolutionary Tribunal).[1] Criminal was the seventy-four-year-old retired playwright Michel-Jean Sedaine for having failed to write a *pièce de circonstance* hailing the Revolution.[2] Criminal was the actor who likewise chose to stay silent when an opportunity presented itself to draw a parallel between the play and current debates, even if it meant breaking out of character: "Quand un acteur parle de la paix, si celui qui est en scène avec lui, ne lui répond: *Point de paix tant que les ennemis souilleront notre territoire: point de paix tant que les tyrans n'auront point rendu hommage à notre république: point de paix jusqu'au moment où la république sera vengée*, alors l'acteur a tort, et on peut l'accuser de modérantisme." (When an actor speaks of peace, if the

151

one who is onstage next to him does not respond: *No peace so long as enemies sully our land; no peace so long as tyrants have not paid homage to our republic; no peace until our republic is avenged*—then the actor is wrong, and one can accuse him of a treasonous moderation.)[3] Is it any surprise, then, that Revolutionary audiences so often regarded the theater less as a site of artistic judgment than as a forum in which to discuss, loudly and freely, contemporary issues?[4]

The above anecdotes, while hardly unique, do, of course, represent extreme cases. *Pièces de circonstances* were not the only plays of the French Revolution, nor were they even the most attended. Emmet Kennedy has shown that the most regularly performed works during the Revolution lacked explicitly political content, with lighthearted, escapist fare being especially popular.[5] As I argue elsewhere, however, this does not diminish the significance of the period's much better-known topical plays.[6] While the latter had fewer performances (although perhaps not during the Terror),[7] their impact was far greater, both on the central debates and events of the Revolution and on subsequent depictions of Revolutionary culture. Indeed, this partitioning of Revolutionary drama along two poles—political propaganda versus escapist diversion—should not conceal the innovation that makes theater from the period so fascinating: its direct engagement in the present through the dramatization of current events and figures. Focusing on topicality makes it possible to transcend the propaganda-versus-diversion binary (after all, topical plays are not always political, nor are lighthearted comedies necessarily atopical) and to explore instead a conception of the stage that is unique, revolutionary, and uniquely Revolutionary.

Scholars have long been fascinated with the topicality of Revolutionary drama, studying it from a variety of perspectives.[8] What connects all these studies is an awareness that many of the works that premiered during the Revolution lacked attributes that we traditionally associate with "play"—in the sense of both a theatrical performance and a game. Significant similarities exist between these two meanings of play, from the collective acceptance of specific, invariable rules to the preservation of a boundary between the play world and the real world intended to prevent confusion between the two, and transformation of the latter by the former. Revolutionary drama, by contrast, is famous for challenging the rules and conventions that structured ancien régime theater, its embrace of liberty most visible in the construction of dozens of new theaters, the creation of countless innovative genres, and the rejection of classical precepts limiting what could be shown onstage and how. Foremost among the conventions defied by the theater of the Revolution is the frontier between play and reality. As Judith Schlanger notes, Revolutionary drama "n'est pas perçu comme une diversion étrangère à l'actualité politique mais comme un redoublement qui appartient au même champ" (is not viewed as a diversion foreign to the political present but as a doubling of it belonging to the same field).[9] For the authors, actors, and spectators of the Revolution, a theatrical work is akin to a speech before a club, a tribunal, or an assembly; it *is* current events, "belonging to the same field" rather than a remote, self-enclosed world that echoes or comments on the present. Stories abound of participants in crucial events being invited to watch and even perform their own roles, thereby further blurring the tenuous border between reality and fiction. This collapsing of real world and play world into a single field gives the latter great power and efficacy.[10] In the traditional vision of play, a performance or game does not seek to transform the world outside it directly; it operates in the mode of the "as if," of the "just for fun." Of course, this does not mean that a performance or game can never have an impact on the real world (on the contrary, as we will see, many believed the impact could be all the greater for being indirect), but it does suggest that play rests on the fundamental notion that what happens during it will not lead to direct consequences for those involved as participants or characters. Compare this to the tragic fate of the actor Arouch, guillotined for having shouted "Long live the king!" *while in character* (as the script required), or to the multiple plays that set out to influence the outcome of the king's trial while it was still unfolding, to see how deeply efficacious—how much more than just a game—the theater had become during the Revolution.[11]

Although Revolutionary drama has received a great deal of scholarly attention, the overwhelming focus has been on the period between 1789 and 1795.[12] As a result, many have studied the topical theater of the Revolution and its departure from earlier visions of play, but few, if any, have looked at its disappearance. While it would be impossible to connect the decline of topical theater to a single event or decree, I contend that 1797 deserves pride of place in that still unwritten history.[13] It was then that there began a press campaign calling for the revival of the (allegedly) lost practice of booing actors and playwrights during a performance.[14] That same year, the legislature entered into a debate concerning the impact of the Revolution on the theater and of the theater on the Revolution.[15] Taken together, these arguments reveal that journalists and politicians alike had grown uneasy with the popularity of *pièces de circonstances*, which they deemed harmful both to the aesthetic quality and, more surprisingly, to the political value of the stage. Although this innovative, multifaceted critique of topicality resulted in few immediate reforms, it set in motion the gradual disappearance, in the name of play, of Revolutionary theater.

In Praise of Booing

The year 1797 marks a turning point in the portrayal in the press of topical theater. This is not to say there were no critiques before then. Writing in *La chronique de Paris*, Aubin-Louis Millin de Grandmaison lamented the vogue of *pièces de circonstances* as early as 1791, warning his readers that "de longues déclamations sans intérêt, dans lesquelles on répète trois cents fois les mots citoyens et liberté, finiront par anéantir l'art dramatique en France. Il est temps d'arrêter ce débordement d'ouvrages de circonstances" (long declamations of no interest, in which one repeats three hundred times the words citizens and liberty, will end up destroying the dramatic arts in France. It is time to stop this flood of topical works).[16] As the Terror—the heyday of topical theater—came to an end, periodicals such as *La décade philosophique*, *Le journal des théâtres*, and *La feuille du salut public* returned to this early critique, developing it through accusations that will sound familiar to anyone aware of the ways that Revolutionary theater as a whole was discredited for centuries.[17] Briefly, the authors of *pièces de circonstances* write too much and too quickly, so as to keep up with current events.[18] They prefer the money and celebrity easily obtained through topical allusions to the lasting glory that only hard work and good taste can provide.[19] As a result, their plays are doomed to disappear as quickly as the events that inspired them, such is their lack of originality:

> Qu'ont été, jusqu'à ce moment, nos pièces révolutionnaires? Des tragédies comiques où les interlocuteurs se sont bornés à dire, le premier: *c'est une abominable chose que la tyrannie, il faut exterminer les rois, vive la liberté*. Le second: *vous avez raison*. Le troisième: *je suis de votre avis*. Après quoi, l'on tue un despote, quand on croit n'avoir pas besoin d'un volcan pour ça, et la pièce est finie.

> What have, until now, been the plays of our Revolution? Comic tragedies whose characters have contented themselves with saying, the first: *Tyranny is an abominable thing; kings must be exterminated; long live liberty*. The second: *You are right*. The third: *I agree with you*. After which one kills a despot, unless one feels the need to use a volcano for that, and the play is done.[20]

Before 1797, however, witty critiques of this sort did not signal an unmitigated rejection of topical theater but rather hope for its improvement. Hence, the same author for *La décade philosophique* who had condemned the haste of Revolutionary playwrights encouraged them in the same article to continue to retrace "d'une main hardie les hauts faits de la Révolution" (with a bold hand the great feats of the Revolution);[21] such was his confidence, expressed in a later article, that "il n'est pas impossible de faire de la bonne comédie sur des sujets de circonstances" (it is not impossible to write good plays on contemporary subjects).[22]

By 1797 this optimism had all but vanished, punctured by the rise of a band of reactionary critics who published a stream of articles, notably in two newly created journals, *Le courrier des spectacles* and *Le censeur dramatique*, mocking topical theater as intrinsically devoid of good taste. Indeed, while critics in 1797 leveled the same accusations as their predecessors, they presented the flaws of *pièces de circonstances* as inevitable consequences of their topicality. For instance, Édouard Marie-Joseph Le Pan, an author for *Le courrier des spectacles*, frequently lamented the decadence of the dramatic arts in France, which he blamed on everything from the proliferation of theaters to the popularity of bourgeois and topical drama, "ce genre d'ouvrage dont la facilité séduit les auteurs, et qui, en frappant vivement l'âme du spectateur, ne lui permet pas d'apercevoir les vices de l'ouvrage" (the kind of work that seduces playwrights through its easiness and that, by striking the spectator's soul deeply, does not let him see the work's flaws).[23] To Le Pan, even if a *pièce de circonstance* could be beautifully written, original, and faithful to classical rules, it would still remain harmful to French theater because of the ability of topicality to capture the spectators' attention so thoroughly that they can no longer see the flaws in the work. The unique strength of topical theater—its contiguity to reality, giving the audience the thrill and pleasure of a direct engagement—thus also represents the source of its weakness. A spectator cannot give simultaneous consideration to both form and content. An emotional and ideological response to the latter makes the former invisible, impeding the very possibility of an aesthetic improvement, be it of the play, its author, or the genre as a whole. Le Pan's rejection not just of topical plays but of topicality itself signals a more profound rethinking of the theater, an attempt to revive it as play—that is, as an event distinct from reality, possessing its own set of rules and expectations that participants need to know and heed in order to find diversion in it.

Looking back to the theatrical world before the Revolution, journalists identified many ways that 1797 audiences could be trained to assume a more aesthetic relationship to the stage: limiting the number and types of theaters, rewarding gifted artists with government pensions, and refining the audiences and repertoires of existing playhouses by modeling them on the *grand siècle* (masterpieces by Pierre Corneille, Molière, and Jean Racine performed nightly before educated and wealthy elites).[24] Of all their strategies, one strikes me as particularly revealing: the 1797 campaign to reintroduce booing. According to a wide range of newspapers, booing had, if not disappeared, at least greatly diminished during the Terror. *La feuille critique et littéraire* regretfully noted this decline in vocal expressions of disapproval as far back as 1794: "à propos des sifflets, nous témoignerons au public combien nous sommes fâchés qu'il ait cessé d'en faire usage, tant pour les pièces, qu'à l'égard des mauvais acteurs" (as regards booing, we shall let the public know how upset we are that it has ceased to make use of it, as much for plays as toward bad actors).[25] By 1797 the decline was such that *Le courrier des spectacles* could claim that many people no longer even knew they were allowed to jeer, and that when better-informed spectators did try to express their displeasure with a play, they were told, "Contentez-vous de ne pas applaudir." (Just content yourselves with not applauding.)[26] A week earlier, the same journal had already lamented that it had become customary to eject from the theater spectators who dared to boo.[27]

What might explain this alteration in spectatorial behavior? For *La feuille critique et littéraire*, the answer was clear: it came from the tendency among

Revolutionary audiences to consider "plutôt l'intention que l'exécution" (more
the intention than the execution).[28] This is a reasonable hypothesis, for in the
first five years of the Revolution, spectators were widely encouraged to focus
primarily on the intentions of playwrights and actors: "L'homme de goût ne
trouvera point ce qui distingue la bonne comédie, il fera grâce aux défauts dramatiques en faveur de l'intention." (A man of taste will not find here that which
distinguishes good comedy; he will forgive the dramatic flaws in favor of the
intention.)[29] This distinction between intention and execution (and the valuing
of the former over the latter) appears repeatedly in theatrical criticism prior to
1797—as, for instance, when *Le moniteur universel* defended the lenient response
of the audience to a poor but patriotic play: "[Le public] a vu les intentions de
l'auteur . . . on lui a donné sur tout cela des applaudissements plus relatifs à son
but qu'à la manière dont il l'a executé." (The public saw the author's intentions . . .
he received applause related more to his aim than to the manner in which he
had executed it.)[30] Newspaper reports from the period suggest indeed that the
overt topicality of the theater during the Revolution inspired a new relationship to the stage—one in which, to quote a government spy during the Terror,
audiences judged as "citizens" rather than as "spectators."[31] These "citizen" audiences attended the theater not to engage in an aesthetic judgment, nor to lose
themselves in the story through the power of illusion, but rather for the chance
it gave them to express their opinion on contemporary events and public
figures.

Such a relationship to the stage altered the nature of booing, from an aesthetic
judgment leveled at bad acting or writing to an ideological judgment targeting
the principles expressed onstage. Numerous newspapers reported instances in
which spectators had abstained from booing for fear that it would be interpreted
as a rejection of the values expressed by the characters and plot. Indeed, at the
height of the Terror, how could a patriot jeer a play, however flawed, that reenacted a sublime moment of Republican virtue or heroism? Talentless playwrights
understood this and took full advantage:

> La sublimité du sujet que traitent les auteurs a l'air d'être pour eux un motif
> de confiance et de sécurité qui les fait complaire dans la négligence. C'est ainsi
> que le spectateur devenu patriote, dans l'hésitation de ne pouvoir séparer du
> talent de l'auteur le respect dû au sujet qu'il a embrassé, laisse aller impuné-
> ment jusqu'à la fin une pièce qui devrait tomber en route.

> The sublimity of the authors' subjects appears to give them a sense of confi-
> dence and security that makes them wallow in negligence. It is thus that the
> spectator turned patriot, unsure that he will be able to dissociate the talent of
> the author from the respect owed to the subject that he espoused, allows a play
> that should have flopped midperformance to reach its conclusion with
> impunity.[32]

A year later, the tables had turned, and plays now targeted the same patriots who had once cheered the Terror. Yet the same problem remained, since spectators watching a play deriding known Terrorists could hardly do anything other than applaud the artists' intentions: "Leurs intentions sont excellentes; mais qu'ils n'abusent pas de l'ascendant que leur donne la circonstance; qu'ils songent que personne n'ose les huer de peur d'être soupçonné de prendre parti pour des monstres." (Their intentions are excellent; but they should not exploit too much the ascendancy that circumstances give them; they should consider that no one dares boo them, for fear of being suspected of siding with monsters.)[33] Be they a celebration of the current regime or a denunciation of the previous one, topical plays fostered a one-sided ideological response that shielded actors and playwrights alike from criticism of their talents as artists.

The campaign to revive booing constituted a rebellion against this Revolutionary form of judgment—an attempt to redirect the focus of theatrical audiences from intention to execution, and from content to form. As we have seen, *Le courrier des spectacles* was particularly outraged by the notion, accepted by the majority of modern spectators, that the absence of applause was somehow equivalent to booing. This is clearly not the case, for withholding applause indicates at best a general disapproval of the play, one that only truly becomes evident upon its completion, whereas booing can condemn a specific flaw, directly and immediately, without necessarily rejecting the play as a whole. It was this ability to interrupt and fragment the performance that made booing such an essential instrument of artistic improvement in the eyes of the journalists. Several noted that the return of booing would allow spectators to dissociate the quality of the writing from the political content of the play, thereby making it easier to weed out playwrights motivated only by a desire for money or fame rather than by a true passion or talent for the theater. As *Le courrier des spectacles* concluded,

> On sifflait autrefois les mauvais ouvrages; voilà ce qui nous a produit les chefs-d'œuvre de la scène. Cette indulgence mal entendue est sans doute contraire aux auteurs qui négligeraient moins leurs ouvrages; mais elle est encore plus nuisible à l'art qu'elle tue. . . . Que le public soit sévère, il y aura moins d'auteurs, mais tant mieux: est-il nécessaire qu'il y en ait tant?

> We used to boo bad plays; that is what produced the masterpieces of our stage. Today's misguided indulgence is without a doubt harmful to authors, who would neglect their works less, but it is even more damaging to art, which it kills. . . . Let the public be severe, there will be fewer authors, but so much the better: is it necessary there be so many?[34]

Likewise, booing could help restore the distinction between actor and character that was so often blurred during the Revolution. In an article titled "Réflexions sur l'utilité de la critique au théâtre," one journalist defended the necessity of jeering young authors to train them, noting that new performers who give weak but regular performances, suggesting less a lack of effort than one of talent, should be booed gently, whereas special scorn should be reserved for those who ignore tradition and listen only to their youthful imaginations.[35]

Indeed, the problem with topicality, journalists noted again and again, is that it leaves no room for tradition. The focus on an ever-changing present as a source of content, instead of on long-standing character types and formulas, means there is no need to learn from the insights and conventions passed down by actors and playwrights from generation to generation. Additionally, the near certainty that a *pièce de circonstance* will disappear as quickly as the event that inspired it all but guarantees that it will yield no tradition of its own. Booing constitutes the best way to combat topical theater because it shifts the focus of actors and spectators onto the existence of preexisting rules, a shared past against which the play's execution, not its immediate intention, must be evaluated, with the aim of identifying what to avoid in future performances. In so doing, booing reinserts theater into history, into a relationship to time not solely defined by the present. It helps ensure that the theater never strays too far from the great tradition of pre-Revolutionary times, thereby forestalling the alleged decadence of the dramatic arts. Its aim is to revive the past and project it onto the future, to return theater to what it was under the ancien régime: a form of play with its own specific rules, fixed by ancient, wise tradition, not a spectacle so enthralled by the present that it finds in it both its origin and its goal.

The Politics of the Circumstantial

The idea that topicality produces bad art seems almost intuitive to us, so accustomed have we become to hearing the claim that it condemned Revolutionary drama to mediocrity. Far more surprising is the notion that topicality weakens the political impact of theater instead of (as early Revolutionaries believed) strengthening it. Such was, however, the conclusion increasingly reached by journalists and politicians of the Directory (the period between November 1795 and 1799, named after the five-member committee that ruled over France) during a fascinating debate on the state of the dramatic arts under the Revolution. The terms of the debate were set by Ange-Étienne-Xavier Poisson de La Chabeaussière and Amaury Duval, who both wrote for *La décade philosophique* and served (successively) as "chef du bureau des théâtres" in the Ministry of the Interior.[36] This dual occupation—composing negative reviews of *pièces de circonstances* and surveying the theaters for the government[37]—perfectly illustrates the way that the aesthetic critique of topicality we saw above was echoed and supported by a political critique. Indeed, the Council of Five Hundred soon took up La Chabeaussière and Duval's proposals, following the motion by Marie-Joseph Chénier (once known, ironically, for his passionate plea for a free stage) that his fellow deputies examine whether the time had come to place the theater under state management.[38] The lengthy debates that ensued in the Council of Five Hundred and the Council of Ancients proposed many potential reforms—limiting the number of theaters and assigning them exclusive genres, censoring certain words or subjects, rewarding commendable authors with state honors, and reversing the theater's capitalistic turn through a system of governmental patronage—all of which sought to address both the perceived decadence of the dramatic arts and their political impotence, with the latter partly blamed, as the former had been, on the period's obsession with topicality.

La Chabeaussière, Duval, and the twelve deputies who joined in the debate all justify the need for reform on the basis that plays have become too implicated in current political affairs. La Chabeaussière thus notes that "tout le monde sait que les spectacles, pendant les divisions intestines, deviennent de petits rassem-blements, des espèces de clubs; que chaque théâtre adopte bientôt un parti; qu'il a en conséquence ses principes, ses auteurs, ses spectateurs; et qu'ils sont ainsi de petits foyers de guerre civile" (everyone knows that theaters, in times of inter-nal discord, become small gatherings, akin to political clubs; that each soon adopts a party and, consequently, its principles, authors, and spectators; and that they are therefore little hotbeds of civil war).[39] Nearly all the deputies echo this fear that the theaters are giving support to clashing factions, a grave concern for a government always seeking a middle ground between royalists and radicals. The partitioning of theaters into political clubs strengthens extremist groups— notably, the royalists whose ideas and traditions they preserve—and weakens the instable consensus on which the Directory rests, by inspiring constant clashes in the parterre.[40] According to the deputies, this factionalization of the theaters could be blamed on the law of January 13, 1791, that had introduced liberty (no censorship) and competition (no privileges) to the French stage. Dozens of the-aters had come into existence, creating such a pressing need for actors and play-wrights that none, however inept, were rejected—especially not those who realized that anyone could make easy money by writing a topical play (hence, the attempt to foster competition by allowing more than one privileged stage per genre paradoxically produced even less competition by yielding too many stages for all genres). It is fascinating to note that this particular type of politicization came to be regarded during the Directory as an obstacle to the theater's true political impact, not as an illustration of it. As one journalist noted, "il parut suffisant alors de décréter la liberté illimitée des théâtres; et, en effet, il s'en est élevé à la fois un tel nombre, que se combattant et se neutralisant l'un l'autre, leur action sur l'esprit public avait perdu presque entièrement son effet" (it seemed enough [in 1791] to decree the unlimited liberty of the theaters; and, indeed, there arose so many at once that, fighting and neutralizing one another, their action on the national spirit had almost lost all impact).[41] The law of January 13, 1791,

under a monarchical government with the backing of privileged theaters, had
served a valuable purpose by ensuring that a multiplicity of voices could be heard,
but now, under a Republic, too many voices at once bred not only conflict but
uncertainty, destroying the general impact of the stage. The once necessary liberation of the theater had turned it into "l'arme banale des factions" (the banal
weapon of factions)—so aggressively political, so nakedly topical, that it lost the
ability to impart deeper political truths.[42]

By repudiating the law of January 13, 1791, and placing the nation's theaters
under state management, the deputies sought not, therefore, to depoliticize the
French stage but to politicize it differently. That much is clear from Pierre Jean
Audouin's rhetorical question in his report to the Council of Five Hundred:
"Pourquoi, sous le régime républicain, ne les élèverait-on pas à la dignité
d'institutions politiques?" (Why, under a republican regime, would we not elevate theaters to the dignity of political institutions?) Such institutions would not
foster partisan disputes but would instead "identifier les mœurs des Français avec
la forme de leur gouvernement" (unite the mores of the French with the form of
their government). Prior to 1797, this rather vague program—republican mores
are never defined beyond bromides about love of liberty, law, and nation—would
not have necessarily excluded topical plays. In fact, some of the deputies still seem
open to the idea that the reenactment of current affairs could inspire a general
love of the Republic and of its values. Most, however, bar *pièces de circonstances*
from their dream of a state-managed theater, noting that the pensions they would
bestow on select authors would give them the financial security necessary to
write a play over an extended period of time, without present circumstances
(theirs and that of the nation) shaping their art. Audouin thus cautions against
"[ces] pièces *ridiculement* patriotiques . . . où l'on représente avec deux petits
canons de bois la plus grande action militaire" (ridiculously patriotic plays . . .
representing the greatest military triumph with two little wooden canons).[43]
Likewise, *Le journal de Paris* warns against "ces mauvaises pièces d'un jour
appelées de circonstances" (poor topical plays forgotten in a day),[44] and La Chabeaussière against "[ces] rapsodies dégoutantes déguisées sous un titre patriotique" (disgusting rhapsodies disguised under a patriotic title).[45] The examples
the deputies give of acceptable political plays also speak volumes: not a single
pièce de circonstance but repeated references to *Brutus, Guillaume Tell*, and the
works of Corneille, Molière, and Racine. As these examples suggest, it is not
political themes they wish to see disappear but direct engagement in the here
and now.

What explains this rejection of topicality? Under the Directory, the authorities appear to have grown increasingly skeptical that the political impact of a
pièce de circonstance could be controlled. A review in *La décade philosophique*
of the play *La pauvre femme* suggests why: "[Cette pièce] contient plusieurs mots
réprobatifs appliqués aux terroristes . . . qui, par la manière dont ils sont placés,

pourraient s'appliquer aux amis de la patrie et de la liberté, et fournir aux roy-
alistes des occasions de hasarder leurs scandaleux applaudissements." (This play
contains several disparaging words targeting terrorists . . . which, by the way they
are placed, could be applied to friends of the nation and of liberty, and could
provide royalists with opportunities to venture their scandalous applause.)[46]
Even a topical play with a clearly progovernment message could serve as a pretext for partisan conflict, on account of the spectators' ability to inverse the
meaning of a political observation. Any reference to the recent past, be it praise-
ful or disapproving, was liable to inspire the spectators to voice their opinions
on the present. In other words, it was not just the liberty and multiplicity of the
theaters under the Revolution that made playhouses a privileged site of discord
and sedition; it was also their fixation on current events. As *Le censeur dramatique* concluded, the Council of Five Hundred's dream of a single voice or political message in praise of general republican mores would remain unattainable
so long as topicality governed the creation and the reception of plays, turning
any work it touched into a weapon that could be used and abused by not just
one but multiple factions.[47]

 Not only did topicality threaten the unity of the Directory's political vision
(by lending itself too readily to conflicting interpretations), it also challenged its
generality. A paragraph from a report by the Commission d'instruction publique best captures this fear:

> À ne considérer ces productions que du côté politique, . . . on ne peut discon-
> venir que leur but général, leur marche commune, ne soient de saisir le goût
> du moment plutôt que la pensée publique et éternelle, d'imiter plus que de
> créer, de ne conquérir enfin que des applaudissements de circonstance. De là
> leur nullité politique.
>
> Examining these performances from a political perspective only, . . . one can-
> not deny that their general aim, their common progress, is to capture the
> taste of the moment rather than public and eternal thought, to imitate more
> than to create, to conquer, lastly, only circumstantial applause. Hence their
> political nothingness.[48]

The leap from "circumstantial applause" ("applaudissements de circonstance")
to "political nothingness" ("nullité politique") is fascinating. Its logic lies perhaps within that strange term, "circumstantial," and its two seemingly unrelated
definitions: "secondary, incidental" but also "detailed, particular." Taken
together, these two meanings perfectly capture the nature of a *pièce de circonstance*, which exists in the realm of the particular, offering specific, familiar
details, yet often lacks as a result more important, general lessons—"la pensée
publique et éternelle"—thereby becoming incidental, mere nothingness. In arguing that immediate, political engagement was incompatible with the theater's

ability to impart broader civic lessons, politicians and journalists were in fact
reviving one of the ancien régime's leading arguments against topical theater.
Classical thinkers believed that staging recent events elicited from the spectators an unmediated, visceral involvement in the particularities of the story,
thereby preventing them from recognizing and reflecting upon its more universal, timeless message.[49] If, as previously noted, it proved nearly impossible for a
spectator attending a play mocking known Terrorists to focus on its aesthetic
quality, it was no easier to engage in a reasoned examination of the need for an
independent justice system or of the pros and cons of denunciation in a republic.
What was missing, in either case, was distance, the kind of distance that would
have made it possible to boo a character—say, Maximilien de Robespierre—as
a character (that is, as an artistic creation, well or poorly written and interpreted)
or as a symbol (illustrating a greater truth), and not simply as a stand-in for the
real Robespierre. In her study of theatrical laughter in the eighteenth century,
Stéphanie Fournier provides numerous examples of the Directory demanding
that parts of comedies—a character, a couple of sentences, sometimes just a few
words—be rewritten to prevent all possible "applications" (an eighteenth-century
term referring to the common practice among spectators of giving a new, topical meaning to a play or line in a play via a well-placed interjection). As a result,
Fournier notes, "on ne peut pratiquement plus se moquer de rien, sauf de types
immatériels, peu ancrés dans l'actualité" (one can practically no longer mock
anything, aside from immaterial types, disconnected from current affairs).[50]
The trend, in other words, was to return to the ancien régime's strict separation between the characters and events onstage and those beyond the audito-
rium doors. The journalists and politicians of the Directory never abandoned
the belief that the theater should have a political impact on the present; they
simply came to the conclusion that staging the present would diminish, not
heighten, this impact, by collapsing the distance on which comparison and reflection depend.

The End of Topicality

The proposals by the Council of Five Hundred met broad opposition in the
Council of Ancients, dooming them to failure. Yet these debates, along with
those in the press, elaborated a wide-ranging critique of topicality that would
have a profound and lasting impact. After 1797 it became ever easier and common to argue that topicality undermined the proper function of theater, however one chose to define that function—aesthetic enjoyment, civic instruction,
or both. More than just the theater's function, in fact, it was its very nature that
was perceived to be at stake: many members of the Directory—and, later, of the
Consulate and the French Empire—felt a responsibility to revive the theater as
play, by requiring once more, as under the ancien régime, that the world onstage

be clearly distant and different from the world offstage. There is much evidence to suggest that they were successful. Reading through reports by theater critics and state censors in the last few years of the eighteenth century, it becomes clear that dramatic audiences grew increasingly reluctant to use applications to transform plays into commentaries on current affairs. Hence, *Le journal de Paris*, having cautioned that a play, *Auguste et Théodore*, would produce frequent applications, was surprised and pleased to report instead, "Le calme qui a régné sur la représentation entière est de bon augure, il faut espérer que nous pourrons restituer aux théâtres les chefs-d'œuvre des grands maîtres, trop longtemps abandonnés." (The calm that reigned over the entire performance is a good omen; we must hope that we will thus be able to revive in the theaters the chefs-d'oeuvre of the great masters, for too long abandoned.)[51] This change in audience behavior was so widespread, according to one state official, that it amounted to no less than "une véritable métamorphose; la chose publique y est respectée; on y omet les applications injurieuses au gouvernement" (a veritable metamorphosis; public affairs are respected, and applications injurious to the government are omitted).[52] This avoidance of direct references to political matters inspired playwrights to do the same, even in the historically subversive genre of vaudeville: "Ceux qui gouvernent aujourd'hui sont plus imposants ou plus irréprochables, sans doute, car le vaudeville les ménage avec une prudence qu'il n'eut jamais sous le règne de nos anciens despotes." (Those who govern today are more imposing or irreproachable, no doubt, since vaudeville spares them with a prudence it never showed under the reign of our former despots.)[53] Tellingly, it was not just political allusions but any form of topicality that grew undesirable. In December 1798 a censor congratulated the author of *Léonore ou L'amour conjugal* for having written "[une pièce] absolument étrangère à la Révolution" (a play utterly unrelated to the Revolution), adding, "Ou du moins elle paraît n'y avoir aucun rapport, quoique le fait qui lui sert de fondement se soit passé en France, pendant le règne de la Terreur. Pour éviter toute application, l'auteur a transporté en Espagne le plus beau modèle de la piété conjugale." (Or at least it appears to have no relation to it, even though the fact that serves as its foundation happened in France during the Reign of Terror. To avoid any application, the author transported it to Spain.)[54] Just a few years earlier, the plot's origin in a recent true story would have been highlighted—the real prisoner or his heroic wife might even have been invited to attend the premiere, as Joseph Cange and others had been— but by 1798, such topicality was deliberately concealed by transposing the events to a distant land or era, precisely the kind of fiction that was once imposed to ancien régime playwrights.

This shift away from topicality, undertaken mostly willingly (if under close surveillance), would become far more compulsory in 1800 following a directive from the minister of police, Joseph Fouché, to all theater directors. Written in response to a play praising the Coup of 18 Brumaire, the directive demanded that it and other plays like it be banned, even when their political message coincided with the current regime's. Fouché denounced the topical theater of previous Revolutionary governments, which had been so full of gratuitous insults for defeated parties and craven flattery for the victors that it had only strengthened factiousness among the French by fomenting resentment and keeping alive the memory of past divisions. As Fouché understood, reviving a coup, even to praise it, meant opening it to the applications, debates, and possible disapproval of an inherently uncontrollable public. This was the lesson of Revolutionary drama: the too explicitly political undermines the greater political good. For Fouché, this greater good resided in the national unity, moderation, and stability that the Coup of 18 Brumaire had supposedly engendered, and which would be lost were it too aggressively politicized in topical plays.[55] The solution—to eschew topicality altogether, whatever the message—harks back to the ancien régime, a parallel made all the more conspicuous by Napoleon Bonaparte's decision on July 29, 1807, to limit the number of theaters in Paris to eight. If the proliferation and lax surveillance of theaters after January 13, 1791, had inspired a wave of *pièces de circonstances* in the early years of the Revolution, the inverse would now lead to their decline, just as the Council of Five Hundred had predicted. Of course, this decline did not result in a complete disappearance of topical theater. Never again, however, would the latter possess anywhere near the centrality and influence that it did between 1789 and 1797. In short, plays were, once again, play. As proof, one need only look at the *bataille d'Hernani*, where the boos rained down on everything except the play's clear links to the present, as if topicality had taken a fall down the famous "Escalier / Dérobé."

NOTES

Unless noted otherwise, all translations are my own.

1. *La feuille du salut public*, October 25, 1793. The same newspaper condemned an Arlequin play in similar terms: "Elle est étrangère à la chose publique, donc elle est coupable" (The play is unrelated to public affairs; thus it is guilty.) *La feuille du salut public*, February 19, 1794.

2. *Le journal des spectacles*, August 14, 1793.

3. *La feuille du salut public*, October 30, 1793.

4. The image of the theater as a Roman forum is a common one among both Revolutionaries and modern scholars. See, for instance, Annette Graczyk, "Le théâtre de la Révolution française, média de masses entre 1789 et 1794," *Dix-huitième siècle* 21 (1989): 396.

5. Emmet Kennedy, Marie-Laurence Netter, James P. McGregor, and Mark V. Olsen, *Theatre, Opera, and Audiences in Revolutionary Paris: Analysis and Repertory* (Westport, CT: Greenwood, 1996).

6. Yann Robert, *Dramatic Justice: Trial by Theater in the Age of the French Revolution* (Philadelphia: University of Pennsylvania Press, 2019).

7. According to Philippe Bourdin, 160 of the 239 plays that premiered in Parisian theaters at the Terror's peak (September 1793–July 1794) contained clearly politicized themes; see Philippe Bourdin, *Aux origines du théâtre patriotique* (Paris: CNRS Editions, 2017), 95. Serge Bianchi, "Théâtre et engagement sur les scènes de l'an II," in *Littérature et engage-*

ment pendant la révolution française, ed. Isabelle Brouard-Arends and Laurent Loty (Rennes, France: Presses universitaires de Rennes, 2007), 33, cites an even higher tally: more than two hundred topical plays in year II.

8. See, for example, Robert, *Dramatic Justice*; Bourdin, *Aux origines*; Judith Schlanger, *L'enjeu et le débat* (Paris: Éditions Denoël, 1979); Mark Darlow, "Staging the Revolution: The *Fait historique*," *Nottingham French Studies* 45, no. 1 (2006): 77–88; Suzanne Jean Bérard, "Une curiosité du théâtre à l'époque révolutionnaire, les 'Faits historiques et patriotiques,'" *Romanistische Zeitschrift für Literaturgeschichte* 3 (1979): 250–77; and Pierre Frantz, "Pas d'entracte pour la Révolution," in *La Carmagnole des muses: L'homme de lettres et l'artiste dans la Révolution*, ed. Jean-Claude Bonnet (Paris: Armand Colin, 1988).

9. Schlanger, *L'enjeu*, 135.

10. Schlanger, *L'enjeu*, 138, observes, "[Le théâtre] constitue à l'intérieur de la réalité globale un secteur homogène au reste mais puissamment actif et doué d'une intense efficience." (The theater constitutes, within global reality, a field homogeneous with the rest but powerfully active and endowed with an intense efficiency.)

11. Robert, *Dramatic Justice*, 191–262.

12. This is, thankfully, starting to change. For instance, two book-length studies of Revolutionary theater extend into the Directory and beyond. See Bourdin, *Aux origines*; and Stéphanie Fournier, *Rire au théâtre à Paris à la fin du XVIIIe siècle* (Paris: Garnier, 2016).

13. Bourdin begins writing that history at the end of his book (even if, as the title *Aux origines du théâtre patriotique* suggests, most of the book's focus lies earlier).

14. The dramatic criticism of the Directory has received little scholarly attention, in contrast to its precursor from the early years of the Revolution (1789–94). For a good overview, see Michel Biard, "Thalie et Melpomène face à leurs juges: La critique théâtrale sous le Directoire," in *La République directoriale*, ed. Philippe Bourdin and Bernard Gainot (Clermont-Ferrand, France: Société des études robespierristes, 1998). On *Le censeur dramatique* and its ambivalent views on topicality, see Sophie Marchand, "Le temps du théâtre d'après le 'Censeur dramatique,'" *Studi Francesi* 169 (2013): 123–35. On one of the period's most important newspapers, *La décade philosophique*, and its depiction of post-Thermidorian theater, see Marc Régaldo, *Un milieu intellectuel: "La décade philosophique" (1794–1807)*, 5 vols. (Lille: Atelier de reproduction des thèses, 1976).

15. One study is entirely devoted to this debate; see Michèle Sajous D'Oria, "Les tréteaux de la corruption," in *La scène bâtarde: Entre Lumières et romantisme*, ed. Philippe Bourdin and Gérard Loubinoux (Clermont-Ferrand, France: Presses universitaires Blaise Pascal, 2004), 269–82. A few other works mention it briefly, including Emmet Kennedy, *A Cultural History of the French Revolution* (New Haven, CT: Yale University Press, 1989), 183–85; and Bourdin, *Aux origines*, 402–6.

16. Aubin-Louis Millin de Grandmaison, *La chronique de Paris*, October 2, 1791. See also his articles in *La chronique de Paris*, March 20 and September 26, 1791.

17. On dramatic criticism between 9 Thermidor and the start of the Directory (1794–95), see Emmet Kennedy, "Taste and Revolution," *Annales canadiennes d'histoire* 32, no. 3 (1997): 375–92. Kennedy's article differs from this chapter in that it focuses on an earlier time period and does not connect accusations of bad taste to topical theater.

18. As was noted in *La décade philosophique*, May 19, 1794, "Fabriquées à la hâte, tout leur mérite est de nous indiquer l'intention patriote de l'auteur." (Written in haste, their only merit is to show us the patriotic intention of their author.)

19. *La décade philosophique*, November 20, 1794. See also *La feuille du salut public*, April 7, 1794.

20. *Le journal de Paris*, November 29, 1793.

21. *La décade philosophique*, May 19, 1794. See also *La décade philosophique*, June 18, 1794.

22. *La décade philosophique*, March 20, 1795.

23. Édouard Marie-Joseph Le Pan, *Le courrier des spectacles*, February 9, 1797.

24. As we will see, deputies engaged in a lengthy debate in 1797 about the need to reestablish a system of privileged theaters and state-pensioned artists. In this they followed and amplified earlier proposals in the press (see Biard, "Thalie et Melpomène"). Likewise, the desire for refined audiences and repertoires was not limited to the press. Ling-Ling Sheu, *Voltaire et Rousseau dans le théâtre de la Révolution française* (Brussels: Éditions de l'Université de Bruxelles, 2005), 11, has noted the return during the Directory of a more educated and wealthy audience, following an increase in seat prices in 1795. According to Bianchi, "Théâtre et engagement," 43, this social revolution in the parterre led to the renewed popularity of the classical repertoire, more suited to the taste of the cultural elites.

25. *La feuille critique et littéraire*, December 5, 1794.

26. *Le courrier des spectacles*, February 9, 1797.

27. *Le courrier des spectacles*, February 3, 1797.

28. *La feuille critique et littéraire*, December 5, 1794.

29. *La feuille du jour*, January 25, 1794.

30. *La gazette nationale, ou Le moniteur universel*, February 14, 1790.

31. The spy's report can be found in *Tableaux de la Révolution française*, vol. 2, ed. Adolf Schmidt (Leipzig: Veit, 1867), 67. It states that "à de telles pièces, le Français est encore plus citoyen qu'il n'est spectateur" (at plays of the sort, the French are more citizens than they are spectators).

32. *La feuille du salut public*, April 7, 1794.

33. *La décade philosophique*, March 20, 1795.

34. *Le courrier des spectacles*, February 2, 1797.

35. *Le courrier des spectacles*, February 16, 1797.

36. La Chabeaussière wrote articles in *La décade philosophique* on August 7, August 17, and September 16, 1797, calling for theatrical reforms months before Chénier's legislative motion in November. Amaury Duval published a pamphlet describing similar reforms that he conceived, or so he claimed, long before La Chabeaussière and Chénier; see Amaury Duval, *Observations sur les théâtres* (Paris: Imprimerie des sciences et arts), 1.

37. Régaldo, *Un milieu intellectuel*, 3:1462–63.

38. Marie-Joseph Chénier, *Corps législatif. Conseil des Cinq-Cents. Motion d'ordre par Chénier sur les théâtres, séance du 26 brumaire an VI* (Paris: Imprimerie nationale, 1797).

39. *La décade philosophique*, August 7, 1797.

40. See François Lamarque, *Opinion de F. Lamarque sur les théâtres: Séance du 2 germinal an 6* (Paris: Imprimerie nationale, 1798), 16.

41. *Le journal de Paris*, March 18, 1798.

42. *Le journal de Paris*, March 18, 1798.

43. Pierre Jean Audouin, *Rapport fait par Audouin, sur les théâtres, séance du 25 pluviôse an 6* (Paris: Imprimerie nationale, 1798), 3, 2, 10, 13.

44. *Le journal de Paris*, March 18, 1798.

45. Ange-Étienne-Xavier Poisson de La Chabeaussière, *La décade philosophique*, December 20, 1797.

46. *La décade philosophique*, April 19, 1795.

47. As was noted in *Le censeur dramatique*, April 9, 1798, "Il n'est aucune tragédie qui ne put fournir ainsi des armes à tous les partis, et le plus innocent des plaisirs deviendrait, dans les mains de l'imprudence, un continuel sujet de discorde, de divisions, de proscriptions et même de massacres." (There is no tragedy that could not thereby supply weapons to all the factions, and the most innocent of pleasures would become, in imprudent hands, a continual subject of discord, of divisions, of proscriptions, and even of massacres.)

48. *Procès-verbaux du Comité d'instruction publique de la Convention nationale*, vol. 4, ed. James Guillaume (Paris: Imprimerie nationale, 1901), 712.

49. Robert, *Dramatic Justice*, 24–27.

50. Fournier, *Rire au théâtre*, 645.

51. *Le journal de Paris*, January 27, 1797.

52. *Paris pendant la réaction thermidorienne et sous le Directoire*, vol. 4, ed. François-Alphonse Aulard (Paris: Cerf, 1902), 384.

53. Jean-Marie-Bernard Clément, *Journal littéraire*, March 9, 1797.

54. The censor's report can be found in Odile Krakovitch, "Le théâtre de la République et la censure sous le Directoire," in *Le théâtre sous la Révolution: Politique du répertoire (1789–1799)*, ed. Martial Poirson (Paris: Desjonquères, 2008), 183.

55. See Bourdin, *Aux origines*, 411.

CHAPTER 10

Video Games as Cultural History

PROCEDURAL NARRATIVE AND THE
EIGHTEENTH-CENTURY FAIR THEATER

Jeffrey M. Leichman

This chapter describes an experimental approach to writing the history of the eighteenth-century Fair theater, a flourishing venue for performing arts (including singing, dancing, acrobatics, and theater) that has consistently been marginalized in cultural histories of this period, as well as within canonical European theater histories. Academic interest in Fair theater has been revived in the past few decades, notably through the work of the Centre d'études sur les théâtres de la foire et de la comédie italienne (CETHEFI), based at the Université de Nantes, where masters theses and doctoral dissertations, scientific editions of manuscript plays, and multiyear collaborative digital humanities projects have greatly increased the visibility of a cultural phenomenon that had the rare virtue of appealing to a wide cross-section of the highly stratified society of ancien régime Paris.[1] The project under discussion here seeks to build on this work by leveraging the affordances of playable digital environments as a serious research tool for professional academics, while at the same time making eighteenth-century cultural history accessible—and enjoyable—for a larger public through the medium of the video game.

Video game itself is a loaded term, meeting Raymond Williams's definition of a "keyword" in which "certain uses bound together certain ways of seeing culture and society" and "certain other uses . . . open up issues and problems."[2] This is particularly true with respect to the intersection of historical scholarship and video games, in which academic deontology is often held to be incompatible with the ludic imperative of games, not least when the field is restricted to products created for worldwide distribution by the commercial video game industry.[3] Yet as one might expect in a domain of cultural production as mature and widespread as video games, the term encompasses a wide range of human-computer interactive environments, many of which explicitly recuse the essentially accumulative logic of the most profitable video game franchises.[4] The narrative architecture of both first-person-shooter and resource-management-style games that dominate the world of historical gaming often put the goals of the video game at odds with those of the historian. Yet the emergence of digital humanities as both an object of study and a loosely defined set of methodologies has opened up a far wider understanding of how video games might fit into this field, including those designed and constructed by and for scholars.[5] This kind of game clearly has a different audience in mind than do the blockbusters designed by major studios, and as a result it is able to explore design and gameplay options that might be unavailable to products principally designed for a highly competitive commercial industry. Such is the case for the game being developed in the Virtual Early Modern Spectacles and Publics, Active and Collaborative Environment (VESPACE) project, which, as the anticipated research outcome of a publicly financed international research collaboration, is unconstrained by sales considerations that might drive interface and content decisions in an industrial setting.[6] As a result, rather than submitting our development decisions to this kind of commercial logic, the VESPACE project aims to explore the implications of advanced immersive graphic environments and procedural rhetoric on the conceptualization and construction of the past, both for professional scholars and the wider public. What is at stake when making history playable?

Narrative Trouble

One immediate consequence of positing games as a valid mode of historical storytelling is to again focus scholars' attention on the role of narrative in the creation of modern historical "truth." The advantages and pitfalls of narrative representation have been a particular focus of historiographic theory from the second half of the twentieth century onward. This discursive reflexivity was accompanied—not necessarily causally, but perhaps not coincidentally—with a suspicion of "grand narratives" that were increasingly disparaged as vehicles of ideological control dressed up in the rhetoric of objectivity in order to consolidate status quo power relations by endowing them with an historic inevitability. In partial response to this, the institutional study of history turned to memory as an archival source with at least as much validity as official records and individual artifacts, privileging micronarratives (and their attendant biases) as an essential source for understanding the present as the expression of a shared, and contested, past.[7] Within this already fractured landscape, digital technologies have in turn exploded previous constraints on both the preservation and accessibility of all kinds of documents. From oral histories of eyewitnesses to handwritten notarial records, digital copies of nearly anything can be accessed from nearly anywhere, bringing a flood of information that has revealed further challenges to the conceptualization of history as a discretely containable story. The vertical hierarchy imposed by the historian's narrative gives way to an "open world" horizontality that privileges jumping from document to document, a hypertextual mode that obliterates the standard view of history as an analytical object that can be encompassed by a univocal, unidirectional, spatially contained narration. In this context, Ann Rigney argues that "the 'book' should no longer provide the exclusive model for theoretical reflection on narrativity and the production of historical knowledge."[8] Rather, in our current context, *data* (disconnected points of information, not necessarily subjected to verification or contextualization) compete with and often overwhelm *historical facts* (intellectual constructs that take their meaning from a theoretical underpinning and a narrative progression) as the source of truth about the past, implicitly asserting the equivalency of all traces and often attributing the greatest authority to the largest accumulation of individual items. While the professional discipline of history is not threatened with extinction any time soon, the internet-enabled proliferation of theories and speculations backed up by mountains of online "proof" illustrates the degree to which historians have been dethroned as the arbiters of truth about the past. In our age of ubiquitous history, what is the value—and what are the values—of history?

The eighteenth century gave rise to a form of history writing whose effects continue to reverberate through the academic history community. Breaking away from the tradition of chronicles and hagiography, in which the past serves primarily as a vast reserve of exempla, a template for understanding all possible present actions as repetitions of an eternal story, Enlightenment historiographers incorporated powerful narrative strategies that borrowed structural features from fiction, in the process endowing history with a teleology of progress.[9] Initially, recording events served to memorialize them such that they could serve as lessons and be recognized when they inevitably occurred again. By contrast, Enlightenment positivism situated the past as prologue rather than iteration, a transitional phase on the way toward a modernity represented by the triumph of reason. Suddenly there was a need for distance and context, for *representations* that make events into evidence pointing toward the present, as opposed to the cyclical reoccurrence of an eternally repeating pattern that proves the essentially repetitive, static nature of a divinely-ordered world. For Claudio Fogu, the current technological environment, with its mutually reinforcing drives toward digitizing documents and replacing textual description with the plasticity of the digital image, has pushed history toward both a *virtualization* (in opposition to late-eighteenth-century "transcendental and immanent conceptions of historical action, representation, and consciousness") and a *spatialization* ("away from the temporal axis of narrative forms of historical consciousness")—two characteristics that are also constitutive of the video game form.[10]

A venerable tradition of video games taking historical subjects as their theme has given rise to perceptive scholarly evaluations and critiques of the historical validity of this model. The focus of most of this work is understandably on commercial releases set in historical eras, including the French ancien régime, in games like *Versailles 1685: Complot à la cour du Roi-soleil* (Cryo Interactive, 1996) and *Assassin's Creed: Unity* (Ubisoft, 2005).[11] Modern history has also proved remarkably fertile territory for video game exploration, with a predilection for armed-conflict games, including the World War II–themed initial installments of the *Call of Duty* series (Infinity Ward, 2003–6), which launched the perennially profitable and popular trend of first-person-shooter historical games. On a more macrohistorical scale, the *Sid Meier's Civilization* series (1991–2016) allows players to control a six-thousand-year progression of world history in a strategy game that emphasizes allocation of resources (and thus a more systemic, and ideological, view of historical processes), as opposed to the inclusion of specific historical data that characterizes simulation-based games that replay discrete events.[12] Historians' interest in these mass-market entertainment products has coincided with the rise of a new academic discipline, game studies, which treats the construction and effects of computer games with the same seriousness that is accorded to literature or film, identifying genre-based characteristics and analyzing the poetics—both narrative and procedural—that have made video games an extremely profitable and massively popular worldwide phenomenon.

In his analysis of computer games and/as history, William Uricchio emphasizes how the distance that separates representation (as in the discursive-textual mode) from simulation (in the visual-digital mode) marks an important epistemological shift away from fixed meaning to player-centered performance.[13] That the representational mode of narrative has remained a gold standard for professional historical practice—despite the well-developed critiques of its reliance on a through line that requires causal linkages between events[14]—testifies to the resilience of a form that has turned the acknowledgment of its shortcomings into the seal of its scientific accuracy: every definitive history contains within it the seeds of the next revision, or renarrativization, that will make a new story of what is otherwise held to be a fixed and stable past. Games, for Uricchio, offer the possibility to elude certain language-based traps with their recourse to visual rhetoric; but, more important, they thematize the instability inherent to historical interpretation by making this the point of entry for the "reader"—now a player—for whom the knowledge of historical constraints conforming to widely accepted "objective" research practices (usually in the form of recourse to period-appropriate primary resources) is the ground on which she will construct a possible sequence of events in the course of gameplay. As Uricchio writes, "a simulation is a machine for producing speculative or conditional representations."[15] This inherently reflexive and subjective mode of history appears to respond to postmodern critiques of historiography's blind spot with respect to narrative, but Uricchio points out that certain problems that confront conventional histories still apply (fixed starting and ending points, a selective definition of the historical "real," etc.). His conclusions call for historians to engage with game form not as consultants whose presence implicitly underwrites the "truth" of the visual representation but in order to "[embed] various historiographic epistemologies as structuring agencies" for the game.[16]

SEEING IS BELIEVING

The importance accorded to visual accuracy and lushly detailed graphic environments underscores the widespread failure of games like the World War II simulation *Brothers in Arms: Road to Hill 30* (Gearbox Software, 2005) to otherwise engage the player's empathy and motivate the kind of investment in the protagonist's journey that is characteristic of film or literature. The attention to external details harks back to the creed of historical reenactment, with the notable exception that most console-based games exclude the reenactor's embodied experience of history, as the controller interface maps recognizable (if not always plausible) character movements to repetitive fine-motor actions involving buttons or levers. In addition to effectively eliminating the body's myriad sensory interfaces from the visual experience of history, the weakly scripted and wooden interpersonal interactions of many video games rob them of emotional impact. Brian Rejack argues that in the absence of emotional engagement, "the developers turn to history and its potential for creating sympathetic identification" by underscoring their fidelity to period details, landscapes, and costume in an effort to paper over both the characters' lack of human qualities and kinetic onscreen action that excludes the gamer's physicality. By way of contrast, Rejack briefly discusses the now-classic game *Façade* (Playabl Studios, 2006), which works with an artificial-intelligence-driven behavioral simulation to create lifelike interactions. Rejack speculates that games that "unite the attention to environments and action with equal focus on dramatic and emotional detail" represent one path forward toward a video game that offers the combination of engagement and veracity that characterizes the best history writing while retaining the unique ludic potential of games whose invitation to active participation exposes the implicit contingencies imposed by narrative structure.[17] Combining visual fidelity grounded in archive-based research with an interactive social world that seeks to provide the same richness of meaningful choice as is habitually accorded to action sequences in major commercial releases, the VESPACE project seeks to leverage contemporary developments in several domains of computer gaming technology.

For the purposes of the VESPACE game, the project team has chosen to model the most prestigious of the Paris fairs, the Foire Saint-Germain, whose eighteenth-century dates were fixed between February 3 and Palm Sunday. Beginning in the late fifteenth century, the Saint-Germain Abbey hosted a commercial bazaar that became an attractive site of social and commercial exchange for the urban population of Paris. The presence of crowds in turn drew performers, and particularly by the time of the regency of Philippe d'Orléans (1715–23), a sophisticated theatrical culture had developed, offering entertainments that ranged from acrobatics and puppetry to the new form of *opéra comique* whose signature "vaudeville" songs recycled well-known tunes, pairing them with new lyrics to advance the plots of the Fair's original comedies and parodies. Combining artistic originality and a carnivalesque rejection of social and esthetic hierarchies, the Fair theater developed into a highly appreciated leisure time activity for audiences whose composition reflected an unusual degree of social diversity for this period.[18] Today there remains no physical trace of this massive covered market that once occupied the heart of Paris; in its former location there is now the Marché Saint-Germain, which includes an Apple Store.

Because the finality of our game is research rather than commercial sales, the choice to work in a virtual reality (VR) graphic environment was not principally motivated by the quest for novel thrills that would incite consumers to purchase consoles or software. Rather, a VR environment allows for the illusion of presence necessary to give appropriate consistency to the period-specific social interactions that comprise the user's point of entry into the computer-modeled world. Furthermore, the physical postures of virtual reality, in which a headset creates an immersive visual and auditory environment whose perspective changes to follow the user's movement through space,[19] simulate a kind of embodiment that might otherwise require the investment in construction and materials associated with historical reenactment.[20] But, perhaps most obviously, VR offers an unparalleled experience of architecture, adjusting the perspective to each user's actual height and eye position, such that the illusion of presence within the graphic representation of the space is complete. For historical restitution, the possibilities seem almost limitless, but the specific case around which our project is articulated also underscores the caution with which professional researchers must approach ever more convincing technologies of illusion. There is nothing left of the Foire Saint-Germain, neither physical remains nor architectural plans; iconographic records, cadastral drawings, notarial documents, and textual descriptions can all provide clues, but each of these sources must be handled with appropriate care, as each responds to particular descriptive codes determined by its representative mode and function. Given the sparseness of these (occasionally unreliable) sources with respect to the Fair theaters, the immense potential of VR as a persuasive medium also emerges as its greatest vulnerability with respect to historical research. The potential weight given to erroneous interpretation is amplified by the exceptionally convincing nature of immersive representation, implicitly underwritten by the academic credentials of its authors. For the VESPACE game prototype, Paul François has modeled a small marionette theater based on a miniature by Louis-Nicolas van Blarenbergh, a restitution that respects the norms of scholarly circumspection and architectural soundness.[21] At the same time, the project team has developed and adopted a design principle called "image depth," which seeks to make the evidence underpinning the visual interpretation available to users within the immersive environment, to serve as a counterbalance to the seemingly incontrovertible evidence provided by the senses.

Yet in theorizing a game that can be used as a tool for historical research, the VESPACE project looks beyond the careful contextualization of the sensory apparatus that, certain technical aspects notwithstanding, closely resembles the work one might find in an interactive museum display that allows for a fully annotated exploration of a digital reconstitution. Rather, the VESPACE project seeks to also engage with the central problem of narrative in the construction of the historical past. Here the video game mode bumps up against the linear cohesion of a classical historical narrative, which Wulf Kansteiner posits as the only "flexible yet sturdy enough hermeneutic tool to acknowledge difference and sublate it within consistent overarching interpretive frameworks which are psychologically and politically useful."[22] Kansteiner's well-founded critique of the effect of video games on the popular understanding of history rests on the rise of immersive technologies (which the VESPACE project specifically attempts to leverage) that foster a perception of nonmediation through the perfection of technologies of illusion, similar to the renaturing artifice of Wolmar's garden in Jean-Jacques Rousseau's *La nouvelle Héloïse*. Just as Rousseau imagines a landscape that perfects nature by erasing all signs of its own facticity, and just as his novel elicited intensely absorptive reactions in its readers, Kansteiner acknowledges that all media tend to fulfill the needs of their historical moment, with each era inventing the most complete illusion it can conceive until the next representational breakthrough again redefines the limits of the perceptual real, immediately invalidating the previous instruments of our fascination—from novels to movies to TV and, finally, in Kansteiner's reading, to video games. By virtue of their perfected technology and the limits of human sensory neurology, Kansteiner posits computer-generated immersive environments as the end of this series (although twelve years and several technological generations after his article, there is certainly room to imagine further improvement).

Yet the sensory aspect of video games is but one half of the equation; unlike an immersive film, the video game disrupts the controlled flow of narrative, inserting the player's agency within the unfolding of the story. For a video game to be successful as an enjoyable ludic experience, there must be the option to make meaningful choices that change the course of the story, giving rise to the thorny problem of counterfactual history. In Kansteiner's dystopian vision, the overwriting of collective memory as a reflection of culture in favor of a set of viscerally engaging (and thus highly memorable) historically-inflected video game experiences unmoors players from the influence of intergenerational, political, or social contexts that help make sense of history and understand its effect on molding the present. In the combination of interactivity and immersion, Kansteiner predicts the end of historical consciousness grounded in a shared sense of time, place, or values, as gamers forge new and more vivid memories within visually persuasive and narratively flexible worlds that can be made to persuasively resemble the historical past. The threat lies specifically in the amputation of the social aspect of historical consciousness, the enclosure within an isolating relationship with the machine that generates an atomized experience of the past susceptible to endless variation and rewriting without input from any of the traditional cultural forces that have helped mold our sense of historical progress since the Enlightenment.

PROCEDURALITY AND CULTURAL HISTORY

Kansteiner's arguments, as well as those of the many other theoretical historians who have engaged with the challenge of interactive narrative to traditional notions of history, tend to focus on the wholesale rewriting of major historical events, in which the counterfactual example of a victorious Third Reich emerges as a kind of ultimate historical disjunction made possible by "playable" historical narrative. Yet this particular scenario has a long and storied history in fiction and media representations (including the Amazon TV series *The Man in the High Castle*, based on a Philip K. Dick novel), and counterfactual history has not waited for digital technology to gain popularity in many quarters, including among professional historians.[23]

In their critique of the narrative problems attendant to interactive media, most historians treat video games themselves as immutable facts, ignoring what game designer and theorist Ian Bogost has termed their "procedural rhetoric," "a technique for making arguments with computational systems and for unpacking computational arguments others have created."[24] While few serious scholars would attempt a critique of written narrative without at least some familiarity with the mechanics of literary rhetoric, there is a similar field of knowledge that can help understand how video games function as arguments (in this case, about history) and thus how they, too, might be used to further scholarship. As nearly all critics mention, the sheer size of the video game industry points to a widespread and durable cultural phenomenon, and thus it seems incumbent on scholars to approach video games with a level of structural scrutiny that is similar to that which they bring to bear on novels and films. At a minimum, turning this attention toward instructional ends may help equip our students—very many of them self-identified gamers—with an awareness of the influence exercised by video games on their understanding of the world as it is and as it was.

The latitude afforded by public funding permits projects like VESPACE to ask how video games can be made to serve the needs of researchers in historical fields. Among other things, this facilitates a focus on cultural history that, despite being a major current in academic history over the last few decades, is conspicuously absent from the treatment of history in mass-market video games. One practical consequence of choosing the eighteenth-century Fair theater as an object of study instead of, say, World War II, is that the scope of the available information is far narrower and has been subjected to far less polemic around its interpretation, in effect lowering the stakes and allowing for a less emotionally charged assessment of the role of procedurality in a digital-interactive restitution. The player is neither a godlike manipulator of global societies seeking to dominate others over the vast sweep of millennia, nor a soldier faced with life-and-death decisions in the heat of battle, but rather a spectator at a popular venue for theatrical performance in the first half of the eighteenth century. The choices that are available relate to the sociability of a particular place and time, which in turn becomes the object of the historical argument advanced by the interactive design of the game.

As Tracy Fullerton shows, even independent producers of "documentary games" tend to assume a conception of history based on widely known events, articulating the gamer's intervention around traumatic moments of spectacular violence (President John F. Kennedy's assassination, the Columbine High School massacre). In such cases, "the inherent tension between the knowledge of an event's outcome and the necessity of allowing player agency to affect that outcome" limits the effectiveness of the video game form for historical research.[25] This incompatibility of interactivity and historical narrative rests on the assumption that the object of historical narrative is always a specific moment—a punctual event or sequence of events whose progress can be corroborated with recourse to archival documents, and whose "outcome" is assumed to be known. Yet many histories—and, in particular, cultural histories—use these same evidentiary standards to describe conditions and mentalities, on the assumption that these excavations are themselves essential to understanding conceptions and practices that are the antecedents of the charismatic events so prominently featured in popular history and game design. By way of example, the first chapter of Jeffrey Ravel's *The Contested Parterre* recounts how an evening might unfold for spectators at the eighteenth-century Paris theater in convincing and vivid detail.[26] Yet this study does not trace a particular outing that can be said to have definitively taken place, even if many thousands of similar experiences would plausibly have occurred in the lives of theatergoers at this time. Rather, in this and similar instances, the historian is describing cultural practices that create the space of possibility for the historical transformations wrought by major events.[27]

The social interactions in the VESPACE game are governed by an artificial intelligence-driven *social physics* engine. Social physics is a computing metaphor that describes a set of rules that determine the volition of characters in a given time and place. Initially developed for the independently produced game *Prom Week*, social physics relies on a weighted utility scoring system to calibrate the reactions of non-player characters to player decisions.[28] In *Prom Week*, which takes place in the days leading up to the end-of-the-year dance at an American high school in the early twenty-first century, characters are assigned traits that can be self-directed, other-directed, or reciprocal, and which can have either Boolean (yes/no) or scalar (numeric) values. The system is guided by thousands of hand-authored rules that determine how particular interactions of different traits—an unrequited desire, a penchant for self-aggrandizement, ownership of a particularly cool gadget, for example—affect others whose traits might make them more or less receptive to the advances of a player's avatar. Each change in the rapport between two characters also ripples through the entire social environment, effecting changes in both intimate and distant acquaintances based on the new status of the relationships that result from each interaction, in turn constituting the new baseline for the next set of interactions.

Social physics attempts to answer several challenges that confront computer games. The first is that of creating plausibly lifelike characters, whose reactions to recognizable human situations come across as emotionally true in a way that the simple decision trees that determine most in-game dialogue do not even attempt to simulate. Linked to this is the idea of collaborative storytelling, in which the player and the program create a narrative that neither could have authored individually. Allowing the human player to drive the interactions relieves programmers from the need to determine each successive step of the story; players can choose whatever social-emotional strategy they wish in order to arrive at their goals, which results in a nearly infinite set of permutations for progressing through the game. Yet the player is only responsible for authoring her individual playthrough, as the framework that governs in-game exchanges has been prewritten by the designer-historian in the form of volition rules that are executed when certain conditions are met, changing the desires (and thus the actions) of characters based on the different traits mobilized by each interaction. Player agency is channeled by a theory of sociability programmed into these rules, an example of procedural rhetoric that is effective to the extent that players come to recognize the coherence and believability of the model and can successfully play within its boundaries.

The potential appeal of this mode of writing cultural history is both obvious and deceptively complex. In the example of *Prom Week*, the rules are derived from an ethnographic reading of popular culture sources representing teenage life in early third millennium America, including the TV series remake *Saved by the Bell* and the movie *Mean Girls* (2004). Aimed at an audience that also brings a certain experience of the situation that is being modeled, *Prom Week* relies on contemporary American gamers' outside knowledge to "bootstrap" play, using their intuition and previous experience to guide them through situations that are either analogous to lived experience or familiar from cultural representations. Applying the computing metaphor of social physics to a historical environment requires game authors to think carefully about both the sources of the rules and the expected level of previous knowledge that players might bring to the experience. Expert users, including researchers with a solid grasp of eighteenth-century French mores, will immediately understand how certain aspects of status (especially with respect to nobility, gender, and wealth) exercised a unique influence over comportment, whereas students with little experience with the culture of this period will be more likely to apply the interpretive frameworks resulting from their own socialization to decisions about interpersonal interactions in the game world. In both instances, the quality of the research underpinning the rules is of paramount importance due to the nature of procedural rhetoric in computer games. Unlike in games where achieving goals depends on the voluntary adhesion of players to rules, "dans les jeux vidéo les règles s'appliquent comme des lois de la nature et non comme des lois politiques" (in video games the rules are applied like natural laws rather than like political laws).[29] When the criteria are met, the rule fires; there is no exception. The interpretive work of changing information about the past into a theory of history takes place in the authoring of the procedures; the game offers users an opportunity to test these rules through performance, to inductively learn about the sociability of the past through a first-person trial-and-error experience that progressively leads to mastery and comprehension. But I contend that the suspicion elicited by video games among professional historians resides primarily in the inalterable nature of rules, the procedural structure that governs the way computers operate. The apprehension, perhaps reasonable, is that the seductive sensory environment can serve as a screen for potentially coercive or ideologically suspect theories of history, embedded in rules whose inflexibility covertly reintroduces discredited visions of a rational, predictable, directional schema of historical progress.

It is in this context that the design principle of image depth again becomes an important methodological stance for scholars working in playable digital media. While one can assume a basic level of digital literacy for most students and colleagues (in the ability to navigate common interfaces for communication, information finding, and entertainment), it is urgent to begin incorporating a certain amount of procedural literacy in humanities instruction, also, in order to understand *how* digital tools increasingly shape our perception of reality. With respect to scholarly gaming, the importance of revealing the archival and interpretive underpinnings of computer-based images flows from both their ubiquity and their persuasiveness, all the more so in immersive virtual reality environments. The same can also be said of the social image, the structure that determines the quality and content of the interactions that constitute the gam-

er's activity in the computer-generated world: an important part of the pedagogical value of the game lies in revealing how it works. Conversely, making video
games—and immersing oneself in the procedural thinking required for this
work—might turn out to be even more important for historians than playing
them.

In this vein, the rules-writing process in the VESPACE project is also conceived as a laboratory for future forms of history writing.[30] Unlike in a traditionally conceived narrative, the transformation of data into history adheres to
different rhetorical codes when designing a video game. For the purposes of this
project, researchers look to primary resources for descriptions of behaviors,
atmospheres, and events that limn the possibilities for comportment in a public
theater space in eighteenth-century France, which then must be made legible,
and actionable, for a computer. Working on a collaborative basis (specifically
including graduate students, the next generation of professional scholars), we are
devoted to elaborating workflows and documentation protocols that can provide
the same level of transparency with respect to sources as the citational practices
characteristic of print-based humanities scholarship. Unlike in mainstream
publications, however, the relational aspect of the individual data points—the
ways in which they interact in order to form a necessary causal relationship with
the outcome of a rule—is determined by an algorithm rather than a paragraph.
Consequently, the outcome is also quite different, leading less to a single interpretation than to a set of conditions waiting to be fulfilled—or not. For every
rule that fires, there are thousands that lie dormant, some of which may never, in
fact, find situations that adequately satisfy the requirements allowing their
expression. This temporality, in which rules (which are not yet narrative) await
a potential future that may or may not come to pass, makes procedural narrative
challenging for historical thought. The story is not only constantly rewritten
in the present moment of playing but also lies in wait, always already present in
the expectation of a "reader" who may never wander into the correct combination of circumstances and choices that allow a particular "sentence" to be written. The resulting game is more akin to an experimental setup than a completed
monograph; the computer environment allows for the gamer's peregrinations
through the "text" to be captured and analyzed, the rules calibrated to test for
particular effects (how do choices change, for example, when the rules are
limited strictly to those derived from police archives, versus those derived from
literary sources, versus a combination?), and the relative weighting of different
elements adjusted. The point of "publication" in this instance becomes the start
of another research process, this one centered around the performance of gamers (including scholars), and the conscious choices to adjust the model as their
iterative and highly personalized playthrough readings reveal the strengths and
weaknesses of the underlying conception. If, as game developer Peter Brinson
asserts, "the player's agency is the story,"[31] a procedural approach to cultural

history implicates a certain kind of remediated historical consciousness around this agency as well.

In an age when postmodern critique has entered into mainstream discourse as a generalized distrust of narratives both great and small—with the often desired political effect of eroding consensus around historical consciousness— thematizing procedural rhetoric by explicitly calling attention to its effects on gameplay may be one way of reasserting the value of historical scholarship within a medium that has often been perceived as a threat to the Enlightenment-era foundations of modern historical practice. To the extent that all history reflects the age in which it is written, the plasticity that video games project onto history, which ironically results from the rigidity of proceduralism, is certainly an appropriate expression of present-day challenges confronting scholarly engagement with the past. Rather than fight this tendency, why not play with it?

NOTES

1. See, for example, Barry Russell, "The Form That Fell to Earth: Parisian Fairground Theatre," *L'Esprit Créateur* 39, no. 3 (1999): 56–63; David Trott, *Théâtre du XVIIIe siècle: Jeux, écritures, regards: Essai sur les spectacles en France de 1700 à 1790* (Montpellier, France: Espaces 34, 2000); Françoise Rubellin, ed., *Théâtre de la foire: Anthologie de pièces inédites, 1712–1736* (Montpellier, France: Espaces 34, 2005); and Françoise Rubellin, "Hiérarchies culturelles et théâtres de la foire: Pour en finir avec le populaire?" *Cahiers de l'Association internationale des études françaises* 70 (2018): 209–29. See also Russell's pioneering website, Foires.net (now archived by the Université de Québec à Montréal, http://www.theatrales .uqam.ca/foires/), as well as the Theaville website (http://www.theaville.org/kitesite/index .php), which provides both a wealth of modern editions of play texts and a searchable database of melodies used in Fair theater vaudevilles.

2. Raymond Williams, *Keywords: A Vocabulary of Culture and Society* (New York: Oxford University Press, 1983), 15.

3. Anecdotally, I have observed a similar resistance among certain scholars in computer science for whom the association of "serious" research with video games elicits similarly vociferous objections, although undoubtedly for different reasons.

4. See David F. Higgins, "Dreams of Accumulation: The Economics of SF Video Games," *Science Fiction Studies* 43, no. 1 (2016): 51–66.

5. Useful overviews of the field of digital humanities and its varied genealogies can be found in Alan Liu, "The Meaning of the Digital Humanities," *PMLA* 128, no. 2 (2013): 409–23; and David M. Berry and Anders Fagerjord, *Digital Humanities: Knowledge and Critique in a Digital Age* (Malden, MA: Polity, 2017).

6. The VESPACE project has been granted the National Endowment for the Humanities awards HAA-255998-17 and HAA-266501-19.

7. Pierre Nora, ed., *Les lieux de mémoire*, 3 vols. (Paris: Gallimard, 1984–92), gave an important theoretical basis to the incorporation of memory into the writing of history, in the process spawning a small industry of memory-based national histories.

8. Ann Rigney, "When the Monograph Is No Longer the Medium: Historical Narrative in the Online Age," *History and Theory* 49, no. 4 (2010): 108.

9. See Johnson Kent Wright, "Historical Thought in the Era of the Enlightenment." In *A Companion to Western Historical Thought*, ed. Lloyd Kramer and Sarah Maza (Malden, MA: Blackwell, 2002), 123–42.

10. Claudio Fogu, "Digitalizing Historical Consciousness," *History and Theory* 48, no. 2 (2009): 115. It is also worth noting that predominance of the visual has been critiqued as reinforcing ableist bias, which institutions have begun to respond to by enforcing the Americans with Disabilities Act requirement that all images on any website be accompanied by textual descriptions; whether this can meaningfully reinstate textuality as the primary arbiter of historical consciousness is far from certain.

11. On the debates surrounding both the development and reception of these games, see Edwige Lelièvre, "Story versus History: The Contentious Creation of the Historical Videogame *Versailles 1685*," *Contemporary French Civilization* 44, no. 1 (2019): 61–79; and Christopher Leffler, "Memory Games: History, Memory, and Anachronism in the Paris of *Assassin's Creed Unity*," *Contemporary French Civilization* 44, no. 1 (2019): 81–99. Ubisoft, responding to persistent critiques that its *Assassin's Creed* series instrumentalizes and distorts history in pursuit of thrills and profits, launched a new mode, dubbed Discovery Tour, with the 2017 release of *Assassin's Creed: Origins* and the subsequent *Assassin's Creed: Odyssey* (2018). Discovery Tour, intended to function like a self-guided museum, has been critiqued in Aris Politopoulos, Angus A. A. Mol, Krijn H. J. Boom, and Csilla E. Ariese, "'History Is Our Playground': Action and Authenticity in *Assassin's Creed: Odyssey*," *Advances in Archaeological Practice* 7, no. 3 (2019): 319, as "a poorly referenced living diorama lacking interactivity," but it clearly represents an attempt by an industry leader to confront accusations of historical misappropriation in violent adventure games.

12. *Civilization* in particular has received a great deal of scholarly attention, not least for its grandiose claims to present an authentic mechanics of world history that is in fact deeply ideological. Fogu, "Digitalizing Historical Consciousness," 121, posits that *Civilization* "is best appreciated as a remediation of the Hollywood historic(al) epic."

13. William Uricchio, "Simulation, History, and Computer Games," in *Handbook of Computer Game Studies*, ed. Joost Raessens and Jeffrey Goldstein (Cambridge, MA: MIT Press, 2005), 328.

14. See, for example, Hayden White, *The Content of the Form: Narrative Discourse and Historical Representation* (Baltimore: Johns Hopkins University Press, 1987).

15. Uricchio, "Simulation," 333.

16. Uricchio, "Simulation," 336. See also Jerremie Clyde, Howard Hopkins, and Glenn Wilkinson, "Beyond the 'Historical' Simulation: Using Theories of History to Inform Scholarly Game Design," *Loading . . . The Journal of the Canadian Game Studies Association* 6, no. 9 (2012): 3–16. See also Jean-Clément Martin and Laurent Turcot, *Au cœur de la Révolution: Les leçons d'histoire d'un jeu vidéo* (Paris: Vendémiaire, 2014).

17. Brian Rejack, "Toward a Virtual Reenactment of History: Video Games and the Recreation of the Past," *Rethinking History* 11, no. 3 (2007): 414, 422.

18. For a concise history of the Fair theater, see Isabelle Martin, *Le Théâtre de la foire Des tréteaux aux boulevards* (Oxford: Voltaire Foundation, 2002). For an economically oriented cultural history of the fairs in eighteenth-century France, see Robert Isherwood, *Farce and Fantasy: Popular Entertainment in Eighteenth-Century Paris* (New York: Oxford University Press, 1986).

19. The VESPACE project is conceived for a commercially available VR headset, the HTC Vive, that tracks user movement within a roughly ten-by-ten-foot area. For movement that goes beyond these (real-world) spatial limits, handsets allow users to teleport to different areas of the virtual world, at which point they again can explore the space through natural movement.

20. Eventually, VESPACE aims to allow for a normative evaluation of gestural codes—correctly executing a greeting, for example—that will place a further emphasis on embodied knowledge as a constitutive element of gameplay. While some theater-based pedagogical applications, notably *Play the Knave*, have successfully leveraged Microsoft Kinect technology

to translate player movement to onscreen avatars, the ability to detect and evaluate the appropriateness or mastery of physical movement remains a technical challenge.

21. See Paul François, Florent Laroche, Françoise Rubellin, and Jeffrey Leichman, "A Methodology for Reverse Architecture: Modelling Space and Use," *Procedia CIRP* 84 (2019): 106–11.

22. Wulf Kansteiner, "Alternate Worlds and Invented Communities: History and Historical Consciousness in the Age of Interactive Media," in *Manifestos for History*, ed. Keith Jenkins, Sue Morgan, and Alan Munslow (New York: Routledge, 2007), 135. Kansteiner's article is a foundational critique of the relationship between narrative history and the immersive worlds of video games that makes a number of predictions about the undermining of historical consciousness that have since been borne out more fully on social media platforms (still in their infancy at the time of the book's publication) than in video games.

23. See the now classic Niall Ferguson, ed., *Virtual History: Alternatives and Counterfactuals* (London: Picador, 1997), which reimagines Western history from 1646 to 1996.

24. Ian Bogost, *Persuasive Games: The Expressive Power of Videogames* (Cambridge, MA: MIT Press, 2007), 3.

25. Tracy Fullerton, "Documentary Games: Putting the Player in the Path of History," in *Playing the Past: History and Nostalgia in Video Games*, ed. Zach Whalen and Laurie N. Taylor (Nashville, TN: Vanderbilt University Press, 2008), 236.

26. Jeffrey Ravel, *The Contested Parterre: Public Theater and French Political Culture, 1680–1791* (Ithaca, NY: Cornell University Press, 1999).

27. Another important area in which narrativized sequences of facts lead to an apparently incontrovertible historical "truth" is in legal proceedings; for an interesting view of how procedurality may also have a place in rewriting courtroom practice, see Lucille Jewel, "The Bramble Bush of Forking Paths: Digital Narrative, Procedural Rhetoric, and the Law," *Yale Journal of Law and Technology* 14 (2011): 66–105.

28. Nonplayer characters, or NPCs, are agents in a game whose actions are controlled by the game system, responding procedurally to gamer choices. For more on how *Prom Week* leverages social physics to create more lifelike NPC reactions, see Ben Samuel, Dylan Lederle-Ensign, Mike Treanor, Noah Wardrip-Fruin, Josh McCoy, Aaron Reed, and Michael Mateas, "Playing the Worlds of *Prom Week*," in *Narrative Theory, Literature, and New Media: Narrative Minds and Virtual Worlds*, ed. Mari Hatavara, Matti Hyvärinen, Maria Mäkelä, and Frans Mäyrä (New York: Routledge, 2015), 87–105.

29. Gauvain Leconte, "Virtualité et interactivité du jeu vidéo," in *Espaces et temps du jeu vidéo*, ed. Hovig Ter Minassian, Samuel Rufat, and Samuel Coavoux (Paris: Questions Théoriques, 2012), 62.

30. VESPACE convened a virtual international workshop during May 17–22, 2020, inviting selected graduate students studying French literature, history, and computer science to participate in experiments in social physics rules authorship protocols. The field report from this workshop is currently under review for publication.

31. Peter Brinson, quoted in Fullerton, "Documentary Games," 234.

Acknowledgments

This volume originated from a session at the 2018 meeting of the American Society for Eighteenth-Century Studies in Orlando, Florida, at which several of our contributors were present either as speakers or auditors. We wish to thank Logan J. Connors for welcoming us to the *Scènes francophones* series along with everyone at Bucknell University Press who assisted us during the editorial process, especially Greg Clingham, Pamelia Dailey, and Suzanne E. Guiod. We also wish to thank Daryl Brower at Rutgers University Press and Mary Ribesky at Westchester Publishing Services for their assistance in production as well as our copyeditor, Brian Bendlin. Our presentation of this book was greatly aided by comments from two anonymous readers of our original proposal to the press. Individual chapters benefitted at a later stage from the advice of two further anonymous readers of the complete manuscript. We are grateful to each of these reviewers for their time and intellectual generosity.

Bibliography

Académie française. *Dictionnaire de l'Académie française*. 4th ed. 2 vols. Paris: Brunet, 1762.

Agamben, Giorgio. *Profanations*. Translated by Jeff Fort. New York: Zone Books, 2007.

Aït-Touati, Frédérique. *Fictions of the Cosmos: Science and Literature in the Seventeenth Century*. Translated by Susan Emanuel. Chicago: University of Chicago Press, 2011.

Allemagne, Henry-René d'. *Sports et jeux d'adresse*. Paris: Hachette, 1904.

Analyse critique de Tarare. Hormuz and Paris, 1787.

Aravamudan, Srinivas. *Enlightenment Orientalism: Resisting the Rise of the Novel*. Chicago: University of Chicago Press, 2012.

Arnold, R. J. *Musical Debate and Political Culture in France*. Woodbridge, UK: Boydell, 2017.

Audouin, Pierre Jean. *Rapport fait par Audouin, sur les théâtres, séance du 25 pluviôse an 6*. Paris: Imprimerie nationale, 1798.

Aulard, François-Alphonse, ed. *Le culte de la Raison et le culte de l'Être suprême (1793–1794): Essai historique*. Paris: Félix Alcan, 1892.

———. *Paris pendant la réaction thermidorienne et sous le Directoire*. Paris: Cerf, 1902.

Aulnoy, Marie-Catherine d'. *Contes des fées, suivis des contes nouveaux, ou Les fées à la mode*. Edited by Nadine Jasmin. Paris: Honoré Champion, 2004.

Bachaumont, Louis Petit de. *Mémoires secrets pour servir à l'histoire de la république des lettres En France, depuis 1762 jusqu'à nos jours, ou Journal d'un observateur*. 36 vols. London: Adamson, 1777–89.

Bahier-Porte, Christelle. *La poétique d'Alain-René Lesage*. Paris: Honoré Champion, 2006.

Bahier-Porte, Christelle, and Régine Jomand-Baudry, eds. *Écrire en mineur au XVIIIe siècle*. Paris: Desjonquères, 2009.

Bakhtin, Mikhail. *Rabelais and His World*. Translated by Hélène Iswolsky. Bloomington: Indiana University Press, 1984.

Barbeyrac, Jean. *Traité du jeu, où l'on examine les principales questions de droit naturel et de morale qui ont du rapport à cette matière*. 2 vols. Amsterdam: Humbert, 1709.

Bawr, Mme de. *Mes souvenirs*. Paris: Passard, 1853.

Bayle, Pierre. *Dictionnaire historique et critique*. 4 vols. Amsterdam: Brunel, 1740.

Beaumarchais, Pierre-Augustin Caron de. *The Barber of Seville and the Marriage of Figaro*. Translated by John Wood. Harmondsworth, UK: Penguin, 1964.

———. "Extrait de la Réponse de l'auteur de *Tarare* au comité de l'opéra." *Journal encyclopédique ou universel* 6 (1790): 462–66.

———. *Œuvres.* Edited by Pierre Larthomas and Jacqueline Larthomas. Paris: Gallimard, 1988.

Bell, David A. *The Cult of the Nation in France: Inventing Nationalism, 1680–1800.* Cambridge, MA: Harvard University Press, 2001.

Belmas, Élisabeth. *Jouer autrefois: Essai sur le jeu dans la France moderne (XVIe–XVIIIe siècle).* Paris: Champ Vallon, 2006.

Bennett, Susan. *Theatre Audiences: A Theory of Production and Reception.* 2nd ed. New York: Routledge, 1997.

Bérard, Suzanne Jean. *Le théâtre révolutionnaire de 1789–1794: La déchristianisation sur les planches.* Paris: Presses universitaires de Paris Ouest, 2009.

———. "Une curiosité du théâtre à l'époque révolutionnaire, les 'Faits historiques et patriotiques.'" *Romanistische Zeitschrift für Literaturgeschichte* 3 (1979): 250–77.

Berry, David M., and Anders Fagerjord. *Digital Humanities: Knowledge and Critique in a Digital Age.* Malden, MA: Polity, 2017.

Béthune, Le Chevalier de. *Relation du monde de Mercure.* 2 vols. Geneva: Barillot, 1750.

———. *The World of Mercury.* Translated by Brian Stableford. Encino, CA: Black Coat, 2015.

Betzwieser, Thomas. "Exoticism and Politics: Beaumarchais' and Salieri's *Le couronnement de Tarare* (1790)." *Cambridge Opera Journal* 6, no. 2 (1994): 91–112.

Bianchi, Serge. "Théâtre et engagement sur les scènes de l'an II." In *Littérature et engagement pendant la Révolution française,* edited by Isabelle Brouard-Arends and Laurent Loty, 27–49. Rennes, France: Presses universitaires de Rennes, 2007.

Biard, Michel. "Thalie et Melpomène face à leurs juges: La critique théâtrale sous le Directoire." In *La République directoriale,* vol. 2, edited by Philippe Bourdin and Bernard Gainot, 663–78. Clermont-Ferrand, France: Société des études robespierristes, 1998.

Bièvre, François-Georges Maréchal de. *Biévriana, ou Jeux de mots du marquis de Bièvre.* Edited by Albéric Deville. 3rd edition. Paris: Maradan, 1814.

———. *Calembours et autres jeux sur les mots d'esprit.* Edited by Antoine Baecque. Paris: Payot, 2000.

Blanco, Mercedes. *Les rhétoriques de la pointe: Baltasar Gracián et le conceptisme en Europe.* Paris: Honoré Champion, 1992.

Bloechl, Olivia. *Opera and the Political Imaginary in Old Regime France.* Chicago: University of Chicago Press, 2017.

Bogost, Ian. *Persuasive Games: The Expressive Power of Videogames.* Cambridge, MA: MIT Press, 2007.

Boileau Despréaux, Nicolas. *Œuvres diverses du Sieur D***; avec Le traité du sublime; ou, Du merveilleux dans le discours.* Paris: Lacoste, 1674.

———. *Satire XII sur l'équivoque.* N.p: n.p., 1711.

Bonnet, Jacques. *Histoire générale de la danse sacrée et profane.* Paris: d'Houry, 1724.

Bouhours, Dominique. *La manière de bien penser dans les ouvrages d'esprit: Dialogues.* Paris: Mabre-Cramoisy, 1687.

Bouissou, Sylvie. *Jean-Philippe Rameau: Musicien des Lumières.* Paris: Fayard, 2014.

Boulay de la Meurthe, Alfred. *Les prisonniers du roi à Loches sous Louis XIV.* Tours, France: J. Allard, 1911.

Boulerie, Florence. "Enquête sur la démarche cognitive des voyageurs philosophes dans les voyages imaginaires au temps de l'*Encyclopédie.*" In *Le philosophe romanesque: L'image du philosophe dans le roman des Lumières,* edited by Pierre Hartmann and Florence Lotterie, 167–77. Strasbourg, France: Presses universitaires de Strasbourg, 2007.

Bourdin, Philippe. *Aux origines du théâtre patriotique.* Paris: CNRS, 2017.

Bourreau, Alain. *La papesse Jeanne.* Paris: Aubier, 1988.

Brazier, Nicholas. *Chroniques des petits théâtres de Paris, depuis leur création jusqu'à ce jour.* 2 vols. Paris: Allardin, 1837.

Brenner, Clarence D. *Le développement du proverbe dramatique en France et sa vogue au XVIIIe siècle.* Berkeley: University of California Press, 1937.

Brillant, Abbé, ed. *Dictionnaire universel françois et latin: Vulgairement appelé Dictionnaire de Trévoux, contenant la signification et la définition des mots de l'une et de l'autre langue: avec leurs différents usages.* 8 vols. Paris: Compagnie des libraires associés, 1771.

Broglie, Gabriel de. *Ségur sans cérémonie (1757–1825).* Paris: Perrin, 1977.

Burke, Peter. *Popular Culture in Early Modern Europe.* Aldershot, UK: Ashgate, 1994.

Burson, Jeffrey D. *The Culture of Enlightening: Abbé Claude Yvon and the Entangled Emergence of the Enlightenment.* Notre Dame, IN: University of Notre Dame Press, 2019.

Byrnes, Joseph F. *Priests of the French Revolution: Saints and Renegades in a New Political Era.* University Park: Pennsylvania State University Press, 2014.

Cahusac, Louis de. *Zoroastre.* 1756. Translated by Adrian Shaw, in accompanying booklet to *Rameau: Zoroastre.* Orchestra and choir dir. William Christie, with Les Arts Florissants. Warner Classics/Erato 0927 43182-2, 2002, compact disc.

Caillois, Roger. *Man and the Sacred.* Translated by Meyer Barash. Urbana: University of Illinois Press, 2001.

———. *Man, Play, and Games.* Translated by Meyer Barash. Urbana: University of Illinois Press, 2001.

Campardon, Émile. *Les comédiens du roi de la troupe française pendant les deux derniers siècles, documents inédits recueillis aux archives nationales.* Geneva: Slatkine, 1970.

Carmontelle, Louis Carrogis. *Proverbes dramatiques de Carmontelle, précédés de la vie de Carmontelle, d'une dissertation historique et morale sur les proverbes et suivis d'une table explicative de l'origine des proverbes.* 4 vols. Paris: Delongchamps, 1822.

———. *Théâtre du Prince de Clénerzow, Russe.* 2 vols. Paris: Jorry, 1771.

Casanova, Giacomo. *Histoire de ma vie.* Edited by Gérard Lahouati and Marie-Françoise Luna. 3 vols. Paris: Gallimard, 2013–15.

———. *History of My Life.* Translated by Willard R. Trask. 12 vols. in 6. New York: Harcourt, Brace and World, 1966–71.

Cassin, Barbara. *L'effet sophistique.* Paris: Gallimard, 1995.

Cassin, Barbara, and Michel Narcy. *La décision du sens: Le livre "Gamma" de la Métaphysique d'Aristote, introduction, texte, traduction et commentaire.* Paris: Vrin, 1989.

Castiglione, Baldassare. *The Book of the Courtier.* Translated by George Bull. New York: Penguin, 1976.

Castle, Terry. *Masquerade and Civilization: The Carnivalesque in Eighteenth-Century English Culture and Fiction.* Stanford, CA: Stanford University Press, 1986.

Cavillac, Cécile. *L'Espagne dans la trilogie "picaresque" de Lesage: Emprunts littéraires, empreinte culturelle.* 2 vols. Talence, France: Presses universitaires de Bordeaux, 1984.

Cerfvol. *Chimérandre l'antigrec, fils de Bacha Bilboquet, ou Les équivoques de la langue française.* N.p.: Balivernipolis, 1766.

Chauvaud, Frédéric. *Le sanglot judiciaire: La désacralisation de la justice, VIIIe–XXe siècles: Séminaire de Royaumont (1993–1994).* Grâne, France: Créaphis, 1999.

Chénier, Marie-Joseph. *Corps législatif. Conseil des Cinq-Cents: Motion d'ordre par Chénier sur les théâtres, séance du 26 brumaire an VI.* Paris: Imprimerie nationale, 1797.

Cherrier, Claude Joseph de. *L'Homme inconnu, ou Les équivoques de la langue dédié à Bacha Bilboquet.* Paris: Quillau, 1713.

———. *Polissoniana, ou Recueil de turlupinades, quolibets, rebus, jeux de mots, allusions, allégories, pointes, expressions extraordinaires, hyperboles, gasconnades, espèces de bons mots, et autres plaisanteries.* Amsterdam: Desbordes, 1722.

Childs, J. Rives. *Casanova, a New Perspective.* New York: Paragon House Publishers, 1988.

Choderlos de Laclos, Pierre Ambroise François. *Les liaisons dangereuses.* Edited by René Pomeau. Paris: Flammarion, 2006.

Cioranescu, Alexandre. *Le masque et le visage: Du baroque espagnol au classicisme français.* Geneva: Droz, 1983.

Clay, Richard. *Iconoclasm in Revolutionary Paris: The Transformation of Signs, 1789–1795.* Oxford: Voltaire Foundation, 2012.

Clyde, Jerremie, Howard Hopkins, and Glenn Wilkinson. "Beyond the 'Historical' Simulation: Using Theories of History to Inform Scholarly Game Design." *Loading . . . The Journal of the Canadian Game Studies Association* 6, no. 9 (2012): 3–16.

Coleman, Charly. *The Virtues of Abandon: An Anti-Individualist History of the French Enlightenment.* Stanford, CA: Stanford University Press, 2014.

Collé, Charles. *Journal historique, ou, Mémoires critiques et littéraires, sur les ouvrages dramatiques et sur les événements les plus mémorables, depuis 1748 jusqu'en 1772.* Edited by Honoré Bonhomme. 3 vols. Paris: Didot, 1868.

Coste, Jean-Claude. "Les 'suppléments' de Jean-Jacques Rousseau." *L'en-je lacanien* 1, no. 4 (2005): 33–45.

Costich, Julia. "Fortune in *Manon Lescaut,*" *French Review* 49, no. 4 (1976): 522–27.

Coulet, Henri. *Le roman jusqu'à la Révolution.* 2 vols. Paris: Armand Colin, 1967–68.

Crowe, Michael J. *The Extraterrestrial Life Debate, 1750–1900: The Idea of a Plurality of Worlds from Kant to Lowell.* Cambridge: Cambridge University Press, 1986.

Curulla, Annelle. *Gender and Religious Life in French Revolutionary Drama.* Liverpool, UK: Liverpool University Press, 2018.

Cussac, Hélène. "L'histoire de Gil Blas de Santillane ou Une littérature du refus." In *L'assiette des fictions: Enquêtes sur l'autoréflexivité romanesque,* edited by Jan Herman, Adrien Paschoud, Paul Pelckmans, and François Rosset, 293–305. Louvain, Belgium: Peeters, 2010.

Cyrano de Bergerac, Savinien de. *Œuvres complètes.* Edited by Madeleine Alcover, Luciano Erba, Hubert Carrier, and André Blanc. 3 vols. Paris: Honoré Champion, 2000–2001.

Darlow, Mark. "Staging the Revolution: The *Fait historique.*" *Nottingham French Studies* 45 (2006): 77–88.

Daston, Lorraine. *Classical Probability in the Enlightenment.* Princeton, NJ: Princeton University Press, 1988.

Daston, Lorraine, and Katharine Park. *Wonders and the Order of Nature.* Cambridge, MA: Zone Books, 1998.

De l'antiquité et de l'usage du bilboquet, par Monsieur C***. Lucerne: n.p., 1714.

Defoe, Daniel. *The Anatomy of Exchange-Alley; or A System of Stock-Jobbing.* London: E. Smith, 1719.

Dejean, Joan. *The Essence of Style: How the French Invented High Fashion, Fine Food, Chic Cafés, Style, Sophistication, and Glamour.* New York: Free Press, 2005.

———. *Tender Geographies: Women and the Origins of the Novel in France.* New York: Columbia University Press, 1991.

Démoris, René. *Le roman à la première personne: Du classicisme aux Lumières.* Geneva: Droz, 2002.

Derrida, Jacques. *De la grammatologie.* Paris: Minuit, 1967.

Dervaux, Sylvie. "'La chambre d'enchantement': *Le bilboquet* de Marivaux (1714)." *Studies on Voltaire and the Eighteenth Century* 323 (1994): 247–69.

Dick, Steven J. *Plurality of Worlds: The Origins of the Extraterrestrial Life Debate from Democritus to Kant.* Cambridge: Cambridge University Press, 1982.

Diderot, Denis. *Contes et romans.* Edited by Michel Delon. Paris: Gallimard, 2004.

———. *Œuvres complètes.* Edited by Herbert Dieckmann et al. 25 vols. to date. Paris: Hermann, 1975–.

———. *Rameau's Nephew and First Satire.* Translated by Margaret Mauldon. Oxford: Oxford University Press, 2006.

———. *The Salon of 1767: Diderot on Art*. Translated by John Goodman. 2 vols. New Haven, CT: Yale University Press, 1995.

Diderot, Denis, and Jean le Rond d'Alembert, eds. *Encyclopédie, ou Dictionnaire raisonné des sciences, des arts et des métiers*. 17 vols. Paris: Briasson, 1751–65.

Didier, Béatrice, and Jean-Paul Sermain, eds. *D'une gaîté ingénieuse: "L'histoire de Gil Blas,"* roman de Lesage. Louvain, Belgium: Peeters, 2004.

Dubin, Nina. *Futures and Ruins: Eighteenth-Century Paris and the Art of Hubert Robert*. Los Angeles: Getty Research Institute, 2012.

Dufrénoy, Adelaïde-Gillette, ed. *Courier lyrique et amusant, ou Passe-temps des toilettes*. Paris: Knapen et fils, 1787.

Dumont de Montigny, Georges-Marie Butel-Dumont, and Jean Baptiste Le Mascrier. *Mémoires historiques sur la Louisiane*. 2 vols. Paris: Bauche, 1753.

Dunn, Richard S. *The Age of Religious Wars 1559–1715*. 2nd ed. New York: W. W. Norton, 1979.

Duval, Amaury. *Observations sur les théâtres*. Paris: Imprimerie des sciences et arts, n.d.

Edwards, Brian. *Theories of Play and Postmodern Fiction*. New York: Garland, 1998.

Ehrmann, Jacques. "Homo Ludens Revisited." Translated by Cathy and Phil Lewis. In *Game, Play, Literature*, edited by Jacques Ehrmann, 31–57. Boston: Beacon, 1971.

Elias, Norbert. *La société de cour*. Paris: Flammarion, 1985.

Eliopoulos, Panos. "Epicurus and Lucretius on the Creation of the Cosmos." *Philosophy and Cosmology* 14 (2015): 249–55.

Escola, Marc, Jan Herman, Lucia Omacini, Paul Pelckmans, and Jean-Paul Sermain, eds. *La partie et le tout: La composition du roman, de l'âge baroque au tournant des Lumières*. Louvain, Belgium: Peeters, 2011.

Faivre, Antoine. *The Eternal Hermes: From Greek God to Alchemical Magus*. Translated by Joscelyn Godwin. Grand Rapids, MI: Phanes, 1995.

———. "Renaissance Hermeticism and the Concept of Western Esotericism," in *Gnosis and Hermeticism from Antiquity to Modern Times*, edited by Roelof van den Broek and Wouter J. Hanegraaff, 109–24. Albany: State University of New York Press, 1998.

Fauconpret, Charles-Auguste de. *La papesse Jeanne, opéra bouffon en vaudevilles, en trois actes*. Paris: Hérissant, 1793.

Ferguson, Niall, ed. *Virtual History: Alternatives and Counterfactuals*. London: Picador, 1997.

Fogu, Claudio. "Digitalizing Historical Consciousness." *History and Theory* 48, no. 2 (2009): 103–21.

Fontenelle, Bernard le Bovier de. *Conversations on the Plurality of Worlds*. Translated by H. A. Hargreaves. Berkeley: University of California Press, 1990.

———. *Entretiens sur la pluralité des mondes*. Edited by Christophe Martin. Paris: Flammarion, 1998.

Fourgnaud, Magali. *Le conte à visée morale et philosophique: De Fénelon à Voltaire*. Paris: Classiques Garnier, 2016.

Fournier, Stéphanie. *Rire au théâtre à Paris à la fin du XVIIIe siècle*. Paris: Garnier, 2016.

Frain du Tremblay, Jean. *Conversations morales sur les jeux et les divertissements*. Paris: Pralard, 1685.

François, Paul, Florent Laroche, Françoise Rubellin, and Jeffrey Leichman. "A Methodology for Reverse Architecture: Modelling Space and Use." *Procedia CIRP* 84 (2019): 106–11.

Frantz, Pierre. "Pas d'entracte pour la Révolution." In *La Carmagnole des muses: L'homme de lettres et l'artiste dans la Révolution*, edited by Jean-Claude Bonnet, 381–99. Paris: Armand Colin, 1988.

Freundlich, Francis. *Le monde du jeu à Paris, 1715–1800*. Paris: Michel, 1995.

Fullerton, Tracy. "Documentary Games: Putting the Player in the Path of History." In *Playing the Past: History and Nostalgia in Video Games*, edited by Zach Whalen and Laurie N. Taylor, 215–38. Nashville, TN: Vanderbilt University Press, 2008.

Furetière, Antoine. *Dictionnaire universel, contenant généralement tous les mots français tant vieux que modernes, et les termes de toutes les sciences et des arts.* 3 vols. The Hague: Leers, 1690.

——. *Dictionnaire universel, contenant généralement tous les mots français tant vieux que modernes, et les termes de toutes les sciences et des arts.* 3 vols. The Hague: Leers, 1701.

Gaillard, Aurélia. "La clé et le puits: À propos du déchiffrement des contes et des fables." *Féeries* 7 (2010): 179–92.

Gallois, Léonard-Charles-André-Gustave, ed. *Réimpression de l'ancien Moniteur, seule histoire authentique et inaltérée de la Révolution française, depuis la réunion des États-Généraux jusqu'au Consulat (mai 1789–novembre 1799), avec des notes explicatives.* 32 vols. Paris: Plon, 1847–50.

Gamboni, Dario. *The Destruction of Art: Iconoclasm and Vandalism since the French Revolution.* New Haven, CT: Yale University Press, 1997.

Ganofsky, Marine, ed. *Petits soupers libertins.* Paris: Société française d'étude du dix-huitième siècle, 2016.

Gaukroger, Stephen. *Francis Bacon and the Transformation of Early-Modern Philosophy.* Cambridge: Cambridge University Press, 2001.

Gell, Alfred. "The Technology of Enchantment and the Enchantment of Technology." In *Anthropology, Art and Aesthetics*, edited by Jeremy Coote and Anthony Shelton, 40–63. Oxford: Clarendon, 1992.

Girard, René. *Deceit, Desire, and the Novel: Self and Other in Literary Structure.* Translated by Yvonne Freccero. Baltimore: Johns Hopkins University Press, 1965.

——. *Mensonge romantique et vérité romanesque.* Paris: Grasset, 1961.

Goodwin, Barbara. *Justice by Lottery.* Chicago: University of Chicago Press, 1992.

Graczyk, Annette. "Le théâtre de la Révolution française, média de masses entre 1789 et 1794." *Dix-huitième siècle* 21 (1989): 395–409.

Granval, Nicolas Racot de. *Le vice puni, ou Cartouche.* Paris: Prault, 1725.

Grélé, Denis. "Escape from Utopia: Love, Religion and the State in Prévost's *Le philosophe anglais, ou Histoire de Monsieur Cleveland*," *Journal of the Association for the Interdisciplinary Study of the Arts* 12, no. 3 (2017): 119–30.

Grimm, Friedrich Melchior, Denis Diderot, and Jacques-Henri Meister. *Correspondance littéraire, philosophique et critique de Grimm et de Diderot, depuis 1753 jusqu'en 1790.* Edited by Jules-Antoine Taschereau and A. Chaudé. 15 vols. Paris: Furne, 1829–31.

Guérin, Daniel. *La lutte de classes sous la première République: Bourgeois et "bras nus," 1793–1797.* 2 vols. Paris: Gallimard, 1946.

Guessart, F. "La censure au commencement du XVIIIe siècle: L'abbé Cherrier, lettres inédites." *La correspondance littéraire: Critique, beaux-arts, érudition* 2, no. 4 (1858): 71–83.

Guillaume, James, ed. *Procès-verbaux du Comité d'instruction publique de la Convention nationale.* Paris: Imprimerie nationale, 1901.

Hannon, Patricia. *Fabulous Identities: Women's Fairy Tales in Seventeenth-Century France.* Amsterdam: Rodopi, 1998.

Hazard, Paul. *The Crisis of the European Mind, 1680–1715.* Translated by J. Lewis May. New York: New York Review of Books, 2013.

——. *La crise de la conscience européenne 1680–1715.* Paris: Fayard, 1961.

Higgins, David F. "Dreams of Accumulation: The Economics of SF Video Games." *Science Fiction Studies* 43, no. 1 (2016): 51–66.

Hodson, Daren. "Beaumarchais' *Tarare*: Courtly Art and Radical Enlightenment." In *Opera Libretti of the Eighteenth Century: Essays on the Libretto as Enlightenment Text*, edited by Pamela Gay-White, 117–48. Lewiston, NY: Edwin Mellen, 2014.

Howarth, William D. *Beaumarchais and the Theatre.* London: Routledge, 1995.

Huchette, Jocelyn. *La gaieté, caractère français? Représenter la nation au siècle des Lumières (1715–1789).* Paris: Classiques Garnier, 2015.

Huizinga, Johan. *Homo Ludens: A Study of the Play-Element in Culture.* Translated by R. F. C. Hull. London: Routledge and Kegan Paul, 1949.

The Hutchinson Unabridged Encyclopedia with Atlas and Weather Guide. Oxford: Credo Reference, 2016.

Isherwood, Robert M. *Farce and Fantasy: Popular Entertainment in Eighteenth-Century Paris.* New York: Oxford University Press, 1986.

Israel, Jonathan. *Enlightenment Contested: Philosophy, Modernity, and the Emancipation of Man 1670–1752.* Oxford: Oxford University Press, 2006.

———. *Radical Enlightenment: Philosophy and the Making of Modernity, 1650–1750.* Oxford: Oxford University Press, 2001.

Jaume, Lucien. *Le religieux et le politique dans la Révolution française: L'idée de régénération.* Paris: Presses universitaires de France, 2015.

Jeanneret, Michel. "'Envelopper les ordures'? Érotisme et libertinage au XVIIe siècle." *Littératures classiques* 55, no. 3 (2004): 157–68.

Jewel, Lucille. "The Bramble Bush of Forking Paths: Digital Narrative, Procedural Rhetoric, and the Law." *Yale Journal of Law and Technology* 14 (2011): 66–105.

Joncourt, Pierre de. *Quatre lettres sur les jeux de hazard, et une cinquième sur l'usage de se faire celer pour éviter une visite incommode.* The Hague: T. Johnson, 1713.

Jones, Christine A. *Shapely Bodies: The Image of Porcelain in Eighteenth-Century France.* Newark: University of Delaware Press, 2013.

Jousse, Daniel. *Traité de la justice criminelle en France.* 4 vols. Paris: Debure, 1771.

Kansteiner, Wulf. "Alternate Worlds and Invented Communities: History and Historical Consciousness in the Age of Interactive Media." In *Manifestos for History*, edited by Keith Jenkins, Sue Morgan, and Alan Munslow, 131–48. New York: Routledge, 2007.

Kareem, Sarah Tindal. *Eighteenth-Century Fiction and the Reinvention of Wonder.* Oxford: Oxford University Press, 2014.

Kavanagh, Thomas. *Dice, Cards, Wheels: A Different History of French Culture.* Philadelphia: University of Pennsylvania Press, 2005.

Kelly, Michael. *Iconoclasm in Aesthetics.* Cambridge: Cambridge University Press, 2003.

Kennedy, Emmet. *A Cultural History of the French Revolution.* New Haven, CT: Yale University Press, 1989.

———. "Taste and Revolution." *Annales canadiennes d'histoire* 32, no. 3 (1997): 375–92.

Kennedy, Emmet, Marie-Laurence Netter, James P. McGregor, and Mark V. Olsen. *Theatre, Opera, and Audiences in Revolutionary Paris: Analysis and Repertory.* Westport, CT: Greenwood, 1996.

Krakovitch, Odile. "Le théâtre de la République et la censure sous le Directoire." In *Le Théâtre sous la Révolution: Politique du répertoire (1789–1799)*, edited by Martial Poirson, 169–92. Paris: Desjonquères, 2008.

La Bruyère, Jean de. *Les caractères.* Edited by Emmanuel Bury. Paris: Librairie générale française, 1995.

La Gorce, Jérôme de, and Pierre Jugie. *Dans l'atelier des menus plaisirs du roi: Spectacles, fêtes et cérémonies aux XVIIe et XVIIIe siècles.* Paris: Archives nationales, 2010.

Lamarque, François. *Opinion de F. Lamarque sur les théatres, séance du 2 germinal an 6.* Paris: Imprimerie nationale, 1798.

Laufer, Roger. *Lesage ou Le métier de romancier.* Paris: Gallimard, 1971.

Le radoteur, ou Nouveaux mélanges de philosophie, d'anecdotes curieuses, d'aventures particulières, etc., publié et mis en ordre par M. de C***, auteur de plusieurs ouvrages connus. Paris: Bastien, 1777.

Leconte, Gauvain. "Virtualité et interactivité du jeu video." In *Espaces et temps du jeu vidéo*, edited by Hovig Ter Minassian, Samuel Rufat, and Samuel Coavoux, 53–72. Paris: Questions Théoriques, 2012.

Leffler, Christopher. "Memory Games: History, Memory, and Anachronism in the Paris of *Assassin's Creed Unity*." *Contemporary French Civilization* 44, no. 1 (2019): 81–99.

Legay, Marie-Laure. *Les loteries royales dans l'Europe*. Villeneuve d'Ascq, France: Presses universitaires du Septentrion, 2014.

Léger, François-Pierre-Auguste. *La papesse Jeanne: Comédie en un acte, en vers et en vaudevilles*. Paris: Cailleau, 1793.

Légier-Desgranges, L.-H. "De la Salpêtrière au Mississippi." *Miroir de l'histoire* 29 (1952): 83–96; and 30 (1952): 35–45.

Lelièvre, Edwige. "Story versus History: The Contentious Creation of the Historical Videogame *Versailles 1685*." *Contemporary French Civilization* 44, no. 1 (2019): 61–79.

Lesage, René. *The Adventures of Gil Blas of Santillane*. Edited by O. M. Brack Jr. and Leslie A. Chilton. Translated by Tobias Smollett. Athens: University of Georgia Press, 2011.

———. *Histoire de Gil Blas de Santillane*. Edited by Roger Laufer. Paris: Garnier Flammarion, 1977.

L'Estoile, Pierre de. *Registre-journal du règne de Henri III*. Edited by Madeleine Lazard and Gilbert Schrenck. 6 vols. Geneva: Droz, 1992–2003.

Lhôte, Jean-Marie. *Histoire des jeux de société: Géométries du désir*. Paris: Flammarion, 1994.

Liu, Alan. "The Meaning of the Digital Humanities." *PMLA* 128, no. 2 (2013): 409–23.

Long, A. A., and D. N. Sedley, eds. *The Hellenistic Philosophers*. 2 vols. Cambridge: Cambridge University Press, 1987.

Loskoutoff, Yvan. *La sainte et la fée: Dévotion à l'enfant Jésus et mode des contes merveilleux à la fin du règne de Louis XIV*. Geneva: Droz, 1987.

Luna, Marie-Françoise. *Casanova mémorialiste*. Paris: Honoré Champion, 1998.

Lyons, John. *The Phantom of Chance: From Fortune to Randomness in Seventeenth-Century French Literature*. Edinburgh: University of Edinburgh Press, 2011.

Mancier, Frédéric. *Le modèle aristocratique français et espagnol dans l'œuvre romanesque de Lesage: L'histoire de Gil Blas de Santillane, un cas exemplaire*. Fasano, Italy: Schena, 2001.

Marchand, Sophie. "Le temps du théâtre d'après *Le censeur dramatique*." *Studi Francesi* 169 (2013): 123–35.

Maréschal de Bièvre, Gabriel. *Le marquis de Bièvre, sa vie, ses calembours, ses comédies, 1747–1789*. Paris: Plon-Nourrit, 1910.

Marivaux, Pierre Carlet de Chamblain de. *Le bilboquet*. Edited by Françoise Rubellin. Paris: Centre national de la recherche scientifique, 1995.

Martin, Christophe, ed. *Fictions de l'origine, 1650–1800*. Paris: Desjonquères, 2012.

Martin, Isabelle. *Le Théâtre de la foire Des tréteaux aux boulevards*. Oxford: Voltaire Foundation, 2002.

Martin, Jean-Clément, and Laurent Turcot. *Au cœur de la Révolution: Les leçons d'histoire d'un jeu vidéo*. Paris: Vendémiaire, 2014.

Martinet, Jean-Luc. "La marquise et la femme de chambre: Le romanesque stendhalien," *Acta Fabula* 8, no. 4 (2007), http://www.fabula.org/revue/document3485.php.

Matytsin, Anton M., and Dan Edelstein, eds. *Let There Be Enlightenment: The Religious and Mystical Sources of Rationality*. Baltimore: Johns Hopkins University Press, 2018.

Mauzi, Robert. "Écrivains et moralistes du XVIIIe siècle devant les jeux de hasard." *Revue des sciences humaines* 90 (1958): 219–56.

———. *L'idée du bonheur dans la littérature et la pensée françaises au XVIIIe siècle*. Paris: Armand Colin, 1960.

Mavidal, Jérôme, and Emile Laurent, eds. *Archives parlementaires de 1787 à 1860, recueil complet des débats législatifs et politiques des chambres françaises*. 188 vols. Paris: Dupont, 1862–1913.

Mäyrä, Frans. *An Introduction to Game Studies: Games in Culture*. London: Sage, 2008.

Maza, Sarah. *Servants and Masters in Eighteenth-Century France: The Uses of Loyalty*. Princeton, NJ: Princeton University Press, 1983.

Mazauric, Simone. *Fontenelle et l'invention de l'histoire des sciences à l'aube des Lumières.* Paris: Fayard, 2007.

McClure, Ellen M. *Sunspots and the Sun King: Sovereignty and Mediation in Seventeenth-Century France.* Urbana: University of Illinois Press, 2006.

Melançon, Benoît. "Oralité, brièveté, spontanéité et marginalité: Le cas du marquis de Bièvre," in *Les marges des Lumières françaises (1750–1789),* edited by Didier Masseau, 215–24. Geneva: Droz, 2004.

Mercier, Louis-Sébastien. *Le nouveau Paris.* Edited by Jean-Claude Bonnet, Anne Le Fur, and Jean Sellier. Paris: Mercure de France, 1994.

Merrick, Jeffrey W. *The Desacralization of the French Monarchy in the Eighteenth Century.* Baton Rouge: Louisiana State University Press, 1990.

Molino, Jean. "Les six premiers livres de l'*Histoire de Gil Blas de Santillane.*" *Annales de la Faculté des lettres et sciences humaines d'Aix* 44 (1968): 88–101.

Momoro, Antoine-François. *Traité élémentaire de l'imprimerie, ou Le manuel de l'imprimeur.* Paris: Momoro, 1793.

Montesquieu, Charles de Secondat. *Persian Letters.* Translated by Margaret Mauldon. Oxford: Oxford University Press, 2008.

———. *The Spirit of the Laws.* Translated and edited by Anne M. Cohler, Basia Carolyn Miller, and Harold Samuel Stone. Cambridge: Cambridge University Press, 1989.

Morin, J. F., and A. Lenoir. *Le nouvelliste littéraire* 91, no. 30 (1799).

Moshenska, Joe. *Iconoclasm as Child's Play.* Stanford, CA: Stanford University Press, 2019.

Murat, Henriette-Julie de. *Contes.* Edited by Geneviève Patard. Paris: Honoré Champion, 2006.

Nora, Pierre. *Les lieux de mémoire.* 3 vols. Paris: Gallimard, 1984–92.

Ordre et marche de la Fête de l'Unité et de l'indivisibilité de la République, qui aura lieu le 10 août, décrété par la Convention nationale. Paris: Gourdin, 1793.

Ozouf, Mona. *Festivals and the French Revolution.* Translated by Alan Sheridan. Cambridge, MA: Harvard University Press, 1988.

———. *La fête révolutionnaire, 1789–1799.* Paris: Gallimard, 1976.

Peden, Knox. "The Politics of Disenchantment: Marcel Gauchet and the French Struggle with Secularization." *Intellectual History Review* 27, no. 1 (2017): 135–50.

Perovic, Sanja, ed. *Sacred and Secular Agency in Early Modern France: Fragments of Religion.* London: Continuum, 2012.

Perrault, Charles. *Contes.* Edited by Catherine Magnien. Paris: Le livre de poche, 2006.

Perrot, Jean. *Tricentenaire Charles Perrault: Les grands contes du XVIIe siècle et leur fortune littéraire.* Paris: Éditions In Press, 1998.

Phalèse, Hubert de. *Les bons contes et les bons mots de Gil Blas.* Paris: Nizet, 2002.

Piron, Alexis. *Œuvres complètes.* Edited by and Jean Antoine Rigoley de Juvigny. 9 vols. Troyes, France: Gobelet, 1799.

Plagnol-Diéval, Marie-Emmanuelle. *Le théâtre de société: Un autre théâtre?* Paris: Honoré Champion, 2003.

Plagnol-Diéval, Marie-Emmanuelle, and Dominique Quéro. *Charles Collé (1709–1783): Au cœur de la république des lettres.* Rennes, France: Presses universitaires de Rennes, 2013.

Politopoulos, Aris, Angus A. A. Mol, Krijn H. J. Boom, and Csilla E. Ariese. "'History Is Our Playground': Action and Authenticity in *Assassin's Creed: Odyssey.*" *Advances in Archaeological Practice* 7, no. 3 (2019): 317–23.

Pomeau, René. *Beaumarchais ou La bizarre destinée.* Paris: Presses universitaires de France, 1987.

Prévost, Abbé. *Cleveland: Le philosophe anglais, ou Histoire de M. Cleveland, fils naturel de Cromwell.* Edited by Jean Sgard and Philip Stewart. Paris: Desjonquères, 2006.

———. *Histoire du chevalier des Grieux et de Manon Lescaut.* Edited by Frédéric Deloffre and Raymond Picard. Paris: Garnier, 1965.

———. *Histoire du chevalier des Grieux et de Manon Lescaut*. Edited by Georges Matoré. Geneva: Droz, 1953.

———. *The Life and Entertaining Adventures of Mr. Cleveland, Natural Son of Oliver Cromwell, Written by Himself*. 3 vols. London: Astley, 1741.

———. *Manon Lescaut*. Translated by Leonard Tancock. London: Penguin, 1991.

———. *Manuel lexique, ou Dictionnaire portatif des mots français dont la signification n'est pas familière à tout le monde*. 2 vols. Paris: Didot, 1750.

———. *Oeuvres de Prévost*. Edited by Jean Sgard. 8 vols. Grenoble: Presses universitaires de Grenoble: 1978–86.

———. *The Story of the Chevalier des Grieux and Manon Lescaut*. Translated by Angela Scholar. Oxford: Oxford University Press, 2004.

Préyat, Fabrice, ed. *Marie-Adélaïde de Savoie (1685–1712), duchesse de Bourgogne, enfant terrible de Versailles*. Brussels: Éditions de l'Université de Bruxelles, 2014.

Procès-verbaux du Comité d'instruction publique de la Convention nationale. Vol. 4. Edited by James Guillaume. Paris: Imprimerie nationale, 1901.

Prosperi, Adriano. *Justice Blindfolded: The Historical Course of an Image*. Leiden: Brill, 2018.

Proust, Jacques. "Lesage ou Le regard intérieur: Recherches sur la place et la fonction de la 'description' dans *Gil Blas*." In *Beiträge zur französischen Aufklärung und zur spanischen Literatur*, edited by Werner Krauss and Werner Bahner, 289–314. Berlin: Akademie-Verlag, 1971.

Racault, Jean-Michel. *L'utopie narrative en France et en Angleterre, 1675–1761*. Oxford: Voltaire Foundation, 1991.

Ravel, Jeffrey. *The Contested Parterre: Public Theater and French Political Culture, 1680–1791*. Ithaca, NY: Cornell University Press, 1999.

Raviez, François, and Éloïse Lièvre. *"Gil Blas" de Lesage: Livres I–VI*. Paris: Atlande, 2002.

Redfern, Walter David. *Calembours, ou Les puns et les autres: Traduit de l'intraduisible*. Oxford: Peter Lang, 2005.

Régaldo, Marc. *Un milieu intellectuel: "La décade philosophique" (1794–1807)*. 5 vols. Lille: Atelier de reproduction des thèses, 1976.

Rejack, Brian. "Toward a Virtual Reenactment of History: Video Games and the Recreation of the Past." *Rethinking History* 11, no. 3 (2007): 411–25.

Rey, Alain, ed. *Dictionnaire historique de la langue française*. Paris: Le Robert, 2010.

Rey, Jean-Michel. *Le temps du crédit*. Paris: Desclée de Brouwer, 2002.

Rigney, Ann. "When the Monograph Is No Longer the Medium: Historical Narrative in the Online Age." *History and Theory* 49, no. 4 (2010): 100–117.

Robert, Raymonde, ed. *Contes: Mademoiselle Lhéritier, Mademoiselle Bernard, Mademoiselle de la Force, Madame Durand, Madame d'Auneuil*. Paris: Honoré Champion, 2005.

———. *Le conte de fées littéraire en France*. Paris: Honoré Champion, 2002.

———. "L'infantilisation du conte merveilleux au XVIIe siècle," *Littératures classiques* 14 (1991): 33–46.

Robert, Yann. *Dramatic Justice: Trial by Theater in the Age of the French Revolution*. Philadelphia: University of Pennsylvania Press, 2019.

Robichez, Jacques. "Le refus de la description dans *Gil Blas*." *Travaux de linguistique et de littérature* 13, no. 2 (1975): 483–89.

Robinet, Jean-Baptiste-René, ed. *Supplément à l'Encyclopédie, ou Dictionnaire des sciences, des arts et des métiers*. 4 vols. Amsterdam: M.-M. Rey, 1776–77.

Roman, Luke, and Monica Roman. *Encyclopedia of Greek and Roman Mythology*. New York: Facts on File, 2010.

Rose, Jenny. *Zoroastrianism: An Introduction*. London: I. B. Tauris, 2010.

Rougemont, Martine de. *La vie théâtrale en France au XVIIIe siècle*. Paris: Honoré Champion, 1988.

Rousseau, Jean-Jacques. *The Collected Writings of Rousseau*. Edited by Roger D. Masters and Christopher Kelly. 13 vols. Hanover, NH: University Press of New England, 1990–2010.

———. *Les confessions*. Edited by Raymond Tousson. Paris: Honoré Champion, 2010.

———. *Correspondance complète de Jean Jacques Rousseau*. Edited by R. A. Leigh. 52 vols. Geneva: Institut et musée Voltaire, 1965–1998.

Rubellin, Françoise. "Hiérarchies culturelles et théâtres de la foire: Pour en finir avec le populaire?" *Cahiers de l'Association internationale des études françaises* 70 (2018): 209–29.

———, ed. *Théâtre de la foire: Anthologie de pièces inédites, 1712–1736*. Montpellier, France: Espaces 34, 2005.

Ruimi, Jennifer. *La parade de société au XVIIIe siècle: Une forme dramatique oubliée*. Paris: Honoré Champion, 2015.

Russell, Barry. "The Form That Fell to Earth: Parisian Fairground Theatre." *L'esprit créateur* 39, no. 3 (1999): 56–63.

Sadler, Graham. "Avant-propos." In *Opera omnia Rameau*, ser. 4, vol. 19, *Zoroastre*, edited by Graham Sadler, xv–xxxviii. Paris: G. Billaudot, 1999.

Saint-Simon, Louis de Rouvroy, *Mémoires du duc de Saint-Simon*. Edited by Adolphe Chéruel and Adolphe Régnier. 20 vols. Paris: Hachette, 1873–77.

Sajous D'Oria, Michèle. "Les tréteaux de la corruption." In *La scène bâtarde: Entre Lumières et romantisme*, edited by Philippe Bourdin and Gérard Loubinoux, 269–82. Clermont-Ferrand, France: Presses universitaires Blaise Pascal, 2004.

Samuel, Ben, Dylan Lederle-Ensign, Mike Treanor, Noah Wardrip-Fruin, Josh McCoy, Aaron Reed, and Michael Mateas. "Playing the Worlds of *Prom Week*." In *Narrative Theory, Literature, and New Media: Narrative Minds and Virtual Worlds*, edited by Mari Hatavara, Matti Hyvärinen, Maria Mäkelä, and Frans Mäyrä, 87–105. New York: Routledge, 2015.

Schlanger, Judith. *L'enjeu et le débat*. Paris: Éditions Denoël, 1979.

Schmidt, Adolf, ed. *Tableaux de la Révolution française*. Leipzig: Veit, 1867.

Segal, Naomi. *The Unintended Reader: Feminism and Manon Lescaut*. New York: Cambridge University Press, 1986.

Sgard, Jean. "Tricher." In *Le jeu au dix-huitième siècle*, 251–58. Aix-en-Provence, France: Édisud, 1976.

Sheu, Ling-Ling. *Voltaire et Rousseau dans le théâtre de la Révolution française*. Brussels: Éditions de l'Université de Bruxelles, 2005.

Spariosu, Mihai I. *Dionysus Reborn: Play and the Aesthetic Dimension in Modern Philosophical and Scientific Discourse*. Ithaca, NY: Cornell University Press, 1989.

Stewart, Philip. "Utopias That Self-Destruct." *Studies in Eighteenth Century Culture* 9 (1979): 15–25.

Strugnell, Anthony, ed. *French Social History: Games in the Eighteenth Century; Happiness in Duclos and Rousseau*. Oxford: Voltaire Foundation, 2000.

Sydenham, Michael J. *Léonard Bourdon: The Career of a Revolutionary, 1754–1807*. Waterloo, ON: Wilfrid Laurier University Press, 1999.

Tillit, Paul. "*Zoroastre* (1749) de Rameau: Droit et utopies dans un opéra franc-maçon du siècle des Lumières." *Droit et cultures* 52 (2006): 85–119.

Townsend, Joseph. *A Journey through Spain in the Years 1786 and 1787: With Particular Attention to the Agriculture, Manufactures, Commerce, Population, Taxes, and Revenue of That Country; and Remarks in Passing through a Part of France; in Three Volumes*. 3 vols. London: Dilly, 1791.

Trinquet, Charlotte. *Le conte de fées français (1690–1700): Traditions italiennes et origines aristocratiques*. Tübingen, Germany: Narr Verlag, 2012.

Trott, David. *Théâtre du XVIIIe siècle: Jeux, écritures, regards: Essai sur les spectacles en France de 1700 à 1790*. Montpellier, France: Espaces 34, 2000.

Uricchio, William. "Simulation, History, and Computer Games." In *Handbook of Computer Game Studies*, edited by Joost Raessens and Jeffrey Goldstein, 327–38. Cambridge, MA: MIT Press, 2005.

Van Kley, Dale K. *The Religious Origins of the French Revolution: From Calvin to the Civil Constitution, 1560–1791*. New Haven, CT: Yale University Press, 1996.

Verba, Cynthia. *Dramatic Expression in Rameau's "Tragédie en musique": Between Tradition and Enlightenment*. Cambridge: Cambridge University Press, 2013.

Villiers, Baron Marc de. "The History of the Foundation of New Orleans (1719–1799)." *Louisiana Historical Quarterly* 3, no. 2 (1920): 214–15.

Voltaire. *Nouveaux mélanges*. Geneva: Cramer, 1765.

———. *Oeuvres complètes de Voltaire*. Edited by Louis Moland et al. 52 vols. Paris: Garnier, 1877–85.

———. *Oeuvres complètes de Voltaire*. Edited by Theodore Besterman et al. 203 vols. Oxford: Voltaire Foundation, 1968–2021.

Vovelle, Michel. *La Révolution contre l'Église: De la Raison à l'Être Suprême*. Paris: Éditions Complexe, 1988.

———. *Les métamorphoses de la fête en Provence de 1750 à 1820*. Paris: Aubier-Flammarion, 1976.

———. *The Revolution against the Church: From Reason to the Supreme Being*. Translated by Alan José. Columbus: Ohio State University Press, 1991.

Wagner, Jacques. "L'ironie des voix superposées dans le *Gil Blas* de Lesage." *Cahiers de narratologie* 10 (2001): 509–24.

White, Hayden. *The Content of the Form: Narrative Discourse and Historical Representation*. Baltimore: Johns Hopkins University Press, 1987.

Williams, Haydn. *Turquerie: An Eighteenth-Century European Fantasy*. New York: Thames and Hudson, 2014.

Williams, Raymond. *Keywords: A Vocabulary of Culture and Society*. Rev. ed. New York: Oxford University Press, 1983.

Williamson, Elizabeth. *The Materiality of Religion in Early Modern English Drama*. Burlington, VT: Ashgate, 2009.

Wolff, Larry. *The Singing Turk: Ottoman Power and Operatic Emotions on the European Stage from the Siege of Vienna to the Age of Napoleon*. Stanford, CA: Stanford University Press, 2016.

Wright, Johnson Kent. "Historical Thought in the Era of the Enlightenment." In *A Companion to Western Historical Thought*, edited by Lloyd Kramer and Sarah Maza, 123–42. Malden, MA: Blackwell, 2002.

Wright, Thomas. *An Original Theory or New Hypothesis of the Universe, Founded upon the Laws of Nature*. Cambridge: Cambridge University Press, 2014.

Yon, Jean-Claude, and Nathalie Le Gonidec. *Tréteaux et paravents: Le théâtre de société au XIXe siècle*. Paris: Créaphis, 2012.

Notes on Contributors

RORI BLOOM is an associate professor of French at the University of Florida. Her contribution to this volume will also appear in her book on Marie-Catherine d'Aulnoy and Henriette-Julie de Murat, forthcoming from University of Nebraska Press.

MARIA TEODORA COMSA is a lecturer in French at Stanford University, specializing in seventeenth- and eighteenth-century French literature with an emphasis on society theater (*théâtre de société*). She is the author of essays on eighteenth-century theater and culture, including "Bâtir une base de données de théâtres de société; Défis et applications" in *Espaces des théâtres de société* and "Casanova's French Networks: Transitioning from a Backstage Coterie to the *beau monde*," in *Networks of Enlightenment: Digital Approaches to the Republic of Letters*. She is currently working on a database of eighteenth-century French society theaters.

ANNELLE CURULLA is an associate professor of French Studies at Scripps College. She is the author of *Gender and Religious Life in French Revolutionary Drama* and of essays on eighteenth-century theater and aesthetics. Her research currently involves Rosalie de Constant and Olympe de Gouges.

FAYÇAL FALAKY is an associate professor at Tulane University, where he specializes in eighteenth-century French literature, culture, and politics. He is the author of "The Cloche and Its Critics: Muting the Church's Voice in Pre-Revolutionary France," in the *Journal of the History of Ideas*, and *Social Contract, Masochist Contract: Aesthetics of Freedom and Submission in Rousseau*.

ZEINA HAKIM is an associate professor of French at Tufts University. Her research mainly focuses on eighteenth-century French literature and intellectual and cultural history in Early Modern France. She is the author of *Fictions déjouées: Le récit en trompe-l'oeil au XVIIIe siècle* and the coauthor, with Marc André Bernier, of a collective book titled *Mémoires et roman: Les rapports de vérité et de fiction au XVIIIe siècle*. She recently published articles in *Lumen, FLS, Diderot Studies, French Forum* and *Rousseau Studies* on Rousseau, Diderot, and Courtilz de Sandras, as well as on the ethics of emotions in the eighteenth century.

KATHARINE HARGRAVE is currently an instructor of French and director of the Foreign Language Lab at the College of Charleston. She specializes in early modern French and Francophone literature and civilization, with a particular emphasis on the intersections between music and society. Her current project, "Lyric Tragedy and Libretto Print Culture in Early Modern France," argues for the study of operas as literary texts used by the French to serve both political and colonial goals.

JEFFREY M. LEICHMAN is Jacques Arnaud Associate Professor in the Department of French Studies at Louisiana State University. His research interests include the theatricality of French Enlightenment thought and the theorization of stage acting in contemporary world cinema. He is principal investigator on the National Endowment for the Humanities–sponsored digital humanities project VESPACE, and coeditor of *Colonialism and Slavery in Performance: Theatre and the Eighteenth-Century French Caribbean*.

ERIKA MANDARINO received her doctorate in French studies from Tulane University. Her scholarly interests lie in eighteenth-century science and literature, and especially in the evolution of scientific literature from that era to today. She currently works in the field of academic publishing.

REGINALD MCGINNIS is a professor of French at the University of Arizona. He is the author of *Essai sur l'origine de la mystification* and coauthor, with John Vignaux Smyth, of *Mock Ritual in the Modern Era* (2022). His current projects include a book on the abbé Edme Mallet.

JEAN-ALEXANDRE PERRAS is a Marie Skłodowska-Curie Research Fellow at the European University Institute in Florence, where he focuses on eighteenth-century French hairdressers' innovation strategies as well as the question of value during the ancien régime as considered through different projects on frivolity, ephemerality, perfume, and fashion. He is the coeditor, with Marine Ganofsky, of *Le siècle de la légèreté: Émergences d'un paradigme du XVIIIe siècle français,* and one of the coeditors of a special issue of the journal *Littérature,* "*Sociabilités du parfum.*"

YANN ROBERT is an associate professor in the Department of French and Francophone Studies at the University of Illinois at Chicago and the author of *Dramatic Justice: Trial by Theater in the Age of the French Revolution*. His current research focuses on vigilantism and popular justice in the literature and culture of the Enlightenment and Revolutionary France.

MASANO YAMASHITA is an associate professor of French at the University of Colorado–Boulder. She is the author of *Jean-Jacques Rousseau face au public: Problèmes d'identité* and has also published articles on women's lives, poverty, and the public sphere in the eighteenth century. She is currently at work on a book on accidents and inequality in eighteenth-century France.

Index

absolutism, 103
Académie royale de musique, 79n19,
   104, 111
acrobatics, 168, 173
acrobats, 9, 16
acting, 156; amateur, 116; playacting,
   115–122, 124, 126–131; social, 116–118,
   120–122, 124–131
actors, 6–7, 130–131; amateur, 115–117, 124;
   professional, 116; in Revolutionary
   theater, 151–153, 155–59
Agamben, Giorgio, 6, 136–137, 148
agency, 66, 68, 77, 112, 174, 176–177, 179–180
agôn, 138
Aït-Touati, Frédérique, 95n9
alchemy, 92, 94
alea, 69, 77, 112, 138. See also chance
algorithm, 179
alienation, 6, 116–118, 123
allegory, 76, 78n11, 89–90, 92, 106, 146
amphigories, 40
antiphrasis, 125–126
Aravamudan, Srinivas, 99
arbitrariness, 4, 66, 74, 77–78, 105, 108
Argenson, René-Louis de Voyer, marquis
   d', 35, 78n5
Arnold, R. J., 109
Arouch (actor), 153
artificial intelligence, 172, 176
artisans, 13, 17, 20
Assassin's Creed, 171, 181n11
atomism, 95n8
Audouin, Pierre Jean, 160
Aulard, François-Alphonse, 135

Aulnoy, Marie-Catherine d', 5; and
   jewelry, 10–11; and magic, 12; and
   marionettes, 14; and marriage, 19; and
   playfulness, 9; and playthings, 15; and
   toys, 12, 20, 21n5, 21nn11–12
authority, 77, 84, 133, 137, 142, 148, 170;
   crises of, 66
auto-da-fé (ritual burnings), 135
automata, 2, 85

Bakhtin, Mikhail, 134
ball, masked, 97–98. See also masquerade
Barbeyrac, Jean, 2–3, 64–65
basset, 15, 22n21
Bawr, Alexandrine-Sophie Goury de
   Champgrand, Baronne de, 41
Bayle, Pierre, 32
Beaumarchais, Pierre-Augustin Caron de,
   6, 97–98, 104–112
Bennett, Susan, 102
Béricourt, Étienne, 139–142, 145, 147–48
Béthune, Chevalier de, 6; biography of, 83;
   and calumny, 94n4; and gambling, 87;
   and materialism, 88; critique of monar-
   chy, 84, 94n7; and religion, 85, 89, 92
Betzwieser, Thomas, 106–107
Bianchi, Serge, 164n7, 166n24
Bièvre, François-Georges Maréchal de,
   36–43
bilboquet: and calembours, 34–44;
   "Chanson nouvelle, sur l'air du
   bilboquet," 27–30; and laces, 25, 44n3,
   44n6; origins of, 26–34; and sexuality,
   30, 32